Book I:
The Discovery — evolution of the stress concept.

Book II:
The Dissection — an analysis of the mechanism through which our bodies are attacked by, and can defend themselves against stress.

Book III:
The Diseases of Adaptation—maladies which result largely from failures in the stress-fighting mechanism.

Book IV:
Sketch for a Unified Theory — how the knowledge of stress can further an understanding of the theory of life.

Book V:
Implications and Applications — how the knowledge of stress can be applied medically, psychosomatically and philosophically to insure a better and happier life.

"The omission of strictly technical details and the paraphernalia of evidence keeps the whole work from foundering in the mass of data of questionable relevance characteristic of some other discussions of the subject. Read it—it is very readable—but try to maintain balance amid Dr. Selye's persuasive enthusiasm."
American Journal of Public Health.

Original editions:

Stress, 1950
First Annual Report on Stress, 1951
Second Annual Report on Stress, 1952 (in collaboration with A. Horava)
Third Annual Report on Stress, 1953 (in collaboration with A. Horava)
Fourth Annual Report on Stress, 1954 (in collaboration with G. Heuser)
Fifth Annual Report on Stress, 1955–1956 (in collaboration with G. Heuser)
The Story of the Adaptation Syndrome (told in the form of informal illustrated lectures), 1952
Textbook of Endocrinology, 2d edition, 1949
"The Steroids," 4 vols., in *Encyclopedia of Endocrinology,* 1943
"Ovarian Tumors," 2 vols., in *Encyclopedia of Endocrinology,* 1946
"On the Experimental Morphology of the Adrenal Cortex" in *American Lectures in Endocrinology* (in collaboration with H. Stone), 1950

The Stress of Life, 1956

Translations:

Trattato di Endocrinologia, Italian translation of *Textbook of Endocrinology* by Professor Cesare Cavallero, 1952
Endocrinología, Spanish translation of *Textbook of Endocrinology* by Professor José Mª Cañadell, 1952
Stress (Sufrimiento), Spanish translation of *Stress,* and the *First Annual Report on Stress, 1951* by Professor J. Morros Sardá and Professor José Mª Cañadell, 1954
Einführung in die Lehre vom Adaptationssyndrom, German translation of *The Story of the Adaptation Syndrome* by Professor Heinz Köbcke, 1953
L'Histoire du syndrome général d'adaptation, French translation of *The Story of the Adaptation Syndrome* by Dr. Tchékoff and Dr. Caplier, 1954
Japanese version of *The Story of the Adaptation Syndrome,* translated by Doctor Kichinosuke Tatai, 1953
Historia del Syndrome de Adaptation, excerpts from *The Story of the Adaptation Syndrome,* selected and translated by Alexander Gode, 1953
La Sindrome di Adattamento, 1956
Stress, Italian translation by Professor E. Rubino, 1956

McGraw-Hill Paperbacks

The Stress of Life

by Hans Selye, M.D.

McGraw-Hill Book Company
New York
Toronto
London

THE STRESS OF LIFE

Library of Congress Catalog Card Number: 56–10432

1819202122232425 MUMU 765432

ISBN 07-056206-7
ISBN 56205-9

Published by the McGraw-Hill Book Company
Printed in the United States of America

"This book is dedicated to those who are not afraid to enjoy the stress of a full life, nor too naive to think that they can do so without intellectual effort." Dr. Hans Selye

*It is highly dishonorable for
a Reasonable Soul to live in so
Divinely built a Mansion as the
Body she resides in, altogether
unacquainted with the exquisite
structure of it.*

—Robert Boyle, 1627–1691

*Not only will men of science have to grapple with
the sciences that deal with man, but—and this is
a far more difficult matter—they will have to
persuade the world to listen to what they have
discovered. If they cannot succeed in this difficult
enterprise, man will destroy himself by his
halfway cleverness.*

—Bertrand Russell, 1872–

Scope

The main purpose of this book is to tell, in a generally understandable language, what medicine has learned about stress.

No one can live without experiencing some degree of stress all the time. You may think that only serious disease or intensive physical or mental injury can cause stress. This is false. Crossing a busy intersection, exposure to a draft, or even sheer joy are enough to activate the body's stress-mechanism to some extent. Stress is not even necessarily bad for you; it is also the spice of life, for any emotion, any activity causes stress. But, of course, your system must be prepared to take it. The same stress which makes one person sick can be an invigorating experience for another.

It is through the *general adaptation syndrome*, or G.A.S. (the main subject of this book), that our various internal organs—especially the endocrine glands and the nervous system—help to adjust us to the constant changes which occur in and around us.

Life is largely a process of adaptation to the circumstances in which we exist. A perennial give-and-take has been going on between living matter and its inanimate surroundings, between one living being and another, ever since the dawn of life in the prehistoric oceans. The secret of health and happiness lies in successful adjustment to the ever-changing conditions on this globe; the penalties for failure in this great process of adaptation are disease and unhappiness. The evolution through endless centuries from the simplest forms of life to complex human beings was the greatest adaptive adventure on earth. The realization of this has fundamentally influenced our thinking, but there is not much we can do about it. Here we are, such as we are; and whether or not man is pleased with the result, he cannot change his own inherited structure.

But there is another type of evolution which takes place in every person during his own lifetime from birth to death: this is adaptation to the stresses and strains of everyday existence. Through the constant interplay between his mental and bodily reactions, man has it in his power to influence this second type of evolution to a considerable extent, especially if he understands its mechanism and has enough will power to act according to the dictates of human intellect.

Stress.is essentially the rate of all the wear and tear caused by life. It will take a whole book to explain the complex mechanisms through which the body can reduce this type of wear and tear. But let me say here, by way of an introduction, that although we cannot avoid stress as long as we live, we can learn a great deal about how to keep its damaging side-effects to a minimum. For instance, we are just beginning to see that many common diseases are largely due to errors in our adaptive response to stress, rather than to direct damage by germs, poisons, or other external agents. In this sense many nervous and emotional disturbances, high blood pressure, gastric and duodenal ulcers, certain types of rheumatic, allergic, cardiovascular, and renal diseases appear to be essentially *diseases of adaptation.*

In view of all this, stress is undoubtedly an important personal problem for everybody. So much has been written for the general public about my work on stress by others, that I gradually came to feel the need of telling the story in my own words. Writing this book certainly helped me. I hope it will also help you. It helped me because I have spent the last twenty years doing experiments on stress and thinking about their interpretations. I have written six large volumes and several hundred scientific articles about stress in technical journals for specialists. But this is the first chance I have had to put the really salient points together and get a bird's-eye view, not only of the facts discovered in the laboratory, but also of the thoughts and emotions inspired by constant preoccupation with the nature of stress in health and disease. The urge to share with others the thrill of adventure which comes from penetrating, even if ever so slightly, into hitherto unknown depths of life can become a major source of stress in itself. I just had to get this book out of my system, and doing so has certainly helped me.

In a similar sense, I hope this account will help my readers—physicians and laymen alike—who do not have an opportunity of experiencing at first hand all those manifold satisfactions which come from designing experimental plans and acquiring the techniques necessary to solve some of those problems of life which concern us all.

But I should like to think that this book may offer an even more practical kind of help. Psychoanalysis has shown that knowledge about oneself has a curative value. I think this is also true of psychosomatic, and perhaps even of what we call purely somatic, or bodily, derangements. The struggle for understanding is one of the most characteristic features of our species; that is why man is called *Homo sapiens*. The satisfaction of this urge is our destiny.

Structure

It may help you to enter into the spirit of this volume if you keep in mind that I wanted to tell not only what we know about stress but also how we found out about it. This dual task determined the structure of my account and particularly its presentation in the form of five Books.

Book I: The discovery of stress describes the evolution of the stress concept from the earliest records of medical thought on the subject up to the present time.

Book II: The dissection of stress attempts to analyze the mechanism through which our body is attacked by, and can defend itself against, stress-producing situations.

Book III: The diseases of adaptation deals with maladies (cardiovascular diseases, digestive disorders, mental derangements) which we consider to result largely from failures in the stress-fighting mechanism.

Book IV: Sketch for a unified theory explores how our knowledge of stress might help us to appraise those elementary forms of reaction which constitute the mosaic of life in health and disease.

Book V: Implications and applications presents the principal lessons to be learned from this study, not only in medicine proper, but also as regards man's ability to devise a natural, healthy philosophy of life.

Readability

In writing this account it seemed logical to proceed from the discovery of stress (Book I) to the analysis of its mechanism in health (Book II) and disease (Book III), and then to explore how this knowledge could further our understanding of life in theory (Book IV) and in practice (Book V). But, by dealing with my topics in this sequence, I had to intersperse highly technical data between the more easily readable, and perhaps more entertaining, parts of the narrative. I would therefore recommend that only physicians, or readers who are at least reasonably familiar with current problems of physiology and medicine, should read this book from cover to cover. If you are quite unacquainted with this field, it will be better to start with Book V (the practical implications and applications of the stress concept in everyday life), using the Glossary as a guide to technical terms, and perhaps looking up occasional earlier passages to which reference is made. If you turn to Book I after this, you will be able to read about the discovery of stress with more understanding. I would recommend that you then peruse at least the Summary of Book II, all of Book III, and the Summary of Book IV. Books II and IV are particularly technical, and even without them the essence of the volume is quite understandable, although they had to be included to complete the picture.

Finally, it may be well to point out right here at the beginning that, whether or not you already know something of the subject, this is the kind of book that can be read profitably only in small installments of, say, no more than ten to twenty pages at a time. But before I discourage you with too many admonitions, let us now start with the story.

Hans Selye

Université de Montréal
Montreal, 1956

Acknowledgments

My work on stress is but one small step toward a better comprehension of man's nature, and my desire to share this experience with others was largely prompted by the pleasure and inspiration I personally derived from such remarkable works as:

Bernard, Claude: *Introduction to the Study of Experimental Medicine*, Oeuvres Immortelles, Constant Bourquin, Geneva, 1945.

Cannon, W. B.: *The Wisdom of the Body*, W. W. Norton & Company, Inc., New York, 1939.

————: *The Way of an Investigator*, W. W. Norton & Company, Inc., New York, 1945.

Carrel, Alexis: *Man the Unknown*, Harper & Brothers, New York, 1935.

Conant, James B.: *On Understanding Science*, New American Library, New York, 1951.

Darwin, Charles: *The Origin of the Species and the Descent of Man*, Modern Library ed., Random House, Inc., New York, 1955.

Einstein, Albert: *Ideas and Opinions*, Crown Publishers, Inc., New York, 1953.

Freud, Sigmund: *Psychopathology of Everyday Life*, New American Library, New York, 1951.

Gamow, George: *The Birth and Death of the Sun*, New American Library, New York, 1953.

Jeans, Sir James: *The Stars in Their Courses*, Cambridge University Press, New York, 1948.

Sherrington, Sir Charles: *Man on His Nature*, Anchor Book ed., Doubleday & Company, Inc., New York, 1953.

Vallery-Radot, Pasteur: *The Most Beautiful Pages of Pasteur*, Flammarion, Paris, 1943.

Zinsser, Hans: *As I Remember Him*, Little, Brown & Company, Boston, 1940.

May I recommend, therefore, that those who are interested not only in stress but also in understanding the different aspects of nature consult some of these great examples of writing about science by those who made it. None of them can be read easily in bed after a busy day, but their message is accessible to any educated person, whatever his background, and they can give us an understanding of the highest aspirations of man: to know himself and to devise a purposeful way of life.

My sincere thanks are due to Acta, Inc., of Montreal, and M D Publications, Inc., of New York, who permitted me to use a number of passages, as well as illustrations, which first appeared in my more technical books on stress. Other illustrations are reproduced by courtesy of the *Journal of the American Medical Association,* the *British Medical Journal,* the *Canadian Medical Association Journal,* and *The Journal of Clinical Endocrinology and Metabolism.*

All the professional-looking drawings in this volume were prepared by Miss Marie Langlois; the amateurish ones were committed by myself. Mr. Kai Nielsen took the photographs.

Contents

Book IV   Sketch for a unified theory

Book V   Implications and applications

Plates

Book **I:**

The discovery of stress

Summary

In its medical sense, *stress is essentially the rate of wear and tear in the body.* Anyone who feels that whatever he is doing—or whatever is being done to him—is strenuous and wearing, knows vaguely what we mean by *stress.* The feelings of just being tired, jittery, or ill are subjective sensations of stress. But stress does not necessarily imply a morbid change: normal life also causes some wear and tear in the machinery of the body. Indeed, stress can even have curative value, as in shock therapy, bloodletting, and sports.

Research on stress was greatly handicapped because we had no objective, measurable indices to assess it, until it was found, some twenty years ago, that stress causes certain changes in the structure and chemical composition of the body, which can be accurately appraised. Some of these changes are merely signs of *damage*; others are manifestations of the body's *adaptive reactions,* its mechanism of defense against stress. The totality of these changes—the *stress syndrome*—is called the *general adaptation syndrome* (G.A.S.). It develops in three stages: (1) the alarm reaction; (2) the stage of resistance; (3) the stage of exhaustion.

The *nervous system and the endocrine (or hormonal) system* play particularly important parts in maintaining resistance during stress. They help to keep the structure and function of the body steady, despite exposure to stress-producing or *stressor* agents, such as nervous tension, wounds, infections, poisons. This steady state is known as *homeostasis.*

In this section we shall discuss the *evolution of the stress concept,* from antiquity to the present time, and the *psychologic problems* met when chance observations, made at the bedside of patients or in the research laboratory, are to be translated into a precise science.

1:

Precursors of the

stress concept

What is stress? What is a discovery? Witch doctors, evil spirits, and incantations (treatment by pain, terror, fever, shock, and the like). How could damage cure? Pónos—the toil of disease. Homeostasis—the staying power of the body.

What is stress?

The soldier who sustains wounds in battle, the mother who worries about her soldier son, the gambler who watches the races, the horse and the jockey he bet on: they are all under stress.

The beggar who suffers from hunger and the glutton who overeats, the little shopkeeper with his constant fears of bankruptcy and the rich merchant struggling for yet another million: they are also all under stress.

The housewife who tries to keep her children out of trouble, the child who scalds himself—and especially the particular cells of the skin over which he spilled the boiling coffee—they, too, are under stress. What is this one mysterious condition that the most different kinds of people have in common with animals and even with individual cells, at times when much—much of anything—happens to them? What is the nature of stress?

This is a fundamental question in the life of everyone; it touches closely upon the essence of life and disease. To understand the mechanism of stress gives physicians a new approach to the treatment of illness, but it can also give us all a new way of life, a new philosophy to guide our actions in conformity with natural laws.

Perhaps the simplest way to enter into the spirit of this concept will be to follow it through its historic evolution. But I wonder where to begin. It would be natural to start with the discovery of stress, yet it seems as though, in a sense, man always knew about this condition and even now still fails to grasp its essence completely.

Perhaps this is true of every fundamental concept; it is not easy to recognize discovery.

It seems to me that most people do not fully realize to what extent the spirit of scientific research and the lessons learned from it depend upon the personal viewpoints of the discoverers at the time basic observations are made. The painter and the message on his canvas, the musician or poet and the emotional impact of their creations are but different aspects of single natural phenomena. It is surprising to what extent the inseparability of this relationship between work and worker has been overlooked as regards the seemingly more impersonal results of scientific investigation. In an age so largely dependent upon science and scientists, I am convinced that this fundamental point deserves special attention. It should be clearly stated right here at the beginning that to demonstrate the importance of this relationship is one of my major objectives in this account. My book must, therefore, serve the dual purpose of describing not only what has been learned about stress, but also the psychologic processes which led to its discovery. This twin objective is my apology for the many seemingly irrelevant digressions in which I shall try to analyze my own mental reactions to personal laboratory observations.

What is a discovery?

Was America discovered by the Indians, who were here from time immemorial, by the Norsemen who came in the tenth century, or by Christopher Columbus who arrived in 1492? Is it still being discovered, now every day, by anyone who drills a new oil well or finds another deposit of uranium on this continent? It depends upon the particular aspect of America and upon the extent of exploration to which you attach the greatest importance. Discovery is always a matter of viewpoint and degree. Whenever we single out an individual as *the* discoverer of anything, we merely mean that for us he discovered it more than anybody else.

The historian of any exploration is faced with these confusing facts. Usually, the subject of the discovery has been suspected and even more or less fleetingly seen from many angles by many people long before it was "actually discovered." For practical purposes, it is unimportant who made a scientific discovery, as long as we can enjoy its fruits. In this sense, it matters little who discovered America as long as we have been given the use of the country. But it does matter, if we want to share the thrill of a true adventure story or profit by the practical lessons that can be learned from it.

And a great deal can be learned from it. For one thing, it can teach us just what constitutes an important discovery for anyone in his daily life, not only for the professional explorer in his scientific studies.

Take again the discovery of America. Obviously, we consider Columbus to be the discoverer only because he, more than anyone else, was responsible for giving us—by "us" I mean the non-Indians—a new continent. The Indians could certainly not look upon him as the discoverer of America. From their point of view, his arrival was the date on which the white man was discovered.

Those isolated groups of Norsemen who came during the tenth century had the great merit of getting here long before any other European, but although they unwittingly discovered America for themselves, they played no part in discovering it for us. Their exploits were completely forgotten because they failed to establish a workable and permanent connection between the New World and the Old. That is why they did not do us, today's inhabitants of America, any good. The Norsemen did not help Columbus either, because, when he planned his trip centuries later, neither he nor anyone in his surroundings knew anything about those earlier voyages. We have learned about them only quite recently, long after America became part of the civilized world. Columbus had to plan his trip without profiting from previous experiences.

The important difference between the discovery of America by the Indians, by the Norsemen, and by Columbus is that only Columbus succeeded in attaching the American continent to the rest of the world.

It is not to see something first, but to establish solid connections between the previously known and the hitherto unknown that constitutes the essence of scientific discovery. It is this process of tying together which can best promote true understanding and real progress.

The relativity of discovery has impressed many a scientist. For instance, the great American bacteriologist, Hans Zinsser, said: "So often, in the history of medicine, scientific discovery has merely served to clarify and subject to purposeful control facts that had long been empirically observed and practically utilized. The principles of contagion were clearly outlined and invisible microorganisms postulated by Fracastorius over a hundred years before the most primitive microscopes were invented; and the pre-Pasteurian century is rich with clinical observations that now seem a sort of gestation period leading to the birth of a new science." (*As I Remember Him*, p. 139.)

We can learn many things by analyzing discoveries, quite apart from the fact that we find out much about the discovered object itself. It is of definite practical value to learn, by studies in retrospect, what makes a discovery little or great, for this will help to guide our efforts in our own fields; and there is room for discovery in any field of human endeavor. For man it is doubly instructive to analyze explorations into the depths of man's nature, for here he is both the explorer and the explored.

With this in mind, let us now take a look at certain early medical concepts about *stress* as a factor in the production of disease. The reader will probably have asked himself by now just what I mean by the term *stress*. I shall come to this later, but I have purposely avoided giving a formal definition so far, because I think it is more instructive to enter this field without being influenced by any preconceived ideas.

Witch doctors, evil spirits, and incantations (treatment by pain, terror, fever, shock, and the like)

For many centuries disease was considered to be something caused by evil spirits or demons. Consequently—for instance in primitive Aztec medicine, and in Babylonian medicine thousands of years B.C.—disease was treated by *incantations*, and *dances*, or by *strong drugs, poultices,* and *painful bandages*, which were applied by awe-inspiring witch doctors or priest-physicians to frighten and expel the demons.

Bloodletting was another time-honored remedy for a number of diseases. It is difficult to establish precisely when it was used first.

In any event, the process of *venesection* (cutting into a vein to draw blood) is clearly depicted on some Greek vases made around 150 B.C.; and it remained an undoubtedly useful standard procedure in medicine until quite recently. In fact, I remember that when I was a boy, my grandfather and even my father, both of whom were physicians, still punctured veins and applied leeches to treat the most diverse diseases by loss of blood.

Flogging of the insane was a common procedure during antiquity and the Middle Ages to drive the demon or devil out of people who suffered from various mental aberrations.

Paracelsus (whose true, but somewhat bombastic, name was Theophrastus Bombastus von Hohenheim) was a famous Swiss physician who lived during the sixteenth century. In his treatise on "Diseases Which Deprive Man of his Reason," he stated that "the best cure and one which rarely fails is to throw such persons into *cold water.*"

About 100 A.D. the eminent Greek physician, Rufus of Ephesus, made the important discovery that strong *fever* can cure many diseases. From his descriptions, it is obvious that he dealt mainly with malarial fevers; these he found to be beneficial in melancholia and other mental disorders, as well as in certain diseases of the skin, and also in asthma, convulsions, and epilepsy. Fever treatment was not altogether original with him; certain peoples of Africa, he said, drank the urine of a goat to produce fever, and, "I know also that a Greek physician, Euenor, employed this remedy." (Ralph H. Major: *A History of Medicine*, p. 184.)

These observations were soon forgotten and it was not until about seventeen centuries later that the great value of treatment with fever was rediscovered and applied to modern medicine. In 1883 Julius Wagner von Jauregg, a Viennese psychiatrist, had noted the disappearance of mental symptoms in certain patients who accidentally contracted typhoid fever. This made such a great impression upon the young doctor that he continued to think and write about the possibilities of fever-cures for insanity until, ten years later, he decided to infect insane persons with various germs, on purpose. He obtained particularly spectacular results in patients suffering from a syphilitic mental derangement, general paresis, when he inoculated them with malaria germs. The method was then successfully applied by various other physicians throughout the world.

This was soon followed by the development of various types of shock therapy for mental patients. Treatments of this kind depend upon the production of a shock by electric current or by certain drugs, such as Metrazol or insulin. These procedures are still in wide use today.

Nobody really knew how these shock therapies worked. They grew out of chance observations on people in whom diseases were cured after accidental exposure to some kind of shock. It seemed as though the patient was somehow "shaken out of his disease," very much as a child can be made to snap out of a tantrum if you suddenly splash a glass of cold water into its face.

The most peculiar thing about all these treatments was a lack of any relationship between the cause of the disease and the way it was treated. It stands to reason that an infection can be cured by a remedy that kills the causative germs; but why should an infection with malaria or treatment with electric shocks cure a mental derangement that was caused, say, by syphilis? This uncertainty about the way these treatments worked created much uneasiness; but they did work—and often in conditions which could not otherwise be treated—and so they enjoyed considerable popularity.

Then, during the first half of this century, a variety of so-called *nonspecific therapies* had a great vogue. These were not so far removed from fever therapy and shock therapy as one might think. They were based upon the observation that the condition of patients suffering from various kinds of chronic diseases—say, rheumatism—is often improved by injections with various foreign materials (for instance, milk, foreign blood, or certain heavy-metal preparations) which stimulate a strong reaction on the part of the body.

How could damage cure?

What do all these treatments have in common? At first thought, one would say: nothing. But when one thinks it over they do seem to have something in common. The mystic exorcisms of a fear-inspiring priest-physician, the loss of blood, the painful whip, the exhausting fever, the shock of an electric current, and the strong bodily reaction against injections with foreign substances have one thing in common: they all cause wear and tear; they all cause stress.

Could a sudden stress, or push, force the body to "snap out of disease"? One wonders: perhaps it could. If, for instance, the compulsory repetition of certain defensive bodily actions could force some of our vital mechanisms "into a groove," so to speak, a good push might get us out of it. Everyone has had experience with a watch, a radio set, or some other machine: when it suddenly stops, you can often get it to work again by simply shaking it a bit. The same is true of a gramophone that suffers from "compulsory repetition" because the needle has made itself a wrong groove. If this can happen in a machine, why not in a living body?

Quite apart from this passive being-pushed-into-place in man, an extremely threatening treatment might even stimulate active mechanisms of defense. These could be intensified to such an extent that they would overcome not only the damage of the treatment which mobilized them, but, incidentally, also a disease.

Either of these two possible mechanisms would also explain the nonspecific nature of all these treatments. By *nonspecific treatment* we mean one whose benefits are not limited to a single disease. Significantly, none of the treatments so far mentioned are specific for any one malady. They may not be particularly effective, but they can do some good in various apparently unrelated diseases. For instance, an artificially produced fever can improve a mental disease as well as an inflammation of the eyes or a rheumatoid arthritis.

However, we must admit that these are only intuitive feelings, not explanations. The fact that a sudden push could set some derailment right in a machine just helps one to imagine, not to understand, how nonspecific shock treatments and the like might work.

We shall come back to this later, after having studied the actual mechanism of stress in man, as revealed by scientific inquiry. But, until quite recently, this much was all we knew—or, perhaps I should say, felt—about the way nonspecific cures might act. This is why all these types of treatment have gone in and out of fashion throughout history, without ever being able to establish themselves as recognized procedures. Scientifically trained physicians do not like to employ methods which they cannot understand, because usually such procedures are unreliable and dangerous. If we do not know through what pathways (nervous, hormonal, or other) a treatment works in the body, we may unwittingly overstrain some weak spot in the patient's system. If we know the mechanism of a treatment, at least we can withhold it from persons who probably could not take it.

I think this gives us a fair picture of what was known about the nonspecific element—or, as we now call it, *stress*—in medical treatment. Let us now have a look at what was known about nonspecific factors in the production of disease.

"*Pónos*"—*the toil of disease*

Twenty-four centuries ago, Hippocrates, the Father of Medicine, told his disciples in Greece that disease is not only suffering (*pathos*), but also toil (*pónos*), that is, the fight of the body to restore itself toward normal. There is a *vis medicatrix naturae,* a healing force of nature, which cures from within.

Some 160 years ago, John Hunter pointed out that "There is a circumstance attending accidental injury which does not belong to disease—namely, that the injury done has in all cases a tendency to produce the disposition and the means of cure."

This is an important point and one which, despite being constantly rediscovered during the intervening centuries, is not yet generally understood even today. Disease is not mere surrender to disease, but also fight for health; and unless there is fight there is no disease.

Not every deviation from the normal condition of the body is disease. Just because a man has lost a leg as a child, he is not ill for the rest of his life. He may be a cripple and yet be in perfect health despite his physical handicap. A woman born with a malformation, such as a harelip, may be seriously disfigured, but she is not sick. Why? Because there is no *pónos*, no toil; the fight was lost long ago and now there is peace in the body, although it is a scarred body. The very concept of illness presupposes a clash between forces of aggression and our defenses.

"*Homeostasis*"—*the staying power of the body*

During the second half of the nineteenth century, the great French physiologist, Claude Bernard, at the Collège de France in Paris, taught that one of the most characteristic features of all living beings is their ability to *maintain the constancy of their internal milieu,* despite changes in the surroundings. The physical properties and the chemical composition of our body fluids and tissues tend to remain remarkably constant despite all the changes about us. For instance, a man can be exposed to great cold or heat without varying his own temperature. He can eat large amounts of one substance or another without greatly influencing the composition of his blood. Whenever this self-regulating power fails, there is disease or even death.

Walter B. Cannon, the famous Harvard physiologist, subsequently called this power to maintain constancy in living beings *homeostasis* (from Greek *homoios*, like, similar, plus *stasis*, position, standing) the ability to remain the same, or static. You might roughly translate it as "staying power." The word *thermostat* (from Greek *thermē*, heat, plus *stasis*), which is in common use, refers to a gadget that maintains the temperature static—for instance, in a room or oven—by automatically cutting down heat-production when it threatens to become excessive, and vice versa. *Thermostasis* is then the maintenance of a steady temperature; and homeostasis is organic stability, or the maintenance of steadiness in every respect.

Let us now take a look at these concepts and ask ourselves what we can learn from them as regards the nature of stress or disease.

Apparently, disease is not just suffering, but a fight to maintain the homeostatic balance of our tissues, despite damage. There must be some element of stress here, at least, in the sense in which the engineer speaks of stress and strain in connection with the interaction of force and resistance. What we have seen up to now however, gives us no reason to believe that *nonspecific* stress plays any role in this. As far as we can see at this point, each damaging agent —every germ or poison—may be opposed by a special, highly specific defense mechanism. Examples would be the production of anti-sera which are good only against certain germs, or the manufacture by the body of some antidotes specifically neutralizing certain poisons but not others.

All this does not help us as yet to define biologic stress or disease in precise terms; still, it does leave us with a vague feeling that various types of treatment and many, if not all, diseases have certain things in common, have certain nonspecific features.

Could all this vagueness be translated somehow into the precise terms of modern science? Could it point a way to explore whether or not there is some nonspecific defense system built into our body, a mechanism to fight any kind of disease? Could it lead us to a *unified theory of disease*?

Throughout the world and throughout the ages, many physicians must have wondered about this. I am just one of them.

2:

My first glimpse

of stress

A young medical student's first impressions of medicine. The "syndrome of just being sick."

A young medical student's first impressions of medicine

In 1925 I was a student at the Medical School of the ancient German University of Prague. I had just completed my courses in anatomy, physiology, biochemistry, and the other preclinical subjects which were required as a preparation before we saw a patient. I had stuffed myself full of theoretical knowledge to the limit of my abilities and was burning with enthusiasm for the art of healing; but I had only vague ideas about how clinical medicine worked in practice. Then came the great day, which I shall never forget, when we were to hear our first lecture in internal medicine and see how one examines a patient.

It so happened that, on that day, by way of an introduction, we were shown several cases in the earliest stages of various infectious diseases. As each patient was brought into the lecture room, the professor carefully questioned and examined him. It turned out that each of these patients felt and looked ill, had a coated tongue, complained of more or less diffuse aches and pains in the joints, and of intestinal disturbances with loss of appetite. Most of them also had fever (sometimes with mental confusion), an enlarged spleen or liver, inflamed tonsils, a skin rash, and so forth. All this was quite evident, but the professor attached very little significance to any of it.

Then, he enumerated a few "characteristic" signs which might help in the diagnosis of the disease. These I could not see. They were absent or, at least, so inconspicuous that I could not distinguish them; yet these, we were told, were the important changes to which we would have to give all our attention. At present, our teacher said, most of the characteristic signs happened to be absent, but until they appeared, not much could be done; without them it was impossible to know precisely what the patient suffered from; and hence it was obviously impossible to recommend any efficient treatment against the disease. It was clear that the many features of disease which were already manifest did not interest our teacher very much because they were "nonspecific," and hence "of no use" to the physician.

Since these were my first patients, I was still capable of looking at them without being biased by current medical thought. Had I known more I would never have asked questions, because everything was handled "just the way it should be," that is, "just the way every good physician does it." Had I known more, I would certainly have been stopped by the biggest of all blocks to improvement: the certainty of being right. But I did not know what was right.

I could understand that our professor had to find specific disease manifestations in order to identify the particular cause of disease in each of these patients. This, I clearly realized, was necessary so that suitable drugs might be prescribed, medicines having the specific effect of killing the germs or neutralizing the poisons that made these people sick.

I could see this all right; but what impressed me, the novice, much more was that apparently only a few signs and symptoms are actually characteristic of any one disease; most of the disturbances are apparently common to many, or perhaps even to all, diseases.

Why is it, I asked myself, that such widely different disease-producing agents as those which cause measles, scarlet fever, or the flu, share with a number of drugs, allergens, etc., the property of evoking the nonspecific manifestations which have just been mentioned? Yet evidently they do share them; indeed, they share them to such an extent that, at an early stage, it might be quite impossible, even for our eminent professor, to distinguish between various diseases because they all look alike.

The "syndrome of just being sick"

Even now—thirty years later—I still remember vividly the profound impression these considerations made upon me at the time. I could not understand why, ever since the dawn of medical history, physicians should have attempted to concentrate all their efforts upon the recognition of *individual* diseases and the discovery of *specific* remedies for them, without giving any attention to the much more obvious "syndrome of just being sick." I knew that a syndrome is usually defined as "a group of signs and symptoms that occur together and characterize a disease." Well, the patients we had just seen had a syndrome, but this seemed to be the syndrome that characterized disease as such, not any one disease.

Surely, if it is important to find remedies which help against one disease or another, it would be even more important to learn something about the mechanism of being sick and the means of treating this "general syndrome of sickness," which is apparently superimposed upon all individual diseases!!

As an apology for the two exclamation marks, let me point out that I was only eighteen years old at that time. Because of the confusion created in Central Europe by the aftermath of World War I, I was allowed to complete my premedical studies as fast as I could pass the exams, and, with the help of an excellent private tutor, I got to Medical School at an unusually impressionable age.

In view of this I might perhaps also be forgiven for having thought that I could solve all these problems in a jiffy by applying classical research techniques to my problem. For several days, I intended asking our professor of physiology for some lab space, so that I might analyze the "general syndrome of being sick" with the techniques of physiology, biochemistry, and histology which we had learned in our courses. If these methods could be used to clarify such specific things as the normal mechanisms of blood circulation or nervous conduction, I saw no reason why they could not be used with equal success to analyze the "general syndrome of disease" which interested me so much.

My immediate plans to dissect the general from the specific did not materialize, however. I was soon confronted with a problem which did not have the same general importance, but was more urgent specifically for me—the necessity of passing exams. Besides, I never did dare to present my proposition to the professor of physiology for fear of being laughed at. After all, I really had no precise plan; I had no blueprint to guide the work I wanted to do.

Then, as time went by, this whole problem lost its meaning for me. As I learned more and more about medicine, the many specific problems of diagnosis and treatment began to blur my vision for the nonspecific. The former gradually assumed an ever-increasing importance and pushed the "syndrome of just being sick," the question "what is disease in general?" out of my consciousness into that hazy category of the purely abstract arguments which are not worth bothering about.

3:

How to question nature

*The urge to learn.   Great hopes.
Grave doubts.   The great
disappointment.*

The urge to learn

What is disease—not any one disease, just disease in general? This question lingered on in my mind, as it undoubtedly has in the minds of most physicians of all nations throughout history. But there was no hope of an early answer, for nature—the source of all knowledge —rarely replies to questions unless they are put to her in the form of experiments to which she can say "yes" or "no." She is not loquacious; she merely nods in the affirmative or in the negative. "What is disease?" is not a question to which one can reply this way.

Occasionally, if we ask, "What would you do if . . . ?" or, "What is in such and such a place?" she will silently show you a picture. But she never explains. You have to work things out yourself first, aided only by instinct and the feeble powers of the human brain, until you can ask precise questions, to which nature can answer in her precise but silent sign language of nods and pictures. Understanding grows out of a mosaic of such answers. It is up to the scientist to draw a blueprint of the questions he has to ask before the mosaic makes sense.

It is curious how few laymen, or even physicians, understand this.

If you want to know whether a certain endocrine (that is, hormone-producing) gland is necessary for growth, you remove it surgically from the body of a growing young experimental animal. If growth stops, the answer is "yes." If you want to know whether a certain substance extracted from this gland is a growth-promoting hormone, you inject it into the same animal, and, if now the latter begins to grow again, the answer is "yes."

These are the nods of nature.

If you want to know what is in the fat tissue around the kidney, you dissect it and find the adrenal. If your question concerns the shape, size, or structure of this gland, just look at it; you can even examine the finest details of its appearance under a powerful microscope.

Such are the pictures of nature.

But if now you ask, "What is an adrenal?" you will get no reply. This is the wrong question; it cannot be answered by nods or pictures.

Only those blessed with the understanding that comes from a sincere and profound love of nature will, by an intuitive feeling for her ways, succeed in constructing a blueprint of the many questions that need to be asked to get even an approximate answer to such a question.

Only those cursed with a consuming, uncontrollable curiosity for nature's secrets will be able to—because they will have to—spend their lives working out patiently, one by one, the innumerable technical problems involved in performing each of the countless experiments required.

What is disease?—What is stress?

I did not know how to ask the first of these questions; I did not even think of asking the second.

Not until about ten years after hearing my first lecture in internal medicine did these same problems confront me again, although now under entirely different circumstances. At the time, I was working as a young assistant in the Biochemistry Department of McGill University in Montreal, on an entirely unrelated subject: the sex hormones. Still, I must say something about this work because it led me right back to the "syndrome of being sick."

Great hopes

Various extracts prepared from the ovaries (the female sex glands) and the placenta (the highly vascular afterbirth through which the embryo gets nourishment from the mother's womb) are very rich in female sex hormones.

> A *hormone* is a specific chemical messenger-substance, made by an endocrine gland and secreted into the blood, to regulate and coordinate the functions of distant organs. Sex hormones are coordinators of sexual activities, including reproduction.
>
> An *extract* is made by mixing tissue (say, the ovaries of cows) with solvents (water, alcohol, etc.) and taking what goes into solution. The extract is pure when it contains only the desired substance (for instance, a hormone) and impure when it also contains contaminants (for instance, unwanted and perhaps damaging ovarian substances).

Several sex hormones had already been prepared by that time (1935), but I thought there was still another one to be discovered. It would lead us too far afield if I were to explain why I thought so. (Besides, my theory was all wrong anyway, so let us not bother with it.) Still, to prove my point, I injected rats wth various ovarian and placental extracts to see whether the organs of these animals would show such changes as could *not* be due to any *known* sex hormone.

Much to my satisfaction, such changes were produced in my rats even by my first and most impure extracts:

1. There was a considerable enlargement of the *adrenal cortex.*

> The *adrenals* are two little endocrine glands which lie just above the kidneys, on both sides. Each of them consists of two portions, a central part, the medulla, and an outer rind, the cortex. Both of these parts produce hormones, but not the same kind. My extracts seemed to stimulate the cortex, without causing much of a change in the medulla. The cortical portion of the adrenals was not only enlarged, but it also showed the microscopic features of increased activity (such as cell-multiplication and discharge of stored secretion droplets into the blood).

2. There was an intense shrinking (or atrophy) of the thymus, the spleen, the lymph nodes, and of all other lymphatic structures in the body.

> The *lymphatic structures* are made up of innumerable, small white blood cells, similar to the *lymphocytes,* which circulate in

the blood. What a lymphocyte does in solid lymphatic tissue or in the blood is not yet very well known, but it seems to play some part in the defense of the organism against various types of damage. For instance, in people exposed to x-rays, the lymphocytes tend to disappear, and then resistance against all kinds of germs and poisons is much impaired.

The *lymphocytes* are made in the lymph nodes, little nodules in the groins, under the armpits, along the neck, and in various other parts of the body. Lymphocytes also make up most of the tissue in the *thymus* and *spleen*: that is why these organs are called *lymphatic tissues* or *thymicolymphatic system*. The thymus is a huge lymphatic organ just in front of the heart in the chest. In children it is very well developed but, after puberty, it tends to shrink, presumably under the influence of sex hormones.

When I saw that the lymphatic organs had so rapidly disintegrated in the rats, I naturally also examined the lymphocytes in the blood. Their number had also diminished under the influence of my tissue extracts, but while studying them I accidentally found an even more striking change in the blood picture: the almost complete disappearance of the *eosinophil cells.*

These are somewhat larger white blood cells, which have received their name because they stain very easily with a dye called *eosin.* This coloring agent is frequently used for histologic studies to make cells more visible under the microscope. The function of the eosinophils is also still debated, but they seem to be related to allergy, because their number increases remarkably when a person suffers from asthma, hay fever, or allied conditions.

3. There appeared bleeding, deep *ulcers* in the lining of the stomach, and that uppermost part of the gut, just after the stomach, which we call the duodenum.

These three types of changes formed a definite syndrome, because they were closely interdependent in some way. When I injected only a small amount of extract, all these changes were slight; when I injected much extract, they were all very pronounced. But with no extract could I ever produce one of these three changes without the others. This interdependence of lesions is precisely what makes them a syndrome. (*See photograph, Plate 1.*)

Incidentally, a syndrome such as ours, which consists of three types of changes, is usually called a *triad.*

Now, from all this I concluded that my extracts must contain some very active substance, and having been prepared from ovaries, this was first presumed to be an ovarian hormone. In apparent agreement with this view, one major manifestation of the triad was a change in an endocrine gland, the adrenal cortex, and another was the involution of the thymicolymphatic apparatus, a type of tissue known to shrink under the influence of sex hormones.

Of course, to me, the most important thing was that no ovarian hormone, or combination of ovarian hormones, known at that time ever produced adrenal enlargement, thymicolymphatic involution, and ulcers in the intestinal tract. It seemed rather obvious that we were dealing with a *new* ovarian hormone.

You may well imagine my happiness! At the age of 28, I seemed to be already on the track of a new hormone. I even had a perfect method with which to identify it in extracts, namely, the appearance in rats treated with this hormone, of the triad just described. It seemed only a matter of time now to concentrate and isolate the new hormone in pure form.

Grave doubts

Unfortunately, this happiness was not to last long. Not only ovarian, but placental, extracts also produced our triad. This did not worry me very much at first; after all, we knew that both the ovaries and the placenta can produce female sex hormones. I began to be somewhat confused, however, when it turned out subsequently that even pituitary extracts produced the same syndrome.

> The *pituitary* (or hypophysis) is a little endocrine gland embedded in the bones of the skull, just below the brain. It produces a number of hormones, but, as far as we knew, no ovarian hormones.

Yet, even this was not too disturbing, since mine was supposed to be a new hormone and (who knew?) perhaps the pituitary could manufacture this one.

But I really became puzzled when I found, a little later, that extracts of the kidney, spleen, or any other organ would produce the same triad. Was the causative factor some kind of general "tissue hormone" that could be produced by almost any cell?

Another inexplicable fact was that all efforts to purify the active extracts led to a diminution of their potency. The crudest preparations—the most impure ones—were invariably the most active. This did not seem to make sense.

The great disappointment

I shall never forget one particularly dark, rainy afternoon during the spring of 1936, when the great disappointment came. I was sitting in my small laboratory, brooding about the ever-increasing volume of findings which by now had made it quite improbable that my extracts could contain a new hormone, at least in the usual sense of the word. Mine could not be a specific substance of any one endocrine gland; I found about equal amounts of it everywhere. Yet the changes produced with these extracts were very real and constant. There must have been something in these preparations to account for such characteristic effects. What could it be?

It was then that a horrible thought occurred to me: for all I knew, this entire syndrome might be due merely to the toxicity of my extracts, to the fact that I did not purify them well enough.

In this case, of course, all my work meant nothing. I was not on the track of a new ovarian hormone; indeed, I was not even dealing with any specific ubiquitous "tissue hormone," but merely with damage as such.

As I thought of this, my eyes happened to fall upon a bottle of Formalin on a shelf in front of my desk.

> Formalin is an extremely toxic and irritating fluid. We use it in the preparation of tissues for microscopic study, as a fixative. Just as you use fixatives in photography, so for microscopic work, we employ certain agents to *fix* the structure of cells by instantly precipitating their constituents in the natural state.

Now, I thought, if my syndrome is really due only to tissue-damage, I should be able to reproduce it by injecting rats with a dilute Formalin solution. The cells in immediate contact with the Formalin would be precipitated and killed and considerable tissue-damage would result. This seemed to be a good way to formulate the question I wanted to ask: can even a toxic fluid not derived from any living tissue also produce my syndrome?

I immediately undertook such experiments and, within 48 hours, when I examined the organs of my animals, the answer was only too clear. In all the rats there was even more adrenocortical enlargement, thymicolymphatic atrophy, and intestinal-ulcer formation than I had ever been able to produce with any of my tissue-extracts.

I do not think I have ever been more profoundly disappointed! Suddenly all my dreams of discovering a new hormone were shattered. All the time and all the materials that went into this long study were wasted.

I tried to tell myself, "You must not let this sort of thing get you down; after all, fortunately, nothing has been published about the 'new hormone,' so no confusion has been created in the minds of others and there is nothing to retract." I tried to tell myself over and over again that such disappointments are inevitable in a scientist's life; occasionally anyone can follow a wrong track, and it is precisely the vision necessary to recognize such errors that characterizes the reliable investigator. But all this gave me little solace and, indeed, I became so depressed that for a few days I could not do any work at all. I just sat in my laboratory, brooding about how this misadventure might have been avoided and wondering what was to be done now.

Eventually I decided that, of course, the only thing to do was to pull myself together, admit my defeat, and return to some of the more orthodox endocrinological problems that had occupied my attention before I was sidetracked into this regrettable enterprise. After all, I was young and much of the road was still ahead. Yet, somehow I could not forget my triad, nor could I get hold of myself sufficiently to do anything else in the laboratory for several days.

The ensuing period of introverted contemplation turned out to be the decisive factor in my whole career; it pointed the way for all my subsequent work. But much more important than that, it revealed vistas sufficiently alluring in their promise of adventure and fulfillment to inspire that irresistible curiosity about nature's ways which was to be my delightful damnation ever after.

4:

The birth of the G.A.S.

A new point of view. If this were so . . . A change of mind. Discouragement. Encouragement. Plans for future research. What is the scope of this approach? The first semantic difficulties. The first publication on the stress syndrome. The three stages. What do you need in order to do research? More semantic difficulties. Dislike of a word may merely stem from inability to grasp the idea behind it. Still more semantic difficulties! The term stress emerges victorious.

A new point of view

As I repetitiously continued to go over my ill-fated experiments and their possible interpretation, it suddenly struck me that one could look at them from an entirely different angle. If there was such a thing as a single nonspecific reaction of the body to damage of any kind, this might be worth study for its own sake. Indeed, working out the mechanism of this kind of stereotyped "syndrome of response to injury as such" might be much more important to medicine than the discovery of yet another sex hormone.

As I repeated to myself, "a syndrome of response to injury as such," gradually, my early classroom impressions of the clinical "syndrome of just being sick" began to reappear dimly out of my subconsciousness, where they had been buried for over a decade. Could it be that this syndrome in man (the feeling of being ill, the diffuse pains in joints and muscles, the intestinal disturbances with loss of appetite, the loss of weight) were in some manner clinical equivalents of the experimental syndrome, the triad (adrenocortical stimulation, thymicolymphatic atrophy, intestinal ulcers) that I had produced with such a variety of toxic substances in the rat?

If this were so . . .

If this were so, the general medical implications of the syndrome would be enormous! Some degree of nonspecific damage is undoubtedly superimposed upon the specific characteristics of any disease, upon the specific effects of any drug.

If this were so, everything we had learned about the characteristic manifestations of disease, about the specific actions of drugs, would be in need of revision. All the actually observed biological effects of any agent must represent the sum of its specific actions and of this nonspecific response to damage that is superimposed upon it.

If this were so, it would mean that my first classroom impressions about the one-sidedness of medical thinking were quite justified and by no means sterile questions without practical answers. If the "damage syndrome" is superimposed upon the specific effects of all diseases and remedies, a systematic inquiry into the mechanism of this syndrome might well furnish us with a solid scientific basis for the treatment of damage as such.

If this were so, we had been examining medicine—disease and treatment—looking only for the specific, but through glasses tinted with the color of nonspecificity. Now that we had become aware of this misleading factor, we could remove the glasses and study the properties of disease and treatment apart from the color we saw through the glasses.

It had long been learned by sheer experience that certain curative measures were nonspecific, that is, useful to patients suffering from almost any disease. Indeed, such measures had been in use for centuries. One advises the patient to go to bed and take it easy; one tells him to eat only very digestible food and to protect himself against drafts or great variations in temperature and humidity.

Furthermore, there were all these nonspecific treatments that we had learned about in medical school, such as injection of substances foreign to the body, fever therapy, shock therapy, or bloodletting.

They were unquestionably useful in certain cases. The trouble was that often they did not help, and sometimes they did much harm; since one knew nothing about the mechanism of their action, using them was like taking a shot in the dark.

If we could prove that the organism had a general nonspecific reaction-pattern with which it could meet damage caused by a variety of potential disease-producers, this defensive response would lend itself to a strictly objective, truly scientific analysis. By clearing up the mechanism of the response through which nature herself fights injuries of various kinds, we might learn how to improve upon this reaction whenever it is imperfect.

A change of mind

I was simply fascinated by these new possibilities and immediately decided to reverse my plans for the future. Instead of dropping the stress problem and returning to classical endocrinology, I was now prepared to spend the rest of my life studying it. I have never had any reason to regret this decision.

Discouragement

It may be worth mentioning that I often had to overcome considerable mental inhibitions in my efforts to carry on with this plan. Nowadays it is perhaps difficult to appreciate just how absurd this plan seemed to most people before I had more facts to show that it worked. For example, I remember one senior investigator whom I admired very much and whose opinion meant a great deal to me. I knew he was a real friend who seriously wanted to help me with my research efforts. One day, during these busy weeks, he asked me into his office for a good heart-to-heart talk. He reminded me that for months now he had attempted to convince me that I must abandon this futile line of research. He assured me that, in his opinion, I possessed all the essential qualifications of an investigator and that I could undoubtedly contribute something to the generally recognized and accepted fields of endocrinology, so why bother with this wild-goose chase?

I met these remarks with my usual outbursts of uncontrolled youthful enthusiasm for the new point of view; I outlined again the immense possibilities inherent in a study of the nonspecific damage which must accompany all diseases and all but the mildest medications.

When he saw me thus launched on yet another enraptured description of what I had observed in animals treated with this or that impure, toxic material, he looked at me with desperately sad eyes and said in obvious despair, "But, Selye, try to realize what you are doing before it is too late! You have now decided to spend your entire life studying *the pharmacology of dirt!*"

Of course, he was right. Nobody could have expressed it more poignantly; that is why it hurt so much that I still remember the phrase today, almost twenty years later. Pharmacology is the science which explores the actions of specific drugs or poisons and I was going to study nothing but their undesired, incidental, that is, non-specific effects. But to me, "the pharmacology of dirt" seemed the most promising subject in medicine.

Yet I could not say that I never wavered; as time went by, I often doubted the wisdom of my decision. Few among the recognized, experienced investigators, whose judgment one could usually trust, agreed with my views; and, after all, was it not silly and pretentious for a beginner to contradict them? Perhaps I had just developed a warped viewpoint. Was I, perhaps, merely wasting my time?

Encouragement

In such moments of doubt I derived considerable strength and courage from the fact that, right from the beginning, one of the most respected Canadian scientists, Sir Frederick Banting, was manifestly interested in my plans. At that time, he frequently visited university laboratories throughout Canada, since he acted as an adviser to the Canadian National Research Council. When in Montreal, he often dropped quite informally into my somewhat overcrowded little laboratory. There was not much space and he usually settled down on top of the desk, listening attentively to my daydreaming about the "syndrome of being sick."

Nothing could have done me more good! He also helped to secure the first modest financial aid for this kind of research, but that was comparatively unimportant. More than anything in the world, I needed his moral support, the reassuring feeling that the discoverer of insulin took me seriously.

I often wonder whether I could have stuck to my guns without his encouragement.

Plans for future research

The next point to decide was how to go about studying *the new syndrome*. Right from the start a multitude of questions arose:

1. To what extent is this syndrome *really nonspecific?*

2. Apart from those already observed, what *other manifestations* are part of it?

3. *How does it develop in time?* Is the degree of its manifestations merely proportional to the magnitude of the damage at all times, or does the syndrome—like many infectious diseases—go through distinct stages in a certain chronological order?

4. To what extent are the manifestations of the nonspecific syndrome *influenced by the specific actions* of the agents which elicit it? All germs, poisons, and allergens have special characteristics which distinguish their effects from those of all other agents. Yet, when any substance acts upon the body, it automatically mobilizes the nonspecific mechanism also. Hence, the resulting picture would have to be a composite one, consisting of both specific and of nonspecific actions. Could these be separated?

5. What could we find out about the *mechanism,* the "dynamics" of this reaction; that is, the pathways through which the various organ-changes are produced?

These and many other questions not only presented themselves quite spontaneously, but became immediately accessible to objective scientific analysis, as soon as the concept of the "nonspecific syndrome" had crystallized. Now it was only a matter of time to find the answers to all these questions which could not even have been asked before the theory of a single "stereotyped response to damage" had taken a precise form.

What is the scope of this approach?

I thought that our first question should be, "Just how nonspecific is this syndrome?" Up to now, I had elicited it only by injecting foreign substances (tissue-extracts, Formalin). Subsequent experiments showed that one can produce essentially the same syndrome with purified hormones, for instance, with adrenaline (a hormone of the adrenal medulla), or with insulin (a hormone of the pancreas). One can also product it with physical agents, such as cold, heat, x-rays, or mechanical trauma; one can produce it with hemorrhage, pain, or forced muscular exercise; indeed, *I could find no noxious agent that did not elicit the syndrome.* The scope of this approach appeared to have no limits.

The first semantic difficulties

At this point I first became painfully aware of the purely linguistic difficulties arising out of new viewpoints in medical research. Novel concepts require new terms with which to describe them. Yet most of us dislike neologisms, perhaps because—especially in referring to clinical syndromes and signs—new names are so often proposed merely to give a semblance of a new discovery. Of course, a new designation, if badly chosen or superfluous, can confuse more than clarify. However, now I clearly needed terms for two things: first, for the nonspecific syndrome itself, and second, for that which produced it. I could not think of any good name for either.

The first publication on the stress syndrome

My first paper, in which I endeavored to show that the syndrome of stress can be studied independently of all specific changes, happened to come out on American Independence Day, July 4, in 1936. It was published as a brief note of only 74 lines in a single column of the British journal *Nature,* under the title, "A Syndrome Produced by Diverse Nocuous Agents."

Although in conversation and in lectures I had previously often used the term *biologic stress,* in referring to what caused this syndrome, by the time the first formal paper was published—yielding to violently adverse public opinion—I had temporarily given up this term. There was too much criticism of my use of the word *stress* in reference to bodily reactions, because in everyday English it generally implied nervous strain. I did not want to obscure the real issues by such squabbles over words and hoped that the word *noxious* (especially after being refined to *nocuous* by the British editor) would be considered less obnoxious than *stress.*

The three stages

In this same paper I also suggested the name *alarm reaction* for the initial response—that is, in the previously mentioned triad—because I thought that this syndrome probably represented the bodily expression of a generalized call to arms of the defensive forces in the organism.

But this alarm reaction was evidently not the whole response. My very first experiments showed that upon continued exposure to any noxious agent capable of eliciting this alarm reaction (unless it killed immediately), a stage of adaptation or resistance followed. In other words, no living organism can be maintained continuously in a state of alarm. If the body is confronted with an agent so damaging that continuous exposure to it is incompatible with life, then death ensues during the alarm reaction within the first hours or days. If survival is possible at all, this alarm reaction is necessarily followed by a second stage, which I called the *stage of resistance*.

The manifestations of this second stage were quite different from, and in many instances the exact opposite of, those which characterized the alarm reaction. For instance, during the alarm reaction, the cells of the adrenal cortex discharged their microscopically visible granules of secretion (which contain the hormone) into the blood stream. Consequently, the stores of the gland were depleted. Conversely, in the stage of resistance, the cortex accumulated an abundant reserve of secretory granules. In the alarm reaction, the blood became concentrated and there was a marked loss of body-weight; but during the stage of resistance, the blood was diluted and the body-weight returned toward normal. Many similar examples could be cited, but these suffice to illustrate the way one can objectively follow resistance-changes in various organs.

Curiously, after still more prolonged exposure to any of the noxious agents I used, this acquired adaptation was eventually lost. The animal entered into a third phase, the *stage of exhaustion*, the symptoms of which were, in many respects, strikingly similar to those of the initial alarm reaction. At the end of a life under stress, this was a kind of premature aging due to wear and tear, a sort of second childhood which, in some ways, resembled the first.

All these findings made it necessary to coin an additional all-embracing name for the entire syndrome. Since the latter appeared to be so evidently related to adaptation, I called the entire non-specific response the *general adaptation syndrome.* This is usually abbreviated as G.A.S. This whole syndrome then evolves in time through the three stages which I have just mentioned, namely: (1) the alarm reaction (A.R.), (2) the stage of resistance (S.R.), (3) the stage of exhaustion (S.E.).

I call this syndrome *general,* because it is produced only by agents which have a general effect upon large portions of the body. I call it *adaptive* because it stimulates defense and thereby helps the acquisition and maintenance of a stage of inurement. I call it a *syndrome* because its individual manifestations are coordinated and even partly dependent upon each other.

We have seen that the idea of stress goes back to the *pónos* of Greek medicine and that even certain nonspecific effects of drugs had long been known. The practical use of stress-producing measures of treatment had been repeatedly hailed as a panacea, each time only to be rejected a few years later as superstition and charlatanism. The parts of this concept were too elusive to be connected and grasped as a whole, hence it could not be analyzed and understood.

Significantly, in English, we use the word *grasp* as synonymous with *understanding,* precisely because it means "to hold or grasp a physical object with our hands." To *understand* is to "lay hold of with the mind." You can physically grasp something only if you manage to get hold of it between other things, for instance, your fingers, over which you have control.

Understanding is quite similar. It is not a totally new mental experience, essentially different from observation, any more than physical grasping is essentially different from touching. Understanding merely represents the solid fixation of a thing relative to the rest of our knowledge.

Throughout recorded medical history, parts of the stress concept have floated about aimlessly, as loose logs on the sea, periodically rising high on the crests of waves of popularity, then sinking low into the troughs of disgrace and oblivion. First we had to bind the loose logs (observed facts) together by solid cables (workable theories) and then, secure the resulting raft (G.A.S.) by mooring it to generally accepted, solid supports (classical medicine) before we could make use of the timber.

That is what I had in mind when I spoke about the essence of discovery. *To discover does not mean to see, but to uncover sufficiently that many can see and continue to see forever.*

As regards the G.A.S., the process of grasping and attaching it to the rest of our knowledge has progressed by this time in two dimensions: (1) *In space,* three fixed points have been established as being part of a coordinated syndrome: the adrenal, the thymico-lymphatic, and the intestinal changes. These have been described as a triad. (2) *In time,* it had been shown that the G.A.S. goes through three distinct changes: the alarm reaction, the stage of resistance, and the stage of exhaustion. It thus follows a predictable path of evolution.

This picture was woefully sketchy and incomplete. Much had been known before about *pónos.* Much more has been written since on the many additional changes subsequently recognized as belonging to the G.A.S. or the *stress syndrome,* as it is also called now. The only important thing about our fixed points in space and time was that they just sufficed to get a hold on stress; they were just strong enough to prevent the concept from ever slipping through our fingers again; they made it amenable to a precise scientific analysis. We could now draw a blueprint for a systematic plan of research on stress. There will be more to say about this blueprint later; but just to take an example, we could now devise experiments to see whether the effect of stress on lymphatic tissue depends upon adrenal activity. To establish this, we only had to verify whether the thymicolymphatic tissue of experimental animals shrinks during stress even after removal of the adrenals. We could not have formulated such precise questions about the mechanism of stress before our fixed points were established.

Now that we have got that far with the story of stress, it may help to enter into the spirit of this investigation, to stop for a moment to discuss problems of research in general, and the thoughts which pass through the mind of an investigator who does this kind of work in the laboratory all his life.

What do you need in order to do research?

A purely technical description of a discovery is based on measurable intellectual values alone; yet in actual life science is far from being purely a product of conscious thought. Indeed, I think that as a rule the greater a scientific creation, the more it is conceived by instinct and emotions. To make a great dream come true, the first requirement is a great capacity to dream; the second is persistence— a faith in the dream. The much glorified quality of intelligence is so much more common, among people likely to pursue scientific dreams, that it rarely represents the major bottleneck in making discoveries.

Pure intellect is largely a quality of the middle-class mind. The lowliest hooligan and the greatest creator in any field of human endeavor are motivated mainly by imponderable instincts and emotions, especially faith. Curiously, even scientific research—the most intellectual creative effort of which man is capable—represents no exception in this respect. That is why the objective, detached form of an original scientific publication or of a textbook falls so ludicrously short of really conveying the spirit of an investigation.

When one starts out in a research career, it is somewhat discouraging to think that, because through so many centuries so many outstanding minds have explored the salient problems of medicine, presumably most of the important things have already been discovered.

In talking to my students I hear this view expressed again and again. Many beginners are also convinced that to make really interesting discoveries today one would need: large sums of money, modern laboratories equipped with all kinds of complicated, expensive machinery, and preferably a large staff of highly-trained assistants. Some students are often discouraged by the thought that the times have gone when it was possible to make an immortal medical discovery by merely looking at a hitherto unexplored part of the human body.

Take the adrenals, which play such a prominent role in my story: the most important fact about them is that they exist. Without knowing this, we could have discovered nothing else about them. Well, this basic fact was revealed in 1563 by Bartolommeo Eustacchio, physician to Cardinal della Rovere. Because of his connections in high places, Eustacchio managed to get permission to perform dissections in Rome. After that it was easy: merely by prodding about in the fat around the upper pole of the kidneys, he could not help it—he *had* to discover the adrenals. There was nothing to it.

I think it is very wrong to look at things this way. First, it must have taken insatiable scientific curiosity to overcome the prejudices of the sixteenth century sufficiently to ask for and use permission for the dissection of a human body. Second, it required great perspicacity to recognize that the inconspicuous little piece of whitish tissue, embedded in fat of almost the same color, is a separate organ, worthy of being described. We must always measure the importance of a discovery against the background of the times in which it was made; and I should think that each period offers just about the same proportion of facilities and handicaps for scientific investigation. We should not envy the ancient anatomists for having been able to make a great discovery with simple means, any more than we should complain that our research tools are undoubtedly very primitive in comparison with those to be used by the investigators of coming centuries.

Only the future will tell us just how much the G.A.S. concept will promote the understanding of disease and the relief of human suffering. But if in these respects it should prove of some value, let us point out, for the encouragement of beginners, that it was found without any of the luxuries of modern laboratories, and even without the wisdom and experience necessary to use such facilities.

Fortunately, it is not so much the existence of things that we *do not know*, or about which we are too uncertain, that handicaps our research, but the existence of things we *do know* and about whose interpretation we are quite certain—although they may turn out to be false. Lack of equipment, or even lack of knowledge, is much less of a handicap in original research than an overabundance of useless materials or useless (and sometimes false) information which clutters up our laboratories and our brains.

You will recall that the indices of stress upon which the concept of the G.A.S. was based were: adrenocortical enlargement, thymicolymphatic involution, and intestinal ulcers. Then came the realization that this syndrome is triphasic, with the initial appearance of marked acute manifestations (alarm reaction), their subsequent disappearance (stage of resistance) and finally, a breakdown in the organism, with complete loss of resistance (stage of exhaustion). These were the facts upon which the first note on "A Syndrome Produced by Diverse Nocuous Agents" was based. All this is easy to see. Actually, a pair of scissors with which to open my rats was the only instrument I had used up to that time, and the production of stress by toxic substances certainly necessitated no complicated apparatus either.

When the problem arose as to whether or not stress could be produced without injecting anything, I wanted to expose animals to cold. We had no suitable ventilated cold-room. But let me assure you that here, in Canada, this presented no problem during the major part of the year, especially in the McGill Medical Building, with its conveniently wind-swept flat roof.

It is true I did use a syringe for the injection of Formalin, and even then I did have a "staff" in the person of Mr. Kai Nielsen who, at the time, was an untrained laboratory assistant. He helped me by holding the rats steady for injection, but mainly by steadying me during those busy days, through the stabilizing effect of his always friendly, even-minded Scandinavian personality.*

As the years went by, I managed to acquire every available facility that modern science can offer in the way of the most up-to-date techniques of histology, chemistry, and pharmacology. I have been given the means to construct one of the best equipped institutes of experimental medicine and surgery in the world and have acquired a staff of 53 trained assistants, technicians, and secretaries. Yet today, as I look back upon the twenty years that have elapsed

---

* Incidentally, I am glad to report that Mr. Nielsen is still with me today. He has learned a great many complex laboratory techniques and he is now in charge of an entire team of technicians. Yet, in retrospect, when everything is said and done, I feel that, in 1936, when we were both young, as well as in 1956, when we are a little less so, his undoubtedly enormous contribution to the study of stress was very simple. He always was, and still is, an utterly reliable, straightforward person and a warmhearted friend, upon whose levelheaded judgment one can count to keep things straight around the lab. Let me assure you that in the actual practice of research these solid characteristics of an associate can be much more useful than the most highly trained staff of assistants, just as simple thoughts connecting simple observations often help you to come much closer to the real understanding of nature than if you put complexities in the way of an intimate contact with her.

since those early observations in 1936, I am ashamed to say that, despite all this help, I have never again been able to add anything comparable in its significance to those first primitive experiments.

I think any young man at the beginning of his career—whether he wants to become a scientist, an artist, a businessman, or an engineer —should keep in mind that he needs but his eyes to see a whole forest. It is only for the detection of some minute detail in a single cell of one tree within this forest that he requires a microscope.

My advice to any young man at the beginning of his career is to try to look for the mere outlines of big things with his fresh, untrained, and unprejudiced mind. When he is older he may no longer be able "to see the forest for the trees." But cheer up, by that time he will have the money to buy fancy tools and to hire assistants who will exploit the details for him.

There are two ways of detecting something that nobody can see: one is to aim at the finest detail by getting as close as possible with the best available analyzing instruments; the other is merely to look at things from a new angle where they show hitherto unexposed facets. The former requires money and experience; the latter presupposes neither; indeed, it is actually aided by simplicity, the lack of prejudice, and the absence of those established habits of thinking which tend to come after long years of work.

You may feel that all this has nothing to do with the G.A.S. which I am supposed to describe. Don't you believe it! On the contrary, to me, these were the thoughts that really counted; that is why I want to share them with you. Remember that the G.A.S. could have been discovered during the Middle Ages, if not earlier; its recognition did not depend upon the development of any complicated pieces of apparatus, new techniques of observation, nor even upon much training, ingenuity, or intelligence, as far as that goes, but merely upon an unbiased state of mind, a fresh point of view.

Now, let us get on with the story of stress.

More semantic difficulties

As time went by, little by little, the main features of the G.A.S. had been recognized and named, but we still had no precise idea of what produced it, and even less a suitable name to describe its cause. In my first writings I spoke of *nocuous agents,* but this term was evidently inadequate. Even such innocuous physiologic experiences as a brief period of muscular work, excitement, or a short exposure to cold proved sufficient to produce certain manifestations of an alarm reaction, for instance, an adrenocortical reaction. Obviously, these could not be described as strictly nocuous agents; we needed a more fitting name.

In search of one, I again stumbled upon the term *stress*, which had long been used in common English, and particularly in engineering, to denote forces which act against a resistance. For example, the changes induced in a rubber band during traction, or in a steel spring during pressure, are due to stress. Physical stress is certainly nonspecific. In a sense, the nonspecific manifestations of the G.A.S. could be viewed as the biologic equivalents of what had been called the results of stress in inanimate matter. Perhaps one could speak of *biologic stress*.

Another advantage of this term was that, although its meaning had never been defined before, it was not strictly a neologism, even in medicine. For instance, the expressions *nervous stress* and *strain* had often been used by psychiatrists to describe mental tension. Walter B. Cannon, the eminent physiologist who introduced the term *homeostasis*, also spoke in general terms of the stress and strains caused when disease puts pressure on certain specific mechanisms necessary for homeostasis, that is, the maintenance of a normal, steady state in the body.

Although the term had not been previously used for any nonspecific reactions, and of course, even less for a coordinated syndrome, I saw no reason why it should not be employed in this new sense. So, during the subsequent years—despite much initial opposition—that is what I did in all my scientific papers and books.

The layman may think it ridiculous to speak so much about a name. After all, as Shakespeare said, "What's in a name? That which we call a rose/By any other name would smell as sweet." In science names have a much more profound significance, especially when they apply to novel concepts. You can discuss a rose by any name because everybody knows exactly what is meant by a rose, but you cannot discuss, and far less define, a new scientific concept without first identifying it in some way by a name. I have tried to convey the importance of this by speaking about the naming of stress before attempting to define the concept of stress in precise scientific language. That is the order in which events actually develop in science.

One of the greatest objections against my use of the term *stress* was that it might lead to confusion with other possible meanings of the word. For instance, some scientists were afraid that stress, in my sense, might be identified with the specific stresses and strains upon individual homeostatic mechanisms, the "built-in homeostats" (Norbert Wiener), or automatic regulators of certain actions. But Cannon had clearly shown, for example, that the specific stabilizing or *homeostatic reaction* to lack of oxygen is quite different from that with which the body meets exposure to cold; this, in turn, is virtually the reverse of that required to resist heat. These and many other highly specialized adjustments (for example, specific serologic re-actions against certain microbes, the strengthening of individual muscle-groups in response to frequent use) represent precisely *that part of the over-all response to an agent which we have to subtract in order to arrive at our stress syndrome.* The features of the G.A.S. (for instance, the increased production of adrenocortical hormones, the involution of the lymphatic organs, or the loss of weight) are the purely nonspecific residue that remains after this subtraction. Besides, Cannon never proposed the term *stress* as a scientific name for anything in particular; it does not even appear in the subject index of his book and, as far as I know, he used it only figuratively in one semipopular lecture.

Anyway, in practice, the possible other meanings of the word have not led to much confusion. If I had coined a totally new name by just putting letters together at random, its meaning would have been difficult to remember; it seemed preferable to use an existent term in a newly defined connotation. After all, the words *general, adaptation, syndrome, alarm, reaction, stage, resistance,* and *ex-haustion* were not new either. They had all been used before in connection with topics other than the general adaptation syndrome and its three stages. Yet this likewise caused no real difficulties of understanding. Of course, actually, none of these terms was imme-diately well received either, but since they have now become part of the medical vocabulary in every language, we hardly need to go into long semantic discussions in their defense.

Dislike of a word may merely stem from inability to grasp the idea behind it

It is of considerable interest to analyze the reasons for the particularly great resistance against my use of the word *stress*. This aversion is an integral part of the story of stress, because here, rejection of the name was largely dependent upon a failure to grasp the new concept. Again and again, in the discussion periods that followed my lectures before scientific societies, someone would get up and ask why I had to speak of stress, when I actually used Formalin, cold, or x-rays. Would it not be more straightforward to say that the adrenals were stimulated by cold, when it was cold that my experimental animal was exposed to?

I tried to point out that it could not be cold itself that was necessary for adrenal stimulation, since heat or any number of other agents produced the same effect. By way of a comparison, I mentioned that a pharmacologist examining the effects of ether should not look upon adrenocortical enlargement or thymus involution as being the effects of ether in the same sense as anesthesia is. Indeed, I emphasized that now, in my opinion, one would have to reexamine the whole of pharmacology to distinguish the changes due to stress from those caused by specific drug actions.

This same kind of objection was formulated by others in a more articulate manner, by pointing out that, actually, *stress is an abstraction* and does not occur as such in the pure state. In other words, it is just a purely hypothetical thing, which possesses no real independent existence. Hence, my opponents said, it is impossible to isolate stress for the objective, direct, scientific observation and measurement of its own effects, which would be indispensable for any scientific treatment of this problem. You cannot study stress; you can merely explore real and tangible things such as the effects of exposure to cold, injections of Formalin, infections, and so forth. For these reasons, I was told, even if we admitted the existence of stress, it would not lend itself to scientific study.

Of course, the concept of stress *is* an abstraction; but so is the idea of life, which could hardly be rejected as a worthless concept in biology. No one has studied life in a pure, uncontaminated form. It is always inseparably attached to something else which is more tangible and seemingly more real, such as the body of a cat, a dog, or a man; still, the whole science of physiology is built upon this abstraction.

To study the laws of gravity, you must learn to separate the concept of weight from other characteristics of objects, even if weight, as such, does not exist. A beautiful girl and a piece of stone, both weighing 120 pounds, are identical as regards weight, though, in some other respects, the girl may be quite unlike the stone.

Yet, during the first few years, such arguments convinced but very few people. It was only gradually, through habit rather than logic, that the term *stress,* employed in my sense, slipped into common usage, as the concept itself became a popular subject for research.

Still more semantic difficulties!

Even after that, when people began to speak of stress in my sense of the word I was again exposed to severe criticism because of a new terminologic difficulty. It was pointed out that the word *stress* is indiscriminately applied both to the agent which produces the G.A.S. and to the condition of the organism exposed to it. Actually, some people do speak of having applied cold-stress, heat-stress, and— oh, horrors!—even infectious-stress, when referring to cold, heat, or infection employed to produce stress; but they also use the same expressions for the state of stress caused in the body by these agents.

This was a justified criticism and I therefore proposed to substitute the word *stressor* for the agent and retain *stress* for the condition.

A little later, yet another unforeseen complication arose, namely, that the word *stress* cannot be translated accurately into foreign languages. Of course, as always, the Greeks had a word for it, *pónos,* but apparently no modern language has an expression like *stress,* a term which would have suggested the new meaning. I became acutely aware of this in 1946, when the Collège de France honored me by an invitation to give a series of lectures on the G.A.S. in Paris.

Now, I was to speak in this famous research institution where, a hundred years earlier, the great Claude Bernard himself delivered his classical lectures on the importance of maintaining the constancy of the *milieu intérieur* (internal environment). As I was to teach there as a representative of a French-Canadian university, I took great pains to deliver my lectures in good French. This was all the more important, since it is the charming tradition of this venerable institution of learning to honor visiting foreign lecturers—at least on the occasion of their inaugural address—by the presence of all the professors of the Collège de France, irrespective of their personal fields of interest. This meant that, right in the first row, in front of me, sat several of the most illustrious literary men of France. You may well imagine that my linguistic responsibilities weighed heavily upon my shoulders! Yet, I had to use at least one anglicism, the word *stress,* because I could not think of a proper French substitute for it.

After my lecture, there ensued a rather spirited debate about the correct translation of *stress* among these distinguished custodians who watch over the purity of the French language. I feel quite incompetent to give you an adequate account of their scholarly discussions, but you may be interested to learn the result.

The term "stress" emerges victorious

Having eliminated as unsuitable, one by one, such terms as *dommage, agression, tension, détresse,* the unanimous conclusion was that since there was no exact equivalent, one must necessarily be coined. Upon weighing the matter carefully, it was decided first that the gender of stress would have to be masculine. Then it was agreed that the best French term for it would be:

le stress.

Thus a new French word was born, and this experience did much to encourage me during subsequent lectures in Germany, Italy, Spain, and Portugal, to speak without the slightest hesitation of *der Stress, lo stress, el stress,* and *o stress.* This gave me the satisfaction of knowing that even if my scientific accomplishments should prove to be of little value, mine will be forever the glory of having enriched all these languages by at least one word.

The word stress, in this sense, designates the sum of all the nonspecific effects of factors (normal activity, disease-producers, drugs, etc.), which can act upon the body. These agents themselves are called *stressors,* when we refer to their ability to produce stress.

If we are to use this concept in a strictly scientific manner, it is especially important to keep in mind that stress is an abstraction; it has no independent existence. But as we saw, this is true also of many among our most useful other scientific concepts, such as life or weight.

We cannot cause stress without also producing some specific actions characteristic more particularly of the agent which we employ. What we actually see when something acts upon the living body is a combination of stress and the specific actions of the agent.

This again is true also of life. Life likewise has no independent existence; it, also, can be studied only as it manifests itself when attached to the body of something living.

We saw that this is also true of weight. Nothing but an object can have weight, and no object has only weight. The fact that objects of equal weight may be dissimilar in every other respect does not prevent us from studying the laws of gravity, quite apart from the factors which determine the color, the size, or the chemical constitution of objects. In fact, it is only our ability to make such abstractions that permits us to develop the science of biology or physics.

These considerations were important in preparing the basis for the science of stress. Sketching a blueprint to investigate the mechanics of the stress syndrome was our next objective.

Book II:

The dissection of stress

Summary

For scientific purposes, *stress is defined as the state which manifests itself by the G.A.S.* The latter comprises: adrenal stimulation, shrinkage of lymphatic organs, gastrointestinal ulcers, loss of body-weight, alterations in the chemical composition of the body, and so forth. All these changes form a syndrome, a set of manifestations which appear together.

In tissues more directly affected by stress, there develops a *local adaptation syndrome* (L.A.S.); for instance, there is inflammation where microbes enter the body.

L.A.S. and G.A.S. are closely coordinated. Chemical *alarm signals* are sent out by directly stressed tissues, from the L.A.S. area to the centers of coordination in the *nervous system* and to endocrine glands, especially the *pituitary* and the *adrenals*, which produce *adaptive hormones*, to combat wear and tear in the body. Thus the generalized response (G.A.S.) acts back upon the L.A.S. region.

Roughly speaking, the adaptive hormones fall into two groups: the *anti-inflammatory hormones* (ACTH, cortisone, COL), which inhibit excessive defensive reactions, and the *proinflammatory hormones* (STH, aldosterone, DOC), which stimulate them. The effects of all these substances can be modified, or conditioned, by other hormones (adrenalines, or the thyroid hormone), nervous reactions, diet, heredity, and the tissue-memories of previous exposures to stress. Derailments of this G.A.S.-mechanism produce wear-and-tear-diseases, that is, *diseases* of *adaptation*.

In a nutshell, the response to stress has a tripartite mechanism, consisting of: (1) the direct effect of the stressor upon the body; (2) internal responses which stimulate tissue-defense; and (3) internal responses which stimulate tissue-surrender by inhibiting defense. *Resistance and adaptation depend on a proper balance of these three factors.*

This section is intended only for those who are seriously interested in the nature of normal and morbid life. Like Book IV, it is somewhat heavy, but those who would rather skip the details can do so by carefully reading this summary, which will provide the necessary continuity.

5:

Why did we need a

blueprint for the

dissection?

To understand a complex thing
you must take it apart
systematically.   The power of an
abstraction.

To understand a complex thing you must take it apart systematically

To understand the nature of disease is the fundamental object of medicine, for knowledge about a thing is the best way to acquire power over it. Of course, the limited capacities and the unlimited curiosity of the human brain will never permit man to solve this, or any other fundamental question, completely. Yet, if it comes to a subject of such immense importance to mankind, even a few steps toward understanding are very rewarding. Could the stress concept help us to make some progress in this direction? We have learned that stress is an inherent element of all disease. If we manage to understand more precisely what stress really is and through what mechanisms it acts, we may perhaps bring some order into our thoughts about the nature of disease.

Advancement along these lines would not necessarily have to stop at the passive satisfaction derived from understanding; it would probably also yield new means through which we could actively influence disease. The more we understand the workings of inanimate machines—say, an automobile or a typewriter—the better we can use them and repair their flaws when they break down. All this is equally true of living machines, such as our own bodies.

To understand a complex engine you have to take it apart. To understand a human body you have to dissect it. But how does one dissect an abstract concept such as stress? What is the stuff a concept is made of? Its parts are imponderable ties which have no substance of their own; yet we cannot do without them if we are to handle effectively, as one coordinated thing, a mass of ponderable and substantial but disconnected facts.

The power of an abstraction

To appreciate the power of abstraction, let us take an example from another field. Think of the units of a navy—submarines, battleships, aircraft carriers—which, though very different in appearance and geographic position, are nevertheless held together for effective use as one coordinated thing. What makes this possible is one abstraction: the imponderable concept of their nationality. This concept would be difficult to measure; it has no physical reality and yet it is much stronger than the most mighty of the battleships. It dominates the whole navy. Concepts always work through abstractions, for it is only by abstracting from the distinct, individual features of each factual object that we can arrive at some common hold on many of them, through which they can all be coordinated from a single point.

Could the abstraction of stress furnish us with such a common hold by which to grasp all the individual manifestations of the G.A.S. and thus coordinate them for the understanding of the very nature of disease?

To begin with, we must clearly realize that stress is a condition, a state, and, although as such it is imponderable, that it manifests itself by measurable changes in the organs of the body. By using these alterations as indicators of stress, we should be able to come closer to an understanding of stress itself. For instance, we could examine whether the various organ-changes seen in patients during the G.A.S. are closely interdependent, whether removing one or the other organ in experimental animals will block all or part of the stress-reaction, whether treatment with certain drugs can increase or decrease resistance to stress, and so forth.

To assess the possibilities offered by such studies, let us see now what the elements of stress are and what procedures we could use for their analysis. In other words, let us make a complete inventory of every tool at our disposal for the dissection of stress. In essence, our assets are: facts, abstractions, materials, and techniques.

6:

Inventory of assets:

(A) The facts

Earlier observations.

Earlier observations

In discussing the historic evolution of the stress concept, we have mentioned some of the most striking organ-changes which occur during stress. These could be accurately determined, and they acted as solid landmarks in the dissection of the stress-mechanism. It may be well to recapitulate them here. First, there was the alarm-reaction triad. The *adrenocortical enlargement* and the *atrophy of the thymicolymphatic organs* could be objectively measured in terms of the weights of these organs. The *gastrointestinal ulcers* were less easy to appraise accurately, but at least we could see whether they were severe, mild, or absent.

Later, during the course of 1937, many other such nonspecific changes were recognized. Among these the most important ones were the *loss of body-weight,* the *disappearance of eosinophil cells* from the circulating blood and a number of *chemical alterations* in the constitution of the body fluids and tissues.

It was not clear just what part, if any, all these changes might play in the body's *resistance to stress,* but that was precisely what we wanted to find out. Experimental animals and even human beings can die from stress, and much could be gained for practical medicine if we succeeded in determining just what kind of change is necessary to raise stress-resistance. Of course, resistance itself could also be used as an objective indicator of stress. We could measure the survival rate of experimental animals under different conditions.

Finally, perhaps one of the most important indicators of stress proved to be its effect upon *inflammation*. Normally, stress applied to a limited part of the body causes inflammation, but the ability of parts to respond in this way is impaired when the whole body is under stress. In other words, experiments showed that animals exposed to some general stressor (such as a blood-borne infection, intense nervous excitement, or extreme muscular fatigue) failed to react with inflammation at sites where some local stressor (for instance, a substance to which they were allergic) was directly applied to their body. Inflammation is also a tangible fact which can be measured, for example, in terms of the degree of swelling, reddening, or the histologic changes which characterize this local response to injury. Do the general stressors act directly upon all cells to prevent inflammation, or through the intermediary of some hormone produced by a gland, perhaps by the enlarged adrenal?

In another dimension, in time, the *triphasic evolution* of the stress-response can be used as a measurable fact. All the changes just enumerated varied during the three phases of the G.A.S. in a characteristic and predictable manner. This variation of response during exposure to an unvarying stressor made it possible to use the measurable indicators of stress (histologic or chemical changes) for the appraisal of the evolution of the G.A.S. in time.

It is rather significant that this chapter is so short. Its brevity indicates that, at the beginning of this study in 1937, our inventory of assets was particularly short on facts. But the important thing is that all these *changes are measurable* manifestations of stress, and, therefore, suitable indicators of how the various parts of the stress-machine work.

None of these facts had any great inherent value in itself. What turned them into effective tools for the dissection of stress were certain abstractions which gave them a more general meaning. Almost every one of the changes characteristic of stress had been known long before as isolated facts, but in the absence of any unifying concept they could not be interpreted or used for the study of the nature of disease. We must therefore give special attention now to a careful definition of the abstractions which served to turn these observed facts into analytical tools.

7:

Inventory of assets:

(B) The abstractions

What is a definition? Definition of stress. Definition of the stressor. Definition of the G.A.S. Relationship between the G.A.S. and the L.A.S.—The concept of adaptation energy. Relationship between adaptation energy and aging. Definition of the diseases of adaptation.

What is a definition?

Now the time has come when we cannot postpone any longer some attempt to define the abstract concepts with which we are constantly dealing here. In the preceding pages I have spoken of stress, stressors, nonspecificity, the G.A.S., and so forth, but I did not try to define them. All these abstractions gradually acquired some sort of meaning, more or less spontaneously, through the discussion of observations which made it necessary to give them names. It may seem odd to name a thing before we can clearly define it, but this is the way such concepts usually begin to take shape in the mind.

What is a definition and what can we expect from it? It is generally agreed that a definition should be a concise explanation of the meaning of a word. According to Aristotle, it is the statement of the essence of a concept. In textbooks the definition comes first and leads you to the concept; the reverse is true in actual life. Be it ever so vague, you must first have a concept—derived from observation and symbolized by a name—before you can even try to delimit it more precisely by a definition.

If we want to present the story of stress as it actually developed, we have to proceed the same way, from observation to concept, and hence to definition. But it must be realized that, in any event, definitions applied to biologic concepts are never quite satisfactory. In the final analysis, most abstractions of biology—as that of life itself—are embraced by experience rather than by rational delimitation. We all know much better what life is than we know how to define it.

In some disciplines (for instance, in jurisprudence and in mathematics), definitions are rigid laws which make a concept what it is; in biology, definitions can only serve as concise descriptions of the way we perceive phenomena. And we must keep in mind that at any time our concepts may be modified by further observations. It is in this spirit that the following definitions are presented.

Definition of stress

The term *stress* has been used so loosely, and so many confusing definitions of it have been formulated, that I think it will be most instructive to start out by stating clearly what it is *not*. Contrary to some current but vague or misleading statements:

1. Stress is not nervous tension. Stress-reactions do occur in lower animals which have no nervous system. An alarm reaction can be induced by mechanically damaging a denervated limb. Indeed, stress can be produced in cell cultures grown outside of the body.

2. Stress is not an emergency discharge of hormones from the adrenal medulla. An adrenaline-discharge is frequently seen in acute stress affecting the whole body, but it plays no conspicuous role in generalized inflammatory diseases (arthritis, tuberculosis), although they can also produce considerable stress; nor does it play any role in local stress-reactions limited to directly injured territories of the body.

3. Stress is not anything that causes a secretion, by the adrenal cortex, of its hormones, the corticoids. ACTH, the adrenal-stimulating pituitary hormone, can discharge corticoids without producing any evidence of stress.

4. Stress is not the nonspecific result of damage. Normal activities —a game of tennis or even a passionate kiss—can produce considerable stress without causing conspicuous damage.

5. Stress is not any deviation from homeostasis, the steady state of the body. Any biologic function (the perception of sound or light, the contraction of a muscle) causes marked deviations from the normal resting state in the active organs.

6. Stress is not anything that causes an alarm reaction. It is the stressor that does that, not stress itself.

7. Stress is not identical with the alarm reaction or the G.A.S. as a whole. These reactions are characterized by certain measurable organ-changes which are caused by stress and hence could not themselves *be* stress.

8. Stress is not a nonspecific reaction. The pattern of the stress-reaction is very specific. It affects certain organs (for instance, the adrenal, the thymus, the gastrointestinal tract) in a highly selective manner.

9. Stress is not a specific reaction. The stress-response is, by definition, not specific, since it can be produced by virtually any agent.

If we consider these points, we may easily be led to conclude that all this is so confusing and vague that stress cannot be defined. Perhaps the concept itself is just not sufficiently clear to serve as the object of scientific analysis.

But what is vague? The abortive attempts at a definition are, but surely not stress itself. It has a very clear, tangible form. Countless people have actually suffered or benefited from it. Stress is very real and concrete indeed. I think it would be correct to say that *stress is the common denominator of all adaptive reactions in the body*. This is simple and true, but perhaps still too vague.

Let us see now whether the following, more precise, definition will fit all our facts:

STRESS IS THE STATE MANIFESTED BY A SPECIFIC SYNDROME WHICH CONSISTS OF ALL THE NONSPECIFICALLY INDUCED CHANGES WITHIN A BIOLOGIC SYSTEM. Thus stress has its own characteristic form and composition but no particular cause. The elements of its form are the visible changes due to stress, whatever its cause. They are additive indicators which can express the sum of all the different adjustments that are going on in the body at any time.

This is essentially an "operational definition"; it tells what must be done to produce and recognize stress. A state can be recognized only by its manifestations; for instance, the state of stress by the manifestations of the stress syndrome. Therefore, you have to observe a great many living beings exposed to a variety of agents before you can see the shape and stress as such. Those changes which are specifically induced by only one or the other agent must first be rejected; if you then take what is left—that which is nonspecifically induced by many agents—you have unveiled the picture of stress itself. This picture is the G.A.S. Once this is established, you can recognize stress no matter where it turns up; indeed, you can even measure it by the intensity of the G.A.S.-manifestations which it produces.*

It seems to me that this formulation was the password which opened the door to a whole new concept of medicine. Rarely, if ever, has it been possible to say this about a single sentence with more justification. It is true that some physicians who have contributed much to our understanding of stress have used this definition, only subconsciously, and without ever clearly formulating it. Yet, at the root of all research on stress, if you look for it, you find this definition. It gives unity and significance to the many individual observations on the G.A.S., the adaptive hormones, and the diseases of adaptation, which would otherwise remain isolated facts. In any case, the definition of stress is the pivot around which every part of this volume turns. We shall have to analyze our definition carefully now in order to grasp its full meaning.

Stress is a STATE MANIFESTED BY A SYNDROME. We would have no way of appraising the state of stress were it not for the changes it produces. We can say of a man, "He is under stress," but we shall have arrived at this conclusion only by the visible manifestations of his being under stress. The distinction between a state and the changes which characterize this condition is just as important in biology as it is in physics. A rubber band can be in a state of tension, but this is recognizable only by physical changes in the rubber. The condition of biologic stress is essentially an adjustment, through the development of an antagonism between an aggressor and the re-

---

* At first I was tempted to define stress as *the rate of wear and tear* within the body at any one time, because this is the immediate nonspecific result of function and damage. Reactions which tend to repair wear and tear (e.g., corticoid-secretion) are not strictly stress, but rather responses to stress. However, in practice, it is rarely (if ever) possible to distinguish clearly between damage and repair. Hence, this formulation—though theoretically more satisfying—could not have acted as a basis for a truly "operational definition" which we needed to give the concept of stress a solid objective foundation.

sistance offered to it by the body. This quality of tension is probably responsible for the common, but very misleading, error of considering *biologic stress* as equivalent to *nervous tension.*

Stress shows itself as a SPECIFIC syndrome, yet it is NONSPE-CIFICALLY INDUCED. Until quite recently in my technical papers I have often referred to stress as "the sum of all nonspecific changes caused by function or damage." Because of its simplicity this definition became popular, but it led to much confusion. Perhaps its greatest weakness was its failure to point out that the pattern of the stress-reaction (for instance, the mosaic of changes in the adrenals, thymus, and gastrointestinal tract) is highly specific; only its causation is nonspecific. We must clearly distinguish between specificity in the form and in the causation of a change.

A *nonspecifically formed change* is one that affects all, or most, parts of a system without selectivity. It is the opposite of a *specifically formed change* that affects only one, or at most, few units within a system.

A *nonspecifically caused change* is one that can be produced by many or all agents. It is the opposite of a *specifically caused change* that can be produced by only one, or at most, by few agents.

It is particularly important to keep in mind that *specificity is always a matter of degree.* Both among changes and among causes, there are fluent transitions between the least and the most specific. Failure to appreciate this is one of the greatest hurdles in the understanding of the stress concept, not only for laymen but even for physicians. The following simple mechanical analogy explains this point:

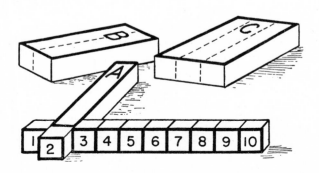

Here we have a row of ten cubes. Let the whole row represent the human body and each of the cubes one of its organs. We also have three blocks which correspond in breadth to one (A), two (B), and three (C) cubes. By pushing with block A, as indicated in the drawing, I can displace a single cube without deranging the others; this is a highly specific action. With block B I could never displace less than two, and with block C less than three cubes at a time. Any intermediate type could be constructed between the block which displaces only a single cube and one which displaces them all. We would need a block ten-cubes wide to produce a wholly nonspecific displacement of all cubes, and even this would be a totally nonspecific change only in this system. In a row of a thousand cubes the displacement of ten would be a comparatively specific change.

As regards the degree of their specificity or nonspecificity, we find the same scale among the various agents (drugs, nervous stimuli, bacteria), which can act upon the human body.

You may feel that if specificity and nonspecificity are such fluid concepts, they could not be of much value in objective scientific research in which all values must be measurable and concrete. This is far from true. The concept of "green" is a very useful one and yet, in a perfect rainbow of colors, no one could say exactly where green starts and where it ends.

Even the most fundamental of all biologic concepts, that of life itself, is relative. As I sit here dictating, I feel very much alive indeed, and yet there are parts of my body which have already died. My hair and my nails definitely belong to my person, but their cells are no longer alive in the usual sense of that word. It would be difficult to prove that the water in my blood is alive. I am sure that my tonsils, which were removed when I was four years old, are dead. Yet all these elements are or were parts of me.

You may argue that I chose poor examples, because the individual as a whole remains alive even if parts of him die. Perhaps we should speak of life and death only with respect to whole individuals; but where are we to draw the line between the parts and the whole? You may take a few cells from my body and make them grow on a nourishing broth in an incubator for many years; in these cells life can continue after I have long been buried. Even without such artificial experiments, through our germ cells we live on indefinitely in our offspring.

So, even life itself is a relative concept.

We have explained that specificity of causation and specificity of form are two essentially different things. Yet, in practice, the two tend to run parallel. Nonspecifically formed effects in large portions of the body are quite common; but highly selective effects upon circumscribed parts of the body are produced by comparatively few agents. For instance, wastage of body tissues is induced by starvation, infectious diseases, emotional upsets, cancer, and by many other conditions, but a truly selective and intense stimulation of the adrenal cortex can be produced only by one hormone: ACTH.

In this respect the stress-response differs from most other biologic reactions, because it is nonspecifically produced and yet, its form is quite specific. There must be some final common pathway through which the same organs can be reached from many directions. To understand this peculiar situation, keep in mind that stress causes two types of change: *a primary change,* which is nonspecific both in its form and in its causation (it can be induced anywhere and by any kind of damage or function), and *a secondary change,* which has the specific pattern of the G.A.S. The first acts as a common signal which can elicit the second from any part of the body.

Let us illustrate the principle of this by an example. Suppose that all possible accesses to a bank building are connected with a police station by an elaborate burglar-alarm system. When a burglar enters the bank, no matter what his personal characteristics are—whether he is small or tall, lean or stout—and no matter which door or window he opens to enter, he will set off the same alarm. This primary change is therefore nonspecifically induced from anywhere by anyone. The pattern of the resulting secondary change, on the other hand, is highly specific. It is always in a certain police station that the burglar alarm will ring, and policemen will then rush to the bank along a specified route according to a predetermined plan to prevent robbery.

It is somewhat difficult, however, even in such a simple siutation, to distinguish clearly between offense and defense, or between primary and secondary change. When the burglar opens the window to enter, this is aggression, but it is also the trigger to set off the alarm which is part of the predetermined defense-pattern. In a complex biologic system such as the human body, it is even more difficult to distinguish clearly between primary change, or damage, and secondary change, or defense. We recognize this difference in principle, but it is often impossible to do so in practice. Hence, it is best to consider the sum of all the changes caused by stress as one syndrome to which the secondary defensive reactions impart a specific pattern or form.

To make our analogy still more applicable to conditions of stress as they exist in the human body, we must now also bring a quantitative aspect into the alarm system. The alarm-response of the body is definitely proportionate to the intensity of the aggression. That is not so with the usual burglar alarms; but, for example, a first fire alarm will bring only a limited number of men and equipment to the scene of conflagration, in comparison with a second or third alarm from the same vicinity. The defensive response is quantitatively adjusted to the number of the alarm signals.

What is here the specific and what the nonspecific part of the alarm-response? In the figure on p. 60, four squares represent boxes from which fire alarms can be set off in four adjacent buildings.

All these trigger mechanisms—like the organs of the human body —are different, as indicated by the different patterns: dots, triangles, rods, and rings. The alarm may be set off by the breaking of a glass in a firebox, the activity of a thermoelectric cell, or any other device. But eventually all these mechanisms act nonspecifically through the same type of electric fire alarm which activates the same bell in the same fire station. No matter where and how the alarm is set off, the result must always be the same. Yet, despite this nonspecificity of causation, the pattern of the resulting defensive response is again highly specific and stereotyped. The bell sends men and equipment to the fire in accordance with a typical standard plan.

In our drawing, the stereotyped, that is, nonspecific trigger mechanism, was set off in the third box through its own particular activation-process indicated by a discharge of the rods; this secondarily mobilized a specific pattern of defense. However, if, simultaneously, fire alarms would also go off at all three other stations, a larger number of firemen and equipment would be sent out. Here we have a definite proportionality between the extent of the damage and the response. The analogy also shows clearly how different interventions (activation of distinct trigger mechanisms at different points) can nonspecifically (always through the same signal) cause a specific pattern of response. It is only the nonspecific part (the signals) that can be summated to bring about a response proportionate to the injury.

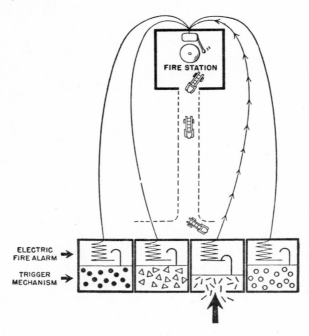

Essentially the same situation exists in the body when the specific pattern of the stress syndrome is induced by the *sum of nonspecific signals* coming from various tissues.

The stress syndrome consists of ALL the nonspecifically induced CHANGES. Why do we have to specify *all* changes? By this we mean that whenever an agent acts upon the body and produces several nonspecifically induced effects, no one of them in itself—but the totality of the changes—is the stress syndrome.

In the triad of the alarm reaction any one change, for instance, the adrenal-stimulation, is not indicative of nonspecific stress. This single change can also be reproduced by a highly specific hormone, ACTH (about which we shall say more later). When thus selectively produced, adrenal-stimulation is a specific action. Only when it is induced by some stressor as an integral part of the triad—that is, simultaneously with thymicolymphatic atrophy and gastrointestinal ulcers—is it a component of the nonspecific stress syndrome.

The general stress syndrome affects the whole body; a local stress syndrome influences several units within a part; but stress always manifests itself by a syndrome, a sum of changes, not by one change. An isolated effect upon any one unit in the body is either damage or stimulation to activity; in either case, it is specific, and hence not stress.

This raises the question, *"What is a biologic unit?"* Can one organ, like the kidney or brain, be called a unit, or should we extend the meaning of this term to include any small group of cells, perhaps even individual cells and cell-parts?

The definition of biologic units capable of selective reaction (*reactons*) is just as fundamental for biology as the definition of elements and subatomic particles is for chemistry and physics. We shall deal with this problem at length in Book IV. All we need to know now is that, no matter what we define as a unit of life—a whole nation, a human being, one region of man's body, or a single cell—we can speak of stress in a living system only as far as several of its constituent parts are nonspecifically affected. If a drug introduced into the general blood circulation causes changes only in the kidney, the action is specifically caused and specifically formed within the body. Very few drugs can thus single out the kidney among all organs of the body (specificity of causation) and, of course, the kidney represents a circumscribed region within the whole individual (specificity in the form or composition of response). On the other hand, if a drug is injected directly into the kidney and causes changes throughout the renal substance, the change is nonspecific, both as regards its form and its causation, because no part of the organ is selectively affected and such an effect can be obtained by innumerable agents. Selective changes in an organ—if they can be produced by almost anything, as long as it is directly applied to this organ—are manifestations of local stress;

whereas the changes which can be produced throughout the body by a great variety of agents, no matter where these are applied, constitute the general stress syndrome.

In this distinction between local and general stress lies the link between specificity and nonspecificity.

Throughout this analysis of our definition, we spoke of biologic *changes.* A change, in this sense, is any deviation from the normal resting state of the body. But what is "normal," and what is the "resting state"?

These are again relative concepts. Clear-cut delimitations are impossible because, in living organisms, there are imperceptible transitions between normal and abnormal, resting and active.

No one is absolutely normal; the slightest scar or freckle is actually an abnormality. No one is ever absolutely at rest either, while alive. Even during sleep, your heart, your respiratory muscles, your brain continue to work. It makes no difference that you are not conscious of this and that these activities require no voluntary effort on your part.

Yet, in the evolution of every species (from the simplest unicellular being to man), of every individual (from embryonic life to maturity), certain types have formed, which we readily recognize as normal for a given species, sex, and age. The manifold adaptations in the evolution of each individual, of each species, have all left their imprints and contributed to the setting of these individual norms. It is normal for certain Peruvian Indians to live in the rarefied air of the Andes Mountains, but it would be highly abnormal and damaging for a man from The Netherlands to do so.

The concept of "resting" is equally relative. Only the dead can tolerate total rest. But the degree and type of activity appropriate for a six-year-old boy would be most abnormal and stressful for a seventy-year-old theoretic physicist, and vice versa.

In our mechanical analogy (p. 56), the cubes were pictured as resting in a straight line during the basic condition of normalcy, before a change occurred. But if we now want to adapt this picture to what we have just learned, we may well imagine that, in the course of time, they may have gradually settled into a V-shaped groove on a constantly vibrating table. In this case, a V-shaped arrangement and vibration would be normal for them, and any enforced deviation from this state—for instance, immobilization in a straight line—would be a change.

The term stress is meaningful only when applied to a PRECISELY DEFINED BIOLOGIC SYSTEM. From all this it is obvious that if a large number of agents produce the same specific reaction-pattern (say, inflammation) in one organ (say, the stomach), they act as stressors for this particular biologic system, and here their effect can be described as a local stress syndrome. But if they act only on one organ, their action is still highly specific with reference to the body as a whole.

Every conceivable agent has both specific and nonspecific actions; every individual, or part of an individual, can be influenced specifically as well as nonspecifically. This is illustrated by the next drawing.

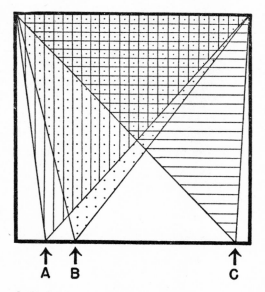

Here the whole field represents the body, and A, B, and C represent three agents which produce specific changes (horizontal lines, vertical lines, or dots) in different sectors of the body. But only with reference to the smallest triangular sector (filled with squares and dots) can we speak of nonspecifically induced changes, because only this sector is affected by all three agents. The changes in this sector correspond to the selective organ-changes (in adrenals, thymus, stomach, etc.) of the general stress syndrome.

Definition of the stressor

Having thus identified the state of stress—at least as far as the limitations of biologic definitions permit—the *stressor* is naturally "that which produces stress." In view of what we have already said about the relativity of stress, it is also self-evident that any one agent is more or less a stressor in proportion to the degree of its ability to produce stress, that is, nonspecific changes.

Definition of the G.A.S.

Now we shall have to bring the important *element of time* into our considerations of nonspecific responses. While stress is reflected by the sum of the nonspecific changes which occur in the body at any one time, the general adaptation syndrome (or G.A.S.) encompasses all nonspecific changes as they develop throughout time during continued exposure to a stressor. One is a snapshot, the other a motion picture of stress.

We saw that a fully developed G.A.S. consists of three stages: the alarm reaction, the stage of resistance, and the stage of exhaustion. There is stress at any moment during these three stages, although its manifestations change as time goes on. Furthermore, it is not necessary for all three stages to develop before we can speak of a G.A.S. Only the most severe stress leads eventually to the stage of exhaustion and death. Most of the physical or mental exertions, infections, and other stressors which act upon us produce changes corresponding only to the first and second stages: at first they may upset and alarm us, but then we get used to them.

In the course of a normal human life, everybody goes through these first two stages many, many times. Otherwise we could never become adapted to perform all the activities and resist all the injuries which are man's lot.

Even exhaustion does not always need to be irreversible and complete, as long as it affects only parts of the body. For instance, running produces a stress-situation, mainly in our muscles and cardiovascular system. To cope with this, we first have to limber up and get these organs ready for the task at hand; then for a while we will be at the height of efficiency in running, but eventually exhaustion will set in. This could be compared with an alarm reaction, a stage of resistance, and a stage of exhaustion, all limited primarily to the muscular and cardiovascular systems. But such an exhaustion is reversible; after a good rest we will be back to normal again.

The same is true of our eyes. When we come out of the dark and try to look into the sun, at first we see nothing. Then we adapt ourselves, but eventually our eyes become exhausted if we keep on looking into the strong light.

Everybody knows this from personal experience for the muscles and for the eyes; it is notoriously true also of various intellectual pursuits. Most human activities go through three stages: we first have to get into the swing of things, then we get pretty good at them, but finally we tire of them.

It is less generally known that this triphasic evolution of adaptation is quite characteristic also of those bodily activities which only the physician can fully appraise; for instance, of inflammation. If some virulent microbes get under the skin, they first cause what we call acute inflammation (reddening, swelling, pain), then follows chronic inflammation (ripening of a boil or abscess), and finally a local disintegration of the tissue which permits the inflamed, purulent fluid to be evacuated (breaking through of an abscess).

Relationship between the G.A.S. and the L.A.S.— The concept of adaptation energy

The selective exhaustion of muscles, eyes, or inflamed tissue all represent final stages only in local adaptation syndromes (L.A.S.). Several of these may go on simultaneously in various parts of the body, and, in proportion to their intensity and extent, they can activate the G.A.S.-mechanism. Only when the whole organism is exhausted—through senility at the end of a normal life-span, or through the accelerated aging caused by stress—do we enter into the terminal stage of exhaustion of the G.A.S.

It is as though we had hidden reserves of adaptability, or *adaptation energy,* in ourselves throughout the body. As soon as local stress consumes the most readily accessible local reserves, local exhaustion sets in and activity in the strained part stops automatically. This is an important protective mechanism, because, during the period of rest thus enforced, more adaptation energy can be made available, either from less readily accessible local stores or from reserves in other parts of the body. Only when all of our adaptability is used up will irreversible, general exhaustion and death follow.

Relationship between adaptation energy and aging

There seem to be close interrelations between the G.A.S. and aging. We have already mentioned that several local adaptation syndromes may develop consecutively or even simultaneously in the same individual. People can get used to a number of things (cold, heavy muscular work, worries), which at first had a very alarming effect; yet, upon prolonged exposure, sooner or later all resistance breaks down and exhaustion sets in. It is as though something were lost, or used up, during the work of adaptation; but what this is, we do not know. The term *adaptation energy* has been coined for that which is consumed during continued adaptive work, to indicate that it is something different from the caloric energy we receive from food; but this is only a name, and we still have no precise concept of what this energy might be. Further research along these lines would seem to hold great promise, since here we appear to touch upon the fundamentals of aging.

It is as though, at birth, each individual inherited a certain amount of adaptation energy, the magnitude of which is determined by his genetic background, his parents. He can draw upon this capital thriftily for a long but monotonously uneventful existence, or he can spend it lavishly in the course of a stressful, intense, but perhaps more colorful and exciting life. In any case, there is just so much of it, and he must budget accordingly.

We shall have more to say about exhaustion when we discuss the actual experiments on which this view is based (see p. 88) and its practical applications to everyday problems (Books III and V). Here I merely wanted to touch upon the theoretic basis of this concept.

Definition of the diseases of adaptation

The last concept which we have to define is that of the "diseases of adaptation." These are the maladies in which imperfections of the G.A.S. play the major role. Many diseases are actually not so much the direct results of some external agent (an infection, an intoxication) as they are consequences of the body's inability to meet these agents by adequate adaptive reactions, that is, by a perfect G.A.S.

This is again a relative concept. No malady is only a disease of adaptation and nothing else. Nor are there any disease-producers which can be so perfectly handled by the organism that maladaptation plays no part in their effects upon the body. Such agents would not produce disease. This haziness in its delimitation does not interfere with the practical utility of our concept. We must put up with the same lack of precision whenever we have to classify any other kind of disease. There is no pure heart disease, in which all other organs remain perfectly undisturbed, nor can we ever speak of a pure kidney disease or pure nervous disease in this sense.

In the preceding passages I have had to lead you through a rather detailed analysis of abstractions, but these concepts are quite indispensable for the understanding of stress as it affects us in everyday life. They had never been precisely formulated before and it is only through them that stress could be explored in the laboratory. Abstract thinking is sometimes quite exhausting, but the very definition of abstraction is "to separate by the operation of the mind." If we want to dissect stress so as to understand its mechanism, we must first expose its integral parts by separating them from confusing, irrelevant incidentals. Such a separation is possible only through an operation of the mind, since the incidentals cannot be materially removed from the true constituents of stress.

In this inventory of all our available assets for an analysis of stress, we have so far listed the facts and the abstractions. Now, let us consider the materials and techniques which can be used for this purpose.

8:

Inventory of assets:

(C) Materials and

techniques

*Experimental animals. Surgical
techniques. Chemical techniques.
Morphologic techniques. Complex
laboratory and clinical techniques.
Techniques for the coordination
of knowledge.*

Experimental animals

If we want to learn something about any aspect of life, we first
need a sample of its pattern as expressed in the body of an animal
or man. The structural organization of life can often be studied by
dissection after death, but vital processes can only be explored in
living beings.

Since it is not justified to perform dangerous operations on man,
experimental animals are quite indispensable for such studies. This
involves what is often called *vivisection*. Literally, the term means
"cutting into a living animal," and it implies to many laymen that
this is done without anesthesia and involves unnecessary suffering.
This misconception is most unfortunate, since it has led many well-
meaning people to attack animal experimentation—the very basis
of medical research—on grounds of cruelty. The *Encyclopaedia
Britannica* concludes an extensive article on the arguments for and
against vivisection with the statement that "either view to be respected must be based upon extensive and accurate knowledge,
accurate statement and sincerity. Unfortunately, these are not always
manifested by protagonists." It is not my purpose to go deeply into
the ethical aspects of animal experimentation, although I hope that
this book will give the reader the understanding necessary to form a
personal opinion. All I should like to say on the authority of a life-

long association with animal experiments and animal experimenters is this:

1. Almost every major step of progress in medicine has been based, at least partly, on animal experiments. Without these Pasteur and his contemporaries could not have discovered the role of microbes in infectious diseases, nor would it have been possible to develop vaccines, sera, or antibiotics against them. Without operating on animals, Ivan Pavlov could not have developed his concept of the "conditioned reflexes," which is still a basic pillar of our knowledge about the nervous system. Banting could not have discovered insulin without making dogs diabetic (by removing their pancreas glands) to test the antidiabetic action of his first extracts. And finally, imagine the unnecessary cruelty to man and loss of human life which would result if every surgeon were to acquire his skill by operating first on patients!

2. I have never met a professional investigator who was not concerned about the question of cruelty to animals and did not attempt to avoid it. Those who claim that animal experiments are never painful simply distort the truth; but every effort is made to diminish pain to the absolutely unavoidable minimum. It is important for the public to realize that, even if an experimental surgeon were a degenerate sadist and wanted to cause pain on purpose, he would nevertheless have to anesthetize his animals for major surgery because delicate operations cannot be performed if the animal struggles.

3. Legislators who pass laws which prohibit or curtail the use of experimental animals for research, or for the teaching of medical students, do so either because of sincere moral considerations or under the pressure of political exigencies. Whatever their motives, they should be recognized as men who have succeeded in reconciling their consciences to the fact that they necessarily inflict untold cruelties upon their fellowmen and seriously interfere with one of the noblest and most human aspirations of man, the desire to understand himself.

The better one understands the nature of life, disease, and suffering, the more one's mind becomes incapable of brutality. This thought was not the least important among the motives which led me to write a book on the nature of disease for those who are not professionally concerned with medicine. In our Institute last year, we used about 400 rats a week for research, but not one of them was exposed to unnecessary pain because of carelessness.

Surgical techniques

Let us see now more precisely what we can gain from the use of experimental surgery and how it is applied in practice to typical problems in the exploration of stress-mechanisms.

Most of these experiments are performed on rats or mice. These animals have a comparatively undeveloped brain and hence presumably (we cannot be really sure of this) feel less anguish and pain than a cat or a dog. Rodents also have the advantage of being small and singularly resistant to infections, which makes them especially suitable for large-scale experimentation.

In a standard experiment a rat is anesthetized with ether, or some other anesthetic, until it is completely unconscious and unable to move or feel pain. Then the experimenter can expose a gland and remove it to learn how the rat will react to stress without this organ. Similarly the experimental surgeon can transect a sensory nerve if, for his studies, he wants to render a certain region of the body insensitive to pain. He can diminish the blood-flow through an artery by putting a constricting loop of thread around it, and so forth. After the operation, the animal wakes up and is then ready for observation.

In most of these instances, the surgical intervention produces a type of deficiency which could spontaneously arise in man. By causing such a selective disturbance, we can appraise the participation of the individual organs in the stress-mechanism.

Chemical techniques

There is much we can learn only through the application of chemical methods. For instance, if we want to study the actions of corticoids, we can get large quantities of beef-adrenals from the slaughterhouse and extract the hormones from these glands. In principle, making an extract means chopping up the glands into fine particles and putting the resulting mush into water or some other fluid in which the hormones are soluble. From this crude extract various fractions can be precipitated out by adding chemicals which make either the hormones or the contaminants insoluble. This process of purification is continued until a hormone is separated from everything else that was in the gland, and emerges in absolutely pure, usually crystalline, form.

Purification is an especially important step, because only pure substances can be analyzed by the chemist who wants to determine their molecular structure, that is, exactly how the individual atoms are arranged within the hormone molecule. After this is accomplished, it usually becomes possible sooner or later to make the natural substance in the laboratory, from its elements or from other simple compounds which are more readily available than glands. This is what we call *synthesis* or putting together.

It is particularly useful to learn how to synthetize hormones, because most of them are valuable remedies which must be made available in quantity for all patients who need them. Such bulk production from animal glands is always costly, and often impossible, because all the slaughterhouses in the world could not furnish enough raw material.

There are, of course, many other problems of experimental medicine which can be solved only by the techniques of biochemistry. The changes, which occur during stress or after treatment with hormones, in the chemical make-up of body fluids and tissues furnish innumerable examples of this.

Morphologic techniques

Morphology literally means "the science of shape" (from Greek *morphē*, shape, form, plus *–logy*, science of). The gross anatomic knowledge gained from merely dissecting and inspecting organs falls into this category; so does the information furnished by the histologic (from Greek *histos*, tissue) structure or cellular pattern of tissues, as revealed through the microscope. By merely looking at them through a microscope we can learn much about the function of certain organs. For example, the resting adrenal is laden with small fat-droplets—readily visible under the microscope—which contain the fat-soluble hormones; the active gland discharges its reserves into the blood and, therefore, contains no such droplets.

Complex laboratory and clinical techniques

We have seen how experimental surgery, chemistry, and morphology furnish us with the basic tools for medical research. It is customary to consider separately the information yielded by *pharmacologic, bacteriologic,* and other experimental techniques or by *clinical* study. Yet, in essence, all these techniques are combinations of surgery, chemistry, and morphology.

Suppose we want to find out whether an excess of adrenal hormones spills over into the urine of a patient under stress. We make an extract from his urine and, after suitable purification, inject it into animals previously subjected to adrenalectomy (from Greek *ectomē,* excision, cutting out). The test animals have to be adrenalectomized to avoid any uncontrollable complications due to the secretion of hormones by their own adrenals. In such adrenal-deficient animals, the thymus is always very big because there are no adrenal hormones which could cause thymus-involution. If we now inject the extract, the degree of the resulting thymus-involution tells us how much adrenal hormone there was in our extract. This pharmacologic method is called a *bio-assay* (short for biological assay), because you test or measure something by its biologic activity.

In essence, this procedure is a combination of chemistry (extraction), surgery (adrenalectomy), and morphology (change in thymus-size).

Most of the changes caused by spontaneous diseases in man or by experimental interventions (treatment with bacteria, allergens, etc.) in animals are revealed through combinations of the three fundamental techniques which we have just outlined.

Techniques for the coordination of knowledge

The volume of medical literature has assumed such gigantic proportions that the mere registration and coordination of the accumulating medical knowledge has become a major task of contemporary research. As Vannevar Bush so aptly said to the American Philosophical Society (*The Atlantic,* August, 1955), if we fail in this task "science may become bogged down in its own product, inhibited like a colony of bacteria, by its own exudations."

Because of its long-standing interest in stress, our Institute has accumulated the world's largest collection of books and pamphlets dealing with this subject. Our G.A.S. Library is virtually complete and its store of information is made accessible through a detailed subject index.

But, to give you an idea of the magnitude and scope of such work, here are a few figures. In 1950, when I published *Stress*, the first technical treatise on this subject, I had to discuss more than 5,500 original articles and books which dealt with various related topics. Since that time, every year, my coworkers and I published a volume entitled *Annual Report on Stress* (and fondly nicknamed AROS in laboratory circles). In each of these books we had to report on between 2,500 and 5,700 publications. Of course all these papers first had to be obtained, read, and carefully indexed before they could be incorporated into our *Reports.* *

Parenthetically, as I dictate these lines and look at the extensive shelf-space occupied by the AROS volumes above my desk, I cannot help thinking with some melancholy about all the fun I missed doing experimental research in the lab (or playing with my children, traveling, listening to music, or reading for relaxation) while I compiled this mountain of information. The same thought must have haunted all the people I talked into helping me with my exacting and monotonous task of registration.

No one who has not done this kind of work himself can realize what it means to go through some 25,000 scientific papers and catalogue their substance so that it may be easy to find when needed. You cannot even fully digest and enjoy information contained in this mass of literature because time does not permit you to do more than skim through the pages with a sharp eye trained to pick out meaningful facts.

Why not read less and take time really to assimilate all we do read? This sounds very sensible; it is what we all should like to do. Unfortunately, it cannot be done in practice because, to judge whether or not a paper is worth reading, it must be virtually catalogued first. To begin with, you have to find it. There are about 8,000 medical journals; you would not have the time to go through

---

* To cope with this task we have developed a "Symbolic Shorthand System for Medicine and Physiology" (H. Selye, Acta, Inc., Montreal, 1956). Here the concepts of medicine are represented by symbols which correspond essentially to the equations of algebra, the formulas of chemistry, or the notes of music. To give the reader some idea of how the system works we have made partial use of it in the INDEX (p. 313).

them all, even if your library could afford to buy them. So, you do the next best thing, and try to find what you want in one of the medical indices. Then you write the author asking for a reprint, or you get a photostat if a reprint is not available (books have to be purchased). After all this, you must at least skim through the publication and mentally catalogue the information in it before you know what it is worth. By that time you might as well write out a catalogue slip and thus make the information permanently available to others as well as to yourself.

Naturally, among the thousands of publications on stress, there were many which I read carefully and with great interest; indeed, some served as a basis for my own experiments. But stress and the adaptive hormones which participate in stress have inspired so many investigations that no one person could really have studied them all. And, yet, it would have been quite impossible to keep the subject together and build it into a science without constructing such an international instrument of information and correlation as the AROS.

It is wasteful to repeat experiments which have already been done elsewhere; it is futile to use obsolete techniques when better ones are available. We cannot see major gaps unless a picture of our knowledge is put together. Hence, this information service became as essential a tool for organized stress research as the experimental animals or the surgical, chemical, and morphologic techniques which we employ in the laboratory.

It is curious that so many governmental and private foundations are subsidizing individual medical research projects, whereas none has been established to aid with the work of registering and correlating the knowledge that is then acquired. In addition to the inherent difficulties of preparing an index of stress research, the problem of financing it always was, and still is, one of our greatest worries.

These are some of the practical points concerning the materials and techniques of medical research in general. While discussing them we have made an inventory of the assets they furnished for our analysis of stress. Let us now try to see how the experimenter actually proceeds when he attempts to analyze biologic mechanisms in general, and how we went about dissecting the stress-machinery in particular.

9:

How does one dissect

a biologic mechanism?

Analogy of the five light-bulbs.
Analysis of interrelations in the
nervous system. Analysis of
interrelations in the endocrine
system.

Analogy of the five light-bulbs

Suppose you are faced with the problem of having to figure out the system of wiring in a complex electric network, in which a battery supplies five light-bulbs with current; the task would be easy but all the wires are hidden in the wall and you can reach them only around the sockets.

In a case like this, after having identified the position of the battery and of the five bulbs, the simplest procedure would be to interrupt the current by disconnecting the wires at each of the possible relay points. This would show us which of the lights go out and which still remain lighted after cutting a certain connection. As a countercheck, we might then—after disconnecting the main battery—supply current at various points by providing an auxiliary source of electricity, to see which of the wires supplies which of the bulbs.

This is illustrated in the drawing on p. 76.

Here, if we could only see the position of the battery and of the five bulbs (numbered 1 to 5), it would be quite impossible to know how they are connected. But we could easily figure it out by a few simple experiments. For instance, if we interrupted the current at point 1, all the lamps, except No. 3, would go out. This means that Nos. 2, 4, and 5 are supplied through a system which must go through point 1, while No. 3 has an independent electric supply directly from the battery.

On the other hand, after turning off the battery and putting on an auxiliary source of electricity just below point 1, it will become evident that bulbs 2, 3, 4, and 5 go on. From this we may conclude that lamp No. 3 has a dual supply of electricity, one coming from somewhere above, the other from below point 1. Now it will only be a matter of patience to demonstrate, with further experiments of the same kind that the three wires leaving point 2 go to bulbs 3,

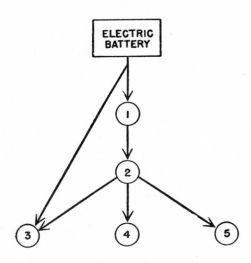

4, and 5. Thus eventually the whole plan of the circuit can easily be determined.

Essentially the same procedure is used by medical investigators when they want to disentangle interrelations in a complex living system, such as the body of an animal or man.

Analysis of interrelations in the nervous system

The nervous system supplies our muscles with the impulses necessary for contraction. It does so through complex cables and filaments: the nerves. The problem of unraveling these connections is quite similar to that posed by an electric network. After cutting certain nerve-cables in an experimental animal, we can see which muscles will become paralyzed. Then, as a countercheck, we can stimulate each nerve-stump with electric current to see which muscle-groups will contract. Some nerves go directly to one muscle or (after branching) to several muscles; others go first to relay stations, the *nerve ganglia*.

Analysis of interrelations in the endocrine system

The situation is very similar in the case of living organs regulated by hormones, the chemical messengers produced by endocrine glands. The principal difference is that the hormones are not carried each through its own separate channels, the way the nerves transmit their impulses through individual fibers or the electric current through separate wires.

Hormones are soluble chemicals poured out by the glands into the blood in which they travel together to all parts of the body. But each hormone carries instructions in a code which only certain organs can read. Therefore, these blood-borne messengers can influence limited parts of the body just as selectively as the nerves can. Each organ responds only to certain hormones which act either directly or through some other endocrine gland (a relay station).

Here the situation is more comparable with radio or television networks, in which the emitting station sends its waves indiscriminately in every direction, but only certain sets are tuned to a particular wavelength. This is what permits the selective reception of certain programs to the exclusion of all others. The comparison can even be carried further, in that some sets will receive a program from the original sender, and others will get it relayed through some local station, just as the hormones of a gland can act upon tissues directly or after first relaying their message through another gland.

Therefore, in the study of endocrinology, which is the science of the endocrine glands and their hormones, we can again use the same analytical procedure. This is illustrated in the next figure by an example taken from the field of stress research. Here we see the effect of a stressor, or stress-producing agent, upon the pituitary gland, the adrenals, the stomach, the lymphatic tissues, and the white blood cells.

It will be remembered that the *pituitary* (or hypophysis) is a small endocrine gland embedded in the bones at the base of the skull just underneath the brain. The *adrenals* are endocrines which lie above the kidneys, one on each side. The *lymphatic tissues* are important defensive organs consisting of small cells, similar to the white blood cells. The lymph nodes in the groins and armpits, the tonsils in the throat, and the thymus in the chest belong to this system. Among the *white blood cells,* some come from the lymphatic organs, others from the bone-marrow. These cells are also important in defense, especially against infections.

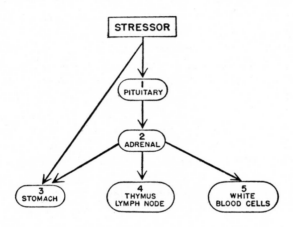

During stress we noticed changes in all these tissues, but we did not know how—through what pathways—they were produced. As far as we could tell, when we began this work, the thymus might have produced some hormone which stimulates the adrenals. But this possibility was soon ruled out. After surgically removing the thymus (point 4 in the preceding figure) of rats, their adrenals (point 2) still became enlarged and overactive during stress. Conversely, however, after the adrenals were removed, the thymus no longer showed the changes characteristic of the stress-reaction. Finally, we found that injections of adrenal extracts (rich in corticoid hormones) produced typical stress-changes in the thymus, even after adrenalectomy. Obviously the pathway went from adrenal to thymus and not from thymus to adrenal.

Now the question arose, "How does the adrenal know when there is stress and, therefore, a need for large amounts of corticoid hormone?" In other words, what is the immediately preceding link in this sequence of events? After unsuccessfully trying various other possibilities, we removed the pituitary and found that, after interruption of the biologic chain-reaction at this point (point 1), exposure to stress now no longer stimulated the adrenal glands (point 2). On the other hand—even without stress, and even in the absence of the pituitary—injection of a pituitary hormone, ACTH (described on page 86), caused typical stress-changes in the adrenal. It became enlarged and produced a great excess of its own hormones. Evidently, the adrenal was a relay station between point 1 and certain points farther down the chain.

It is easy to see how—using this sketch as a blueprint for the dissection of stress—the whole complex endocrine network of the G.A.S. became amenable to scientific analysis. We merely had to interrupt the network by the removal of a gland and then correct the resulting defect by the injection of the gland's special hormone.

This kind of work is still in progress and will have to continue for quite some time. We, like hundreds of other investigators, are busy trying to disentangle the many still mysterious complexities of the stress-machinery. But now let us take stock and see what we have managed to find out about it so far.

10:

Results of the dissection

Outline for report on dissection. Detection of interactions between specific and nonspecific events. How can various agents produce the same specific syndrome? How can qualitatively different reactions be added? The course of the stress-response is triphasic. The defense is antagonistic. The importance of conditioning factors.

Outline for report on dissection

In the preceding chapters I have attempted to give an inventory of all the material and conceptual assets we had at our disposal for the dissection of stress. Now we shall summarize what we have learned from it. Some of our findings have already been touched upon, but a certain amount of recapitulation may not be superfluous whenever we deal with facts remote from everyday experience.

On the other hand, there would be no point in describing at length the techniques used in every experiment that was performed to prove each fact. The principles upon which such an experimental analysis is based have already been reviewed at length; it does not take much imagination to see how they were applicable to our specific problems.

I have subdivided the material into five parts to be discussed in this and the next three chapters:

1. *Generalities.* The principal advances in the understanding of stress and its relationship to disease.

2. *Stress in a nutshell.* The over-all picture of the newly acquired facts.

3. *Stress and inflammation.* The application of the stress concept to the study of this special problem was selected as an example for

more detailed consideration, because inflammation is one of the most fundamental features of disease. Furthermore, it so happens that up to now it has been in this field that knowledge of the stress-mechanism has been most successfully applied to clinical problems.

4. *Synoptic view of the whole stress-mechanism.* A detailed account of the manner in which the various organs cooperate in order to maintain health during stress.

5. *The nature of adaptation.*

Detection of interactions between specific and nonspecific events

We have seen that every conceivable agent which can act upon the human body, from without or from within, does certain things more than others. Those which it does more are relatively specific changes, as compared to those which it does less. The latter, the nonspecific actions, may therefore be viewed as incidental side-effects. But they are incidental only from the standpoint of classical medicine, which is always interested in the specific causes of disease and the specific cures with which to combat them. Stress research is primarily concerned with these nonspecific actions. Whatever our point of view, we must keep in mind that, in actual practice, it is impossible to separate the specific from the nonspecific.

In each of the following drawings the solid arrow represents stress and the other the contaminating specific actions of three agents.

Obviously, the end-result of exposure to any of the agents represented by these double arrows could not be the same, even though their stress-effects are identical. The two types of actions of the same agent can influence one another. In the language of stress research, we say that the nonspecific effects are *conditioned* (modified) by the specific effects of each agent. Indeed, the specific actions of agents can, even totally, block certain nonspecific effects whenever the two happen to be diametrical opposites. This modifying and masking by specific actions was one of the main reasons why it took so long to draw a precise picture of stress.

Of course this state of affairs is encountered whenever we try to make any generalization. For instance, if we want to arrive at a picture of what we mean by a Negro, at first his dark skin strikes us as the most specific indication of his race. It seems safe to generalize by saying, "Negroes have a dark skin." Yet, there are albino Negroes, in whom, due to a hereditary defect, the skin cannot form dark pigment. This does not invalidate our generalization that there is a dark-skinned race. The vast majority of Negroes are dark-skinned and deep pigmentation is a useful, though not an infallible, index in recognizing them. No one indicator suffices to define a race, but even an albino can be recognized as a Negro, because of his other racial features. We can learn to know these other characteristics only by examining a large number of Negroes.

The same is true of stress research. For instance, one of the typical features of the G.A.S. is its characteristic blood-sugar curve, which follows a distinctive triphasic course: it first falls, then rises, and finally declines again. If stress is produced by the injection of insulin (the antidiabetic hormone of the pancreas), the typical blood-sugar response will be obscured because the specific action of insulin is to lower the blood sugar at all times. It would be false to conclude that the blood sugar is no indicator of stress, or that insulin cannot produce a G.A.S. The stress-effect of insulin can still be recognized because, like all other stressors, it causes adrenocortical stimulation, thymus-involution, and so forth. This lesson has been learned by examining many effects of many agents.

How can various agents produce the same specific syndrome?

In the next drawing we see four squares symbolizing potential target areas for stimuli. They might represent whole organs, tissues, or even individual cells. Each of these squares is subdivided into a top part containing alarm signals (arrows) and a bottom part which is constructed to give specific reactions upon stimulation.

Each time a specific agent acts upon any one target, two things happen: there is a specific response (graphically represented here by the discharge of the distinct action-patterns from the lower part of the square), and a nonspecific response (represented by the discharge of the always identical little arrows from the top part of the square).

For instance, light acting upon the eye causes vision, a diuretic induces the kidney to produce urine; a nerve impulse makes a

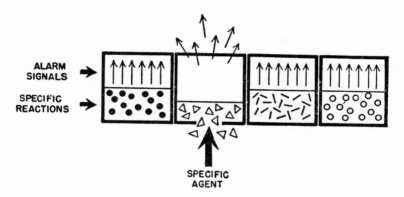

muscle contract. These are specific responses. But, at the same time, the cells of all these organs can also send out some nonspecific alarm signals which merely indicate activity. That the eye, kidney, or muscle each react differently and specifically to stimulation is a self-evident fact. But how can we concretely prove the nonspecific response? The chemical nature of the alarm signals has still not been definitely determined; yet, their existence has been proved beyond doubt.

When, in experimental animals or man, organs are induced to function intensely (for instance, if a large part of the musculature is forced to work), or when tissues are damaged (for example, if the surface of the skin is burned), there is positive evidence of an increased secretion of ACTH, the adrenal-stimulating pituitary hormone. This substance, in turn, stimulates the hormone secretion of the adrenal cortex; consequently, the cortical-hormone content of the blood rises. Evidently, somehow the directly affected organ must have sent out a message notifying the pituitary-adrenal system of an increased cortical-hormone, or "corticoid," requirement.

At first it was thought that such messages would have to travel through nerves. This is not the case. It has been possible to show.

for instance in a deeply anesthetized rat, that if one hind-limb is completely separated from the body (except for its blood vessels) mechanical injury or scalding of that limb can still produce adreno-cortical stimulation. Here, there was no nervous connection between the directly stimulated part and the rest of the body. Obviously, the alarm signals could not have been nervous stimuli; they must have traveled from the limb to the adrenal through the blood stream. Presumably, these messengers are chemical compounds, *fatigue substances*, produced as metabolic by-products during activity or damage.

Experience has also shown that a specific agent acting only on one organ usually causes less of a stress-response than a nonspecific agent acting on many parts of the body. Why?

The explanation of this fact can again be visualized by our anal-ogy of the four squares, as shown in the next figure.

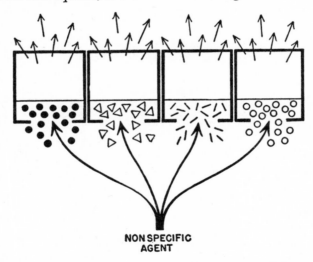

NONSPECIFIC
AGENT

If a nonspecific agent acts simultaneously upon all four targets, each of them will respond in its own characteristic way (a muscle with contraction, a nerve with conduction, and so on). But, of course, these responses cannot be additive, since each target has a different pattern of response. On the other hand, every tissue will also discharge its alarm signals; these are identical throughout and their nonspecific effects are additive.

The hormonal response to the discharge of these alarm signals is a useful adaptive response, in which the pituitary and adrenal glands play a cardinal role. Experiments on animals have shown that if either of these glands is removed before exposure to stressors, resistance is very low. Yet, it can be restored toward normal if suitable substitution treatment is given by the injection of the required hormones.

In all these respects the mechanism of the stress-response is very reminiscent of the events during a fire alarm, which we used as an analogy in the preceding chapter.

In this picture a specific agent acts upon the third square. The

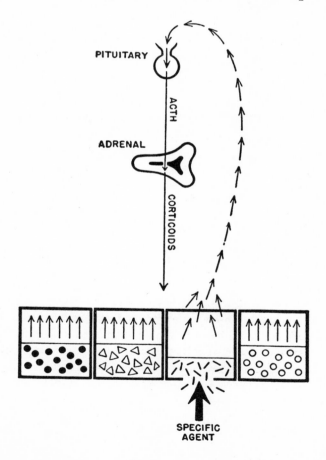

PITUITARY

ACTH

ADRENAL

CORTICOIDS

SPECIFIC
AGENT

target reacts with its own characteristic pattern of response (downward discharge of the rods); but this specific activity automatically discharges alarm signals which travel to the pituitary. The signals are nonspecific, no matter which target they come from; they just say, "Stress." But, from here on, the pattern of response is quite specific.

In the preceding chapters I spoke at length of the adrenal cortex, but the pituitary was barely mentioned. This gland is embedded in bones at the base of the skull and regulates the production of corticoids through its *adrenocorticotrophic hormone* or ACTH. It does not matter that the adrenals are placed above the kidneys, at a great distance from the pituitary, because hormones are carried equally to all organs through the blood. When the pituitary produces ACTH, this trophic (from Greek *trephein,* to nourish) hormone incites the cells of the adrenal cortex to transform all suitable raw materials into corticoids. These are then also discharged into the blood so that they can act throughout the body wherever they are needed.

The selective secretion of ACTH and corticoids under the influence of the alarm signals is a specific form of response. Its ultimate purpose appears to be the increased production of corticoids, which can then act back upon the directly stimulated target, to steady its work and to put out the fire of excessive activity.

How can qualitatively different reactions be added?

If we compare the two preceding drawings, it is easy to see that the more nonspecific the eliciting agent (the less its effect is limited to individual targets), the greater its ability to elicit an intense stress syndrome. Even maximal specific stimulation of any one target can only produce stress corresponding in its intensity to the limited quantity of alarm signals this one activated unit can emit. On the other hand, if a large number of target areas is affected by a nonspecific agent which acts simultaneously in many places, the quantity of the alarm signals discharged can become enormous. Here—as in our analogy of the multiple fire alarms—there is a direct proportionality between the number of signals and the extent of the resulting defensive measures.

This hypothesis is by no means definitely proved as yet, but no other interpretation fits our experimental observations better. We have seen, for instance, that if one rat is exposed to intense sound, another to severe cold, and yet another to scalding of a paw, there is a moderate adrenal enlargement in each of them. There is a definite limit to the adrenal stimulation that can be produced by any one agent, say scalding a small area, no matter how severely. On the other hand, if a rat is exposed to sound, cold, and scalding simultaneously, the resulting adrenal enlargement will be much greater than that produced by any one of these stressors. Obviously these three distinct agents must have had some common effect through which their actions upon the adrenal could be added.

It is apparently the discharge of alarm signals that makes stress the common denominator of the most diverse reactions to all kinds of agents.

The course of the stress-response is triphasic

If we follow the development of the G.A.S. in time, we can see that it goes through a typical triphasic course. To illustrate this I pointed out (in Chapter 2) that if an animal is continuously exposed to some stressor (say, cold), the adrenal cortex first discharges all its microscopic fat-granules which contain the cortical hormones (alarm reaction), then it becomes laden with an unusually large number of fat-droplets (stage of resistance) and finally it loses them again (stage of exhaustion). As far as we can see, the same triphasic course is followed by most, if not all, of the manifestations of the G.A.S.

The next figure illustrates this graphically, using general resistance to injury as an indicator.

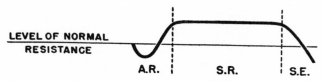

LEVEL OF NORMAL RESISTANCE

A.R.   S.R.   S.E.

In the acute phase of the alarm reaction (A.R.), general resistance, to the particular stressor with which the G.A.S. had been elicited, falls way below normal. Then, as adaptation is acquired, in the stage of resistance (S.R.), the capacity to resist rises considerably above normal. But eventually, in the stage of exhaustion (S.E.), resistance drops below normal again.

You may well ask, "How does one find out about such things in actual practice?"

We exposed large numbers of rats to various stressors over long periods of time and tested the resistance of sample groups among these animals at repeated intervals. For instance, in one experiment we placed a hundred rats in a refrigerated room where the temperature was near freezing. Thanks to their fur coats, they could stand this quite well, although during the first 48 hours they developed the typical manifestations of the alarm reaction. This was proved by killing ten animals at the end of the second day; all of them had large fat-free adrenals, small thymuses, and stomach ulcers.

At this same time—after 48 hours of exposure—twenty other rats were also removed from the cold-room to test their resistance to low temperatures. They were now placed in a still colder chamber, together with normal rats which up to then had lived at room temperature. It turned out that the rats which had already developed an alarm reaction due to moderate cold were even less than normally resistant to excessive cold.

Five weeks later another sample of rats was taken from the cold-room. By that time they had fully adapted themselves to life at low temperature and were in the stage of resistance of the G.A.S. When these animals were placed in the still more refrigerated chamber, they survived temperatures which nonpretreated animals could never withstand. Evidently their resistance had risen above the normal level.

Yet, after several months of life in the cold, this acquired resistance was lost again, and the stage of exhaustion set in. Then the animals were not even capable of further surviving in the comparatively moderate cold of the refrigerated chamber in which they had spent so much time in a state of perfect well-being, even since the initiation of the experiment.

The three waves in the curve (see p. 87) (down, up, and down again) represent a summary of many such observations, because this type of experiment was repeated with various other stressors (forced muscular work, drugs, infections) and the result was always the same.

Adaptability can be well trained to serve a special purpose, but eventually it runs out; its amount is finite.

This was not what I had expected. I should have thought that once an animal has learned to live in the cold, it could go on resisting low temperatures indefinitely. Why shouldn't it, as long as it received enough food to create the internal heat necessary for the maintenance of a normal body-temperature? Naturally, in order to get used to cold, the organism must learn how to produce an excess of heat by the combustion of food. For additional safety the body must also learn to prevent unnecessary loss of heat. It does this through a generalized constriction of the blood vessels in the skin which interferes with the cooling of the blood on the surface. But once all this has been learned and the animal has become well adjusted to life at low temperatures, one would expect that nothing but lack of food (caloric energy) would stand in the way of continued resistance to cold. Observation shows that this is not the case.

Similar experiments have then revealed that the same loss of acquired adaptation also occurs in animals forced to perform intense muscular exercise, or in those given toxic drugs and other stressors over long periods of time. These were the actual observations which led to the concept of "adaptation energy" (see p. 65).

The defense is antagonistic

There are two principal ways of defending yourself against aggression: to advance and attack the foe or to retreat and run out of his reach. Both these techniques are also used by the defensive forces of our tissues against foes inside the body. For instance, there are serologic mechanisms which can defend us against invading microbes. When a germ gets into the blood stream it can be killed by these purely aggressive, chemical substances which we call *antibodies*. There is no element of retreat, no flight in this response. Conversely, if I accidentally put my hand on a hot plate, my muscles will immediately pull the burned hand back. This happens whether I want it to or not, because it is an involuntary reflex of flight. There is nothing aggressive about this; I make no effort to destroy the source of my injury, but merely draw away from it.

To my mind, it is one of the most characteristic features of the G.A.S. that its various defensive mechanisms are always based on combinations of these two types of response: advance and retreat. It is essentially an antagonistic response, that is, one designed to activate two opposing forces. I rather think that it is the subconscious realization of this fact that gave the word *stress* its connotation of "tension" in everyday English. In physics, tension is the result of two balancing forces, and that is very much what antagonistic, nervous, or hormonal, tensions create during stress in the human body. Of course, advance and retreat cannot occur simultaneously and at the same place, but the forces of advance and those of retreat can both be mobilized concurrently at any one place.

Let me illustrate this again by a simple, mechanical analogy, one which incidentally represents a procedure of defense actually used by the human body.

The black rods in this figure represent the two large bones in the arm; the two white spindles correspond to the bending (flexor) and stretching (extensor) muscles. It is evident from this drawing how contraction of the flexor will bend, and how contraction of the extensor will stretch, the arm. If both these antagonistic muscles contract simultaneously with the same force, the arm does not move but becomes tense and hence more steady.

When an irritant touches my wrist I can retreat from it by contracting the flexor muscle (flight); I can push it away by contracting the extensor muscle (advance); or I can steady myself against it by contracting both (tension).

So, we see that actually the two antagonistic mechanisms give us three possibilities of reaction: retreat, advance, or steadiness, all of which can have their uses; and we must choose among them, depending upon the circumstances.

Survival depends largely upon a correct blending of advance, retreat, and standing one's ground. To obtain the best results these three types of reaction must be perfectly coordinated, not only in time but also in space, so as to adjust our reactions to the changing demands of the situation at various times in various parts of the body. Whenever they come in contact with an aggressor, in this coordination lies the art of defense for every organ, for every man, for every nation.

The principal coordinating systems of the body are the nervous and the hormonal systems. In both of these we have pairs of antagonists. As far as the fight for survival is concerned, we might call them the *pro-* and the *antidefense factors.* The former carry the message to act or to advance, the latter to relax or to retreat.

As regards the *nervous system* this had been known for a long time. The voluntary muscles of our limbs are innervated by antagonistic nerve fibers; so are the many involuntary muscles which innervate the stomach, intestines, blood vessels, and other internal organs.

How do nerves act this way? Interestingly, in the final analysis even they act through hormones. At the minute end-points of each nerve-branch, hormonelike chemical substances are discharged, and it is these which act upon the tissues, for instance, upon the muscles to cause contraction.

The so-called *adrenalines* (adrenaline itself and its close relative, noradrenaline) represent one type of such a nerve hormone.

The adrenalines produced by nerves are identical with the hormones secreted by the *adrenal medulla.* Up to now, I have spoken almost solely about the outer part, or cortex, of the adrenal, because it was here that we saw the most striking changes during the alarm reaction. Yet, the central portion, the medulla of the gland, is also important; the adrenalines which it secretes likewise have important functions to fulfill during stress.

One wonders why the body makes these substances, once in a gland and once in nerves. When adrenalines are secreted into the blood by the glandular cells of the adrenal medulla, the hormones are necessarily distributed equally to all parts of the body; this assures widespread effects, but it can give no selectivity of action. On the other hand, when these substances are liberated at nerve-endings, high concentrations of them can be produced in certain circumscribed territories of the body, so that their effects may become very selective. In other words, the hormones produced by the adrenal medulla can best achieve a generalized, uniform effect throughout the body, whereas those locally produced by individual nerves are most effective in causing pronounced changes in one place without disturbing the rest of the body. It depends upon circumstances, which of the two types of reaction is preferable, the generalized or the selective.

The nerve hormone which acts as an antagonist of the adrenalines is called *acetylcholine.* As far as we know, it is not produced and secreted into the general blood stream by any endocrine gland; it is liberated only at nerve-endings.

The *adrenal cortex* makes a large number of hormones. Some of these are sex hormones, quite similar to those produced by the sex glands. They have little or nothing to do with stress research, but they may cause severe sexual derangements. For instance, most of the bearded women who exhibit themselves in circuses, are suffering from an excessive production of male hormones by their adrenals. Three- to four-year-old little girls may develop mature breasts and other sexual characteristics of adult women merely as a result of excessive female-hormone production by their adrenals.

I mention these anomalies only to complete the picture; but in our discussion of stress, it is not with these, but with the so-called vital or life-maintaining hormones of the adrenal cortex that we have to deal. When these are lacking there is no adaptability to change—and lack of adaptability spells death.

At first it was thought that the adrenal cortex produced only one kind of vital hormone; this was called *cortine.* But further research showed that there are at least two types of such hormones. It was at that time—some fifteen years ago—that I proposed the term *corticoid hormones,* as a collective name for this group.

The outstanding effect of one type of corticoid is to inhibit inflammation. Inflammation is a defense reaction of the tissues; so this type of hormone can be regarded as an antidefense hormone, in that it prevents a defensive reaction. There are several such hormones. Let us call them *anti-inflammatory corticoids* (A-Cs). To this group belong cortisone and cortisol, which have become so generally known because of their conspicuous beneficial effects in rheumatoid arthritis, allergic inflammation, inflammation of the eyes, and other inflammatory diseases.

The opposite kind are quite naturally designated as the *proinflammatory corticoids* (P-Cs). These are less well known by the general public, because we are just beginning to learn something about their role in clinical medicine. Aldosterone and desoxycorticosterone are two such proinflammatory hormones.

To follow our argument it is not essential to burden your memory with all these complex names. Remember only that many corticoids have been discovered: some of them are anti-inflammatory (A-C), others proinflammatory (P-C).

If, for the sake of simplicity, we group them this way, we must constantly bear in mind, however, that these terms are merely symbols; they do not tell the whole story. First, it is only under certain conditions that the two types of corticoids inhibit or stimulate inflammation. Second, they do many other things besides acting on inflammation. For instance, the anti-inflammatory corticoids can also raise the blood sugar; therefore, biochemists prefer to call them *glucocorticoids* (from glucose). On the other hand, one of the most outstanding chemical effects of proinflammatory corticoids is to influence mineral metabolism; they are *mineralocorticoids* in that they cause a retention of sodium and an excretion of potassium.

It is somewhat confusing to have several names for the same group of compounds, but this is necessary, even in designating things encountered in everyday life. For instance, the same region may be called *wheat country* or *oil country*, depending upon whether one is interested in the products of the surface or of the depth of the land. Incidentally, in addition to acting on inflammation and on sugar and mineral metabolism, the corticoids have many other effects—for instance, upon the pigmentation of the skin, emotional reactions, and the blood pressure—just as any geographic region has many characteristics apart from producing wheat or oil.

Finally, it must be kept in mind that although the anti- and proinflammatory corticoids do, under certain conditions, diametrically oppose each other's effects on inflammation, this is not always so; nor are these hormones necessarily antagonistic as regards their other actions. In some respects they may actually be synergistic, that is, they may work together and mutually increase each other's effects.

I mention these facts to avoid a distortion of my account by an oversimplified presentation. But let me repeat that all we really must keep in mind meanwhile is that there are two types of corticoids which antagonize each other in many respects and, more particularly, with regard to inflammation.

This simple drawing recapitulates the salient points:

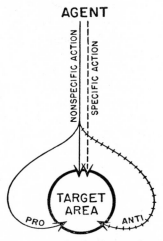

Any agent which acts upon the body produces dual effects. Some are specific and some nonspecific. In this discussion we are not concerned with specific actions, so we shall say no more about them here. The nonspecific component acts three ways:

1. Directly on whatever tissue the agent happens to touch (target area). For instance, microbes on a splinter of wood which gets under our skin can destroy cells in their immediate surroundings by the direct effect of bacterial poisons.

2. Indirectly by mobilizing the antidefensive part of the antagonistic defense system, which is actually a chemical message to retreat from, or at least, ignore, the aggressor.

3. Indirectly by mobilizing the other part of this same system which is prodefensive, that is, a message to advance against and, if possible, to destroy the aggressor.

It is easy to see how a whole human being, or even part of one--

for instance, an arm—could advance against or retreat from an aggressor. But how could these descriptions be applicable to tissue-reactions? We shall try to show this by using inflammation as an example; but first we shall have to become more familiar with the principle of *conditioning,* which I have barely mentioned up to now.

The importance of conditioning factors

Suppose you are given some strawberries to eat, would your reaction depend only upon the quality of the fruit? Certainly not. It would depend upon many other conditions. If you like strawberries and have not had any for a long time, you would welcome them with enthusiasm. If strawberries were all you had had to eat for weeks, they would probably disgust you. If you should happen to be allergic to strawberries, they would make you sick.

The reactions of our tissues to various agents are dependent upon very similar conditioning factors. Generally speaking, we distinguish two types of these: the internal and the external. The *internal conditioning factors* are those which have become part of the body. Heredity and past experiences leave some trace, some "tissue-memories," which influence the way we react to things. For instance, cold is less damaging to a polar bear than it is to a tropical fish whose whole genetic evolution was oriented towards life in a warm climate. But, in any one animal, the reaction to cold will also largely depend upon whether this particular individual has previously been living in a cold or a hot atmosphere. Remember that the same cold, which initially produced an alarm reaction in our rats and decreased resistance to more cold, eventually produced a stage of resistance with an increased cold-tolerance. Thus, both inherited genetic factors and previous exposure of an individual can create internal conditions which alter resistance from within.

On the other hand, whatever acts upon us from without can also influence our response to a simultaneously acting agent, even if it causes no permanent change in our body. The diet we take, the climate we live in are such *external conditioning factors.*

Our discussion of physiologic reactions to stressors would be very incomplete and misleading if we failed to make the importance of conditioning quite clear. Take the case of conditioning by food substances. The same amount of proinflammatory (mineralocorticoid) hormone which causes marked kidney-damage and hypertension in a rat kept on a high salt intake has absolutely no such effect if given to a rat receiving a salt-free diet. It is especially noteworthy that stress itself can act as a conditioning factor for the adaptive hormones produced during stress. For instance, the same amount of cortisone which markedly inhibits inflammation in a patient who has just undergone a major surgical operation will be relatively ineffective in a perfectly healthy person.

At first we thought that this was merely due to increased corticoid-production by the patient's own adrenals. Of course, the effect of the internally formed corticoids is added to that of the injected cortisone. But this is not the whole story. Such conditioning by stress (or, in the previous example, by salt) occurs even in adrenal-ectomized animals in which no corticoids could possibly be produced. Here we must be dealing with some direct interaction between the conditioning factors (the dietary salt, the stress of surgery) and the corticoids.

Stress apparently acts two ways; for instance, to inhibit inflammation, it increases both the production of, and tissue-sensitivity to, anti-inflammatory corticoids. The next drawing shows how:

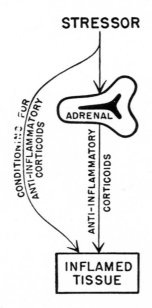

11:

Stress in a nutshell

The essence of the stress-response.

The essence of the stress-response

What we have said up to now is already sufficient to give us a fairly correct picture of the basic mechanisms involved in all types of stress-reactions. They can be visualized by the following sketch:

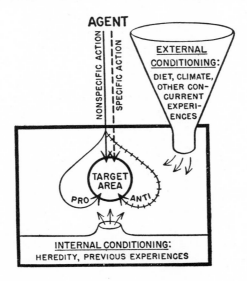

We recognize again the elements of the drawing on p. 94, but now, having learned about conditioning, the diagram can be made much more explicit.

Again we note that the agent produces both specific and non-specific actions, through which it influences the whole body (here represented as a square). But this picture also shows that the agent does not act on the whole body evenly; it usually hits some part, the direct target area, more than other regions.

For example, if I accidentally swallow some corrosive fluid, my whole body suffers to some extent, but no part of it will be as much affected as the tissues between my lips and stomach, which came into direct contact with the poison. These represent the target area in this case. Yet, parts far away from this region are also affected; for instance, the adrenals are stimulated to produce an excess of pro-inflammatory and/or anti-inflammatory corticoids; there are nervous and emotional reactions and various biochemical changes which influence metabolism. As a result of all this, virtually every tissue in the body is eventually affected to some extent.

The drawing also reminds us that the whole development of the reaction largely depends on conditioning factors. These can be in-variables which act upon us from within: our hereditary predis-positions and previous experiences (internal conditioning), as well as variables which influence our body simultaneously with the agent from without (external conditioning). All these are integral ele-ments of the response during stress; they all contribute something to the picture of the G.A.S.

This general view of the stress-mechanism now permits us to consider in more detail the application of our concept to a special problem.

12:

Stress and inflammation

Forms of inflammation.
The structure of inflammation.
The purpose of inflammation.
The regulation of inflammation.

Forms of inflammation

Inflammation has been defined as "a local reaction to injury." It can occur almost anywhere in the body and it can take many forms; yet it is always the same kind of reaction.When fully developed it is always characterized by swelling, reddening, heat, and pain.

If a particle of dust gets under your eyelid, there will be some pain, with reddening and swelling of the membranes around the irritated spot; the eyes become hot, and tears form, which usually succeed in washing the offensive particle away. But while the irritation lasts, it is actually an inflammation of the outer eye-membrane, the conjunctiva; we call it *conjunctivitis*.

If a child develops a sore throat, what usually happens is that certain microbes proliferate in his tonsils and cause local swelling, reddening, heat, and pain. This is an inflammation of the tonsils; we call it *tonsillitis*.

A patient may come down suddenly with violent pain in his abdomen because microbes have gotten out of control in one small part of his intestine, the appendix, and caused swelling, heat, reddening, and pain there; this is *appendicitis*. If the wall of the appendix can no longer resist aggression by the microbes, it perforates. Then the bacteria can attack the whole of the fine membrane which is stretched around the outer surface of our intestines, the peritoneum. The resulting inflammation, if not treated, is usually fatal; we call it *general peritonitis*.

The disorders which I have just mentioned are very different, indeed; yet all of them are examples of what we call *inflammation.* In medicine it became customary to add the suffix *-itis* after the name of the organ affected, to indicate that an inflammation had developed in it. We could mention many other examples, but let us just take a few to show the variety of the disease-conditions in which this fundamental process of defense plays a leading part. Inflammation of the liver is *hepatitis,* of the kidney, *nephritis,* of the joints, *arthritis,* of the nerves, *neuritis.*

Viruses (living beings even smaller than bacteria) which cause paralyzing inflammatory changes in certain portions of the central nervous system, are the cause of *poliomyelitis.* Some larger microbes tend to irritate the inner surface of the heart and produce *endocarditis.* Ingestion of irritating foods can cause an inflammation of the stomach, that is, *gastritis;* and exposure of the skin to allergens or x-rays may lead to *dermatitis.*

Even the mending of the *wound,* if you have cut your hand, will depend on inflammation, and so will the healing of a *tuberculous cavern* in the lung. *Hay fever,* an inflammation of the nasal mucosa, develops in certain persons because something in their bodily structure has made them especially sensitive to certain plant-pollens in the air. The innocuous *sting of a mosquito,* just as an almost fatal *exposure to the atomic bomb,* is met by the body with what we call *inflammation.*

From all this it is evident that virtually any agent can cause inflammation in virtually any part of the body, and the resulting conditions present the most varied aspects. Yet when you examine the affected organs under the microscope, the cellular changes in them are essentially the same in every case.

Surely this gives food for thought. No one can look upon this list of disorders without feeling the need for some unifying explanation. How could so many conditions be so vastly different and yet be the same, in the sense that they are all inflammations? This is undoubtedly a striking instance of nonspecificity in bodily reactions. That is why we think it will serve our purpose well to show, on the basis of one particular example, how the stress concept can be applied to medical problems.

To do so we must first learn a little more about the *nature of inflammation,* the process which seems to bring unity into this diversity of diseases.

The structure of inflammation

We have said, "Inflammation is a reaction to injury." If so, it must be something active; it is not merely the passive result of injury, but a positive reaction against it. By calling it a *reaction,* we also imply that it has a purpose; apparently its object is to repulse the aggressor and mend whatever damage has been caused.

But what is its structure? What does inflammation look like? In going through our long—though still quite incomplete—list of the inflammatory diseases, we have repeatedly pointed out that there is reddening, heat, swelling, and pain. This is the classical syndrome of inflammation.

The reddening and heat are due to a dilatation of the blood vessels in the inflamed area. The swelling is caused, partly, by the leakage of fluids and cells from the dilated blood vessels into the surrounding solid tissues, and, partly, by an intense proliferation of the fibrous connective tissue, whose cells rapidly multiply in response to irritation. The pain is due to an irritation of the sensory nerve-endings which are caught in and invaded by this inflammatory process.

These cardinal signs have long been known to physicians. They were first clearly described in the Third Book of the famous *Treatise on Medicine,* which Aurelius Cornelius Celsus, the great Roman physician, wrote just a few years before the birth of Christ. This volume contains what is probably the most quoted sentence in medical writing: "Indeed, the signs of inflammation are four, redness and swelling, with heat and pain." To this was later added: "and interference with function," because the swelling and the pain always diminish the functional efficiency of inflamed organs.

The salient microscopic characteristics of inflammation can be summarized by a very simple schematic drawing (see p. 102).

On the left side we see the microscopic appearance of a small normal connective-tissue territory. There are spindle-shaped connective-tissue cells and, between them, connective-tissue fibers which surround a branching, small blood vessel. In the latter we notice both red and white blood cells. Connective tissue is the material which cements all our other tissues together. Here we have described its microscopic features, but with your naked eyes you have already seen it. Whenever some friction, or a cut, takes a bit of skin away, the sticky, pinkish material you see beneath is connective tissue.

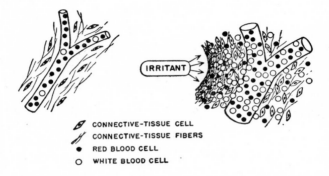

CONNECTIVE-TISSUE CELL
CONNECTIVE-TISSUE FIBERS
RED BLOOD CELL
WHITE BLOOD CELL

After exposure to air, and contact with various irritating substances that we may use to dress the wound, its surface usually becomes granular, and sometimes whitish pus forms on it. That is the naked-eye appearance of inflamed connective tissue. The granules are due to proliferations of connective-tissue cells and fibers. The whitish pus is essentially a mass of white blood cells which have penetrated to the surface—through the vessel walls and the connective tissue—toward the source of irritation.

On the right, we see a microscopic picture of such inflamed tissue. It is actually the same region which has been shown on the left as an example of normal tissue, but now an irritant has acted upon it. The blood vessel became dilated and engorged with blood cells. Many of these, especially the white cells, emigrate into the connective tissue around the vessel, traveling particularly in the direction of the irritant. The connective-tissue cells and fibers proliferate; they tend to form a thick, impenetrable barricade, which prevents the spread of the irritant into the blood.

An important thing which cannot be shown in this drawing is that, from the blood and from the connective tissue, chemical substances are also secreted toward the irritant; they tend to neutralize its poisons and to kill any bacteria that it may contain.

The purpose of inflammation

Judged by its structure, inflammation is undoubtedly an active defense reaction: it represents fight, not flight. There is also an element of repair in it, in that any wound, any tissue-defect caused by an injury, is filled out and mended by the rapidly proliferating connective-tissue cells and fibers. As the fibers mature, they tend to contract; this further helps to abolish the defect.

Once we have thus understood the structure of inflammation, it appears to be self-evident that this reaction is useful for the maintenance of health. This is often true, but not always. If the irritant is really dangerous—say, the deadly microbe of tuberculosis which, if allowed to multiply and invade the blood vessels, would spread throughout the body—then inflammation certainly is useful. It can prevent the irritant from invading farther, by putting a strong barricade of connective tissue around it. If microbes are thus restrained, there is not enough food for them to multiply indefinitely, and eventually they become bogged down by their own exudations. Furthermore, many of the surviving bacteria are killed by the antibacterial chemicals formed by inflammatory tissue, and other microbes are actually engulfed by the white blood cells, which literally eat bacteria.

But what could possibly be the use of responding with inflammation to something like a harmless plant-pollen, which cannot multiply or invade anyway, and which is not damaging to tissue? Yet some sensitive persons react to such plant-pollens with the inflammation which we call *hay fever*. You may say, perhaps nature knows best; perhaps inflammation has a protective value even here. After all, who could tell whether the nasal tissues of a sensitive person would not be destroyed by such plant-pollens if there were no inflammation? This is not so and we can prove it. If a hay-fever-sensitive person is first given large doses of the anti-inflammatory cortisone, contact with plant-pollens will not cause inflammation in his nose; still, under these conditions the nasal structures are not damaged. Indeed a person so protected by cortisone could not even know that he had been exposed to the pollens which normally would produce most distressing symptoms in him. In other words, we might say that here inflammation is no protection against disease: it *is* the disease.

To summarize, we may say that inflammation is undoubtedly a reaction to injury. If the injury is serious, and especially if it threatens life because the causative agent could spread into the blood and throughout the body, then this reaction is useful for the maintenance of health. It essentially consists of putting a strong barricade around the invaded territory, thereby clearly demarcating the sick from the healthy. The diseased part may have to be sacrificed; the destructive cells and fluids of inflammation enter the quarantined area to kill the invader, but usually they also kill the invaded tissues. The pus evacuated from a boil contains the dead bodies of both the microbes and the tissue cells. Other disadvantages are the swelling, pain, and interference with function, which the proliferating inflammatory tissue necessarily produces. This is still a small price to pay for the preservation of life. But if the invader is harmless, there is no point in reacting at all. In this case inflammation does not help, it only hurts.

Now that we have looked at an essentially defensive biologic reaction in a small bit of tissue through the microscope, let us pause for a moment to gain perspective. If we compare inflammation with the defensive reactions of a whole human being, or even of a whole nation, we find striking similarities in the over-all pattern everywhere. By recognizing these we may gain more insight into the mechanism, and even the philosophy, of defense in general, insight which penetrates far beyond the confines of medicine.

If a man comes at you with a knife, obviously with the intent to kill you, it is certainly best to fight. The struggle will be unpleasant; you may be injured; you may even be killed; still, it is undoubtedly better to put up a fight and take your chances than just to wait passively for certain death. But if a ruffian calls you names, why bother about it? His insults cannot hurt you unless you react: either mentally, by worrying about what he said, or physically, by hitting him. In either case what hurts you is the ensuing internal or external fight—your reaction.

This is so even if you consider a whole nation. When an alarm is sounded to announce the approach of the enemy, the threatened nation may immediately stop its peaceful activities to mobilize for war; it may place all available manpower under arms and put up countless barricades of all sorts—or it may do nothing at all. Which course is better depends largely upon the aggressor. If the foe is well-armed and dangerous, it may be preferable to fight. But if the approach of a small band of marauders happened to set off the alarm, a nationwide mobilization of defenses would only hurt the population by unnecessarily interfering with its normal activities.

In all these examples of reactions—whether we deal with the problems of a few cells, with those of a whole man, or of an entire nation—defense may bring salvation or it may bring self-inflicted injuries. Whether to fight or not to fight depends upon circumstances; and, on the whole, cells are more judicious than men, and men wiser than nations, in making this choice. Yet all biologic groups from the microscopic to the geographic are singularly short-sighted when it comes to this alternative. It is, as it were, a difficult selection to make *from within,* for tissues, men, and nations alike. These situations are best appraised by looking at the disturbed unit *from without,* whence you can see its position within a larger complex. This is especially true whenever the result depends largely upon possible help from without.

The regulation of inflammation

Let us analyze now, against the background of these considerations, what we can learn from the mechanism of stress during inflammation about intelligent defense. What regulates inflammatory defense from within the body? How can we help to regulate it from without?

I shall emphasize mainly the role of the endocrines—especially that of the adrenals and of the pituitary—because it is with these that I am best acquainted through personal investigations. Also, it so happens that we have learned more about the role of hormones in the regulation of inflammation than about that of nerves and other factors.

It is easy to see how, by discharging ACTH into the blood, the pituitary can inform the adrenal that a situation of local stress exists somewhere in the body; but how does the pituitary "know" there is stress? This question has still not been fully answered.

ACTH induces the adrenals to produce mainly anti-inflammatory corticoids (such as cortisol and cortisone); hence this chemical messenger of the pituitary can only inhibit inflammatory reactions to injury. What happens when stimulation of inflammation is needed? Intensive work along these lines is still in progress to-day in many laboratories and clinics throughout the world. But we have learned enough about the problem to draw at least a prelimi-nary sketch of stress and inflammation as a part of the G.A.S. blueprint.*

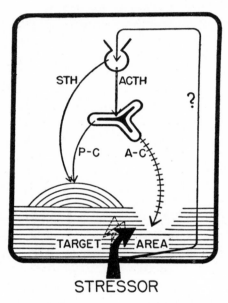

STRESSOR

Here we shall not consider internal and external conditioning, nor the specific actions of agents. These have already been discussed on pages 95–96 and may now be taken for granted. The whole square field represents the body. The funnel-shaped structure on top is the floor of the brain; the round body just beneath it the pituitary. In the middle we see the Y-shaped cross section of one adrenal with its light cortex and dark medulla.

---

* If I may be permitted a small aside before I confront you with this sketch, let me point out that it is taken—without the slightest change—from the 1955 volume of our *Annual Reports on Stress.* It is rather satisfactory to me that in this book written for the general reader it is possible to present all the funda-mental facts necessary to understand this highly technical outline.

The *stressor* (for instance, a colony of microbes) acts upon the *target area* (any part of the body) both directly (thick arrow) and indirectly by way of the pituitary and adrenals.

To begin with, some alarm signal (labeled by a question mark) travels from the directly injured target area to the pituitary. This first mediator of the stress-response undoubtedly exists, but we do not know what it is. Perhaps it is not even always the same signal. In some instances, it may be a chemical substance formed in the directly affected tissue, in others a nervous impulse elicited by pain. It often appears to travel first to the brain and then, through the floor of the brain, to the pituitary, notifying this gland that a condition of stress exists, so that more ACTH is needed.

The subsequent increase in ACTH-secretion stimulates the adrenal cortex to make more anti-inflammatory corticoids (A-Cs). The adrenal can also produce proinflammatory corticoids (P-Cs); but we do not know what stimulates them to do so; it does not seem to be ACTH.

By changing the proportion between pro- and anti-inflammatory stimuli, the body can regulate the ability of tissues to undergo inflammation in response to local injury. This change in reactivity can be accomplished in various ways:

1. Any increase in ACTH-secretion necessarily shifts the balance in favor of an inhibition of inflammation because this hormone stimulates mainly the production of A-Cs.

2. As I said, we still do not know what stimulates the adrenals to produce an excess of P-Cs, but it has been established with certainty that the blood-concentration of these hormones also fluctuates, and quite independently of the A-C-content of the blood. Evidently the production of both types of corticoids can be independently regulated.

3. In order to change the proportion between pro- and anti-inflammatory stimuli in the body, it is not even necessary that the proportion between P-Cs and A-Cs be changed. We found, for example, that if both types of corticoids are very plentiful in the blood (we call this *hormonal tension*) the A-Cs always win the contest. This is so, no matter how much P-C is simultaneously present.

4. Yet another way of changing the inflammability of tissues is

through a pituitary substance which blocks ACTH. This compound is known as the *growth hormone*, because it stimulates the growth of the body as a whole. Most of the giants you can see in circuses are "pituitary-giants," whose growth was stimulated by an abnormal excess of growth hormone. The international scientific name of this substance, *somatotrophic hormone*, is derived from the Greek *soma*, body, plus *trephein*, to nourish, and I have recommended for it the symbol STH (in analogy to ACTH).

Specialists are still divided now in their views on the possible effects of STH upon the adrenals. Some think that STH stimulates proinflammatory-corticoid production, just as ACTH enhances the secretion of anti-inflammatory corticoids; but this is still uncertain. In any event, STH can unquestionably increase the activity of pro-inflammatory corticoids and thereby shift the hormone-balance toward the left. This is accomplished by the direct effects of STH upon connective tissue, as indicated in our drawing on p. 106.

The local response of any directly injured territory to nonspecific stressors, the *local adaptation syndrome* (L.A.S.), is mainly characterized by tissue-death and reactive inflammation. It is clear, from what we have just learned, that this L.A.S. is powerfully influenced by the G.A.S. It is largely dependent upon the balance between proinflammatory and anti-inflammatory hormones secreted by the endocrine glands in reply to alarm signals sent off by the stressor itself.

In our drawing the results of enhancing inflammation are depicted on the left side. Here strong barriers of inflamed connective tissue are shown. They develop under the combined influence of: (1) local irritation by the stressor, and (2) stimulation of defense against the stressor by STH and proinflammatory corticoids. These barriers prevent the spread of the irritant toward the interior of the body. Conversely, on the right side of the diagram, we see the results of an anti-inflammatory-hormone predominance. This manifests itself as an atrophy of connective-tissue elements, a prevention of their inflammatory proliferation, and thus essentially an opening of the way for invasion by the aggressor.

It will largely depend upon the nature of the aggressor which of the two responses is more useful for the maintenance of health.

13:

Need for an over-all picture.
The over-all picture.

Need for an over-all picture

Inflammation is undoubtedly one of the most important features of the response to localized stress-situations during the L.A.S. But the endocrine regulators of general stress-reactions—for instance, the pituitary and the adrenals—also participate in the control of localized inflammation; hence there are close interactions between the L.A.S. and the G.A.S. A primarily local stress, if sufficiently severe, can produce a G.A.S., and general stress influences the L.A.S.

But what happens when a stressor does not act selectively upon any one target organ to produce inflammation? What happens, for instance, when nervous tension (worry, fear, pain), total irradiation of the body with x-rays, or a sudden change in atmospheric pressure, initiates a G.A.S.? None of these agents affects the body through any one limited portal and consequently none of them produces a well-defined L.A.S. Besides, even when there are more or less well-defined direct target areas which react with inflammation, what happens to the other internal organs besides the pituitary and the adrenals? In short, what does the picture of the whole G.A.S. look like? Inflammation is, at the most, a limited part of the whole picture.

Virtually every organ and every chemical constituent of the human body are involved in the general stress-reaction. We should now try to draw a sketch of the whole G.A.S. Of course such an ambitious general map will have to be quite incomplete. In a book of this kind we could not even describe all parts of the human body. Besides, the participation of every organ in the G.A.S. has not yet been fully explored. Still, we badly need a sketch of this kind right now. We must have it, just as an explorer must have some preliminary idea of unknown regions before he can begin to chart them. In medicine, as in geography, or in any other field, we must form some picture of what is known—and even of what can reasonably be suspected—in order to show where further investigation is most likely to be worth the effort.

To draw such a broad picture of the G.A.S., the scientist must start by forgetting all the little problems of detail which happen to occupy him in his daily laboratory work; only then will the well-established fundamental facts stand out clearly.

What are the most important landmarks which necessarily must be in the picture? The *kidney*, for instance, will certainly have to be included, because it plays a central part in maintaining the steady equilibrium of the body during the G.A.S. It regulates the chemical composition of the blood and tissues by selectively eliminating certain chemicals from the body. The kidney can also adjust blood pressure—which is essential for the normal life of all tissues—by secreting renal pressor substances (RPS) into the blood.

The renal mechanism of *blood-pressure regulation* is complicated and still only partially understood; but we have learned many important facts about it, mainly through animal experiments performed by three distinguished scholars: H. Goldblatt and I. Page of Cleveland, and E. Braun-Menendez of Buenos Aires. We have learned, for instance, that when the renal arteries are partially constricted, the kidney produces an excess of renal pressor substances. It is also known—chiefly thanks to Arthur Grollman of Dallas—that the blood pressure also rises if we remove both kidneys from an experimental animal. Here we have a curious paradox: both too much and too little renal activity can result in high blood pressure. It seems that the kidney can both secrete and destroy blood-pressure-raising substances.

We have seen that in general P-Cs and A-Cs antagonize each other; yet large amounts of both these hormones can raise the blood pressure and cause renal damage. Animals injected with large amounts of a P-C develop a kidney disease of the kind which also occurs spontaneously in man and is called *nephrosclerosis*. No matter whether this disease is produced in animals by overdosage with such corticoids, or whether it develops spontaneously in man, nephrosclerosis is accompanied by a marked rise in blood pressure.

At the same time definite inflammatory changes develop in the walls of the arteries throughout the body. These changes, *arteritis* or *arteriosclerosis*, belong to the group of diseases commonly seen in the aged, presumably as the result of cumulative lifelong stress and strain.

We have already had occasion to speak of the antagonistic effect of P-Cs and A-Cs upon connective-tissue responses, particularly *inflammation*. We have likewise mentioned that during stress the *lymphatic cells* tend to disintegrate in the thymus, the lymph nodes, and even in the circulating blood. At the same time the *eosinophil cells* tend to disappear from the circulation.

All this would somehow have to be fitted into an over-all picture of the G.A.S.

But this is not all. The work of Walter B. Cannon and his school at Harvard University has taught us that during acute emergencies the adrenal medulla and certain nerves secrete an excess of *adrenalines*. The significance of *noradrenaline* became evident in this respect more recently, chiefly through the investigations of Ulf von Euler of Stockholm.

The whole important concept of *neurohumoral transmission* of nerve impulses has been clarified by the classical investigations carried out by Sir Henry Dale in England and Otto Loewi in Austria. These were the men who first showed that both noradrenaline and acetylcholine are produced at nerve-endings, and that through these two fundamentally antagonistic nerve hormones the brain and the nerves exert their manifold actions.

The *thyroid*—a gland which lies just before the trachea in the neck—is also often affected during stress; through special hormones which intensely stimulate the metabolism of every tissue, this organ can influence all the organs in the body.

The *liver* is a sort of central chemical laboratory of the organism;

it participates in most of the biochemical adjustments to stress. It regulates the concentration of sugar, proteins, and other important tissue-foods in the blood; indeed it can even check an excess of corticoid hormones by destroying the surplus when the adrenals make too much.

The white blood cells (particularly the lymphoid cells and eosinophils) regulate *serologic immune reactions* and *allergic hypersensitivity responses* to various foreign substances.

Obviously all these tissues have important parts to play during the G.A.S. A general outline of the stress-response will not only have to include them all but will also have to indicate the manifold interrelations between them. This is not easily accomplished. Just think of it: in our map we shall have to place in their proper positions: brain and nerves, pituitary, adrenal, kidney, blood vessels, connective tissue, thyroid, liver, and white blood cells, showing precisely how all these structures may participate in adaptive reactions.

This is attempted in the following synoptic drawing, but I present this "atlas of stress" with great trepidation, because, despite the enormous mass of available data, the picture is still very incomplete.

Undoubtedly my blueprint will evoke the same condescending smile in future investigators of stress which I have so often seen on the faces of first-year medical students to whom I have shown the early anatomic charts prepared by Andreas Vesalius in 1537. These old drawings erroneously portrayed the liver as having five lobes and the whole venous system as arising from the liver. Worst of all, they gave no indication at all that man has adrenals! If I still presume to present the picture of stress as I see it now, my only excuse is that the perfect anatomic charts of today could not have been drawn without their incomplete and largely erroneous predecessors. The same is true of any chart. The maps of Jacques Cartier may make us smile today, yet he and his mariners made good use of them in their exploration of Canada. The investigator of any subject at any time in history will always have to depend upon contemporary pictures to improve upon them.

But must I apologize? We need an over-all atlas of stress, and we need it now, for orientation. Up to the present time we have had none, good or bad; so here is mine.

STRESSOR

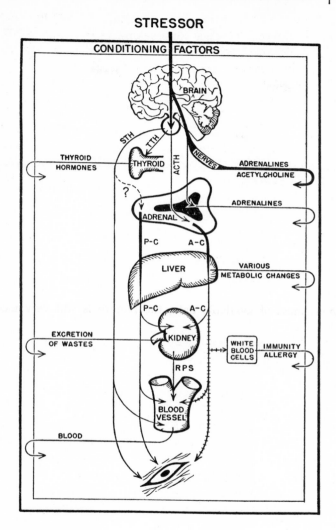

The over-all picture

In this diagram the whole field again represents the entire body. The *conditioning factors* (heredity, previous exposures, diet, etc.) are symbolized by the frame within which all reactions must develop. The main regulators of the stress syndrome (brain, nerves, pituitary, thyroid, adrenals, liver, kidney, blood vessels, connective-tissue cells, white blood cells) are each represented by special symbols. The interactions between these main regulators are shown in the usual way by connecting arrows. But of course no anatomic drawing can, or should be, as complete as the body which it depicts. Only through incompleteness can it emphasize the important and well-established points, differentiating them from everything which is either less important or less certain. To bring this out in our sketch, many arrows do not go specifically to any one organ, but are drawn through the frame, pointing to the body as a whole. The exact pathways through which they act will be the subjects of future research; meanwhile we know only that they can influence the response selectively at various points. It is this possibility of a *selective conditioning* that explains why every person reacts somewhat differently to stress, depending upon his inherited and acquired characteristics.

Since this general diagram attempts to illustrate the fundamental pattern of all stress-situations, the *stressor* is not shown as acting upon any one target area in particular. We merely indicate that, wherever it happened to act first, it eventually produced generalized stress-reactions in the whole body. This generalization of the response can be accomplished by way of the two great coordinating systems: the endocrine and the nervous. Through the floor of the brain the alarm signal reaches the pituitary, the headquarters of hormonal responses; at the same time, by way of the many nerve-ramifications, it influences virtually any organ in the body, without having to go through the endocrine-gland system.

Acting through the *nerves*, stressors produce *adrenalines* and *acetylcholine* which can influence the G.A.S.-mechanism selectively at any point. These two types of nerve hormones generally antagonize each other. For instance, in an inflamed area, the adrenalines can produce circumscribed blood-vessel constriction which interferes with inflammation; whereas acetylcholine has an inverse effect. The movements of the intestinal tract and many other physiologic functions are also antagonistically influenced by nerves through the production of adrenalines or acetylcholine.

A few nerve filaments go directly to the *adrenal medulla*. It is not stimulated by any hormone but by nervous stimuli which cause it to produce adrenalines. These hormones of the adrenal medulla act just like the adrenaline-producing nerve-endings; in fact, the adrenalines made by the gland are chemically identical with those secreted by nerves. The only difference is that the former are secreted into the circulating blood and, therefore, cannot act selectively anywhere, whereas nerves can produce adrenalines in limited tissue-regions without disturbing the rest of the body.

The other great pathway leads through the floor of the brain to the *pituitary* and carries orders for the secretion of ACTH. Here we are in well-known territory. As we have seen before, ACTH stimulates the *adrenal cortex* to produce predominantly A-C (anti-inflammatory corticoid) substances. These, in turn, destroy the *white blood cells* (lymphoid cells, eosinophils) which are necessary both for immunity and for allergic hypersensitivity reactions. Consequently, such immune and allergic responses are inhibited by the cortisonelike hormones.

The A-Cs also influence the *connective tissue* (represented at the bottom of the picture by a single, spindle-shaped connective-tissue cell, surrounded by connective-tissue fibers) to inhibit inflammation no matter how produced. (Inhibition is shown here by cross-hatched arrows.)

The *liver* is perhaps the most important chemical plant in the body. Substances brought to it by the blood can be stored here for later use or transformed into other substances to meet requirements. By means of chemical manipulations the liver can also inactivate a variety of poisonous substances and even hormones. For instance, while the corticoids go through the circulation of the liver, a large part of them is destroyed or transformed into other types of corticoids. Consequently, the liver can change the corticoid-content of the blood, even when the adrenals produce these hormones at a constant rate.

The A-Cs also act upon the *kidney* and—at least under certain circumstances (for instance, when P-Cs are also plentiful)—they can even produce permanent histologic changes in it. Curiously, as regards their known actions upon the kidney, the A-Cs and P-Cs are not antagonistic, although in most other respects they do counteract each other. Among the renal changes produced by the corticoids are certain inflammatory arterial lesions which tend to constrict the blood vessels of the kidney. A change then results, very similar to that which Goldblatt had produced mechanically by putting a constricting ligature around the main renal artery. The main difference is that the hormones, through their chemical actions, put such constrictions upon many minute arteries inside the kidney. We may reasonably assume that such a vessel constriction, no matter how produced, increases the secretion of *renal pressor substances* (RPS). These, in turn, constrict the blood vessels throughout the body and thereby increase the peripheral resistance against which the heart pumps. It is precisely this pumping against great resistance that then raises the blood pressure. Perhaps the ability of the kidney to detoxify pressor substances is also inhibited by certain corticoids; that would, of course, add to the rise in blood pressure.

In any event, the renal changes produced by corticoids—like those elicited by a mechanical constriction of the main renal artery—can produce inflammatory, arteritic, and arteriosclerosislike changes in the *blood vessels* throughout the body. Since A-Cs generally inhibit inflammation, we were not surprised to find that they also prevent this arteritis, at least under certain conditions. I say "under certain conditions" because—as the drawing clearly shows—their ability to do so depends upon the proportion between their kidney-mediated and direct actions. If the kidney is hypersensitized by P-Cs, a concurrent excess of A-Cs may cause renal lesions, and, through these, a rise in blood pressure so pronounced that the arteritis is actually aggravated, although the direct effect of A-Cs is to inhibit it (cross-hatched arrow).

Now, to the left side of the picture. We have reason to suspect that the STH secreted by the pituitary can act upon the adrenal cortex to stimulate P-C (proinflammatory corticoid) production, but this is still uncertain (hence the question mark). In any event, through its direct effect upon connective-tissue cells, STH certainly helps P-Cs to stimulate inflammation. In most other respects STH is also an ally of the P-Cs, due to its direct (not adrenal-mediated) actions. Curiously, it does not appear to act this way on the kidney. STH imitates the kidney-damaging action of P-Cs in intact animals, but not after adrenalectomy. This is one of the main reasons why we also have to consider the possibility of an indirect STH-action which is relayed through the adrenals. We still do not know with certainty what the normal stimulator of P-C production might be. As we have said, these are also called *mineralocorticoids*, because, apart from acting on inflammation, they also influence mineral metabolism. Probably certain minerals in the blood (sodium and potassium) can act back on the adrenal to regulate the production of mineralocorticoids in accordance with requirements.

Finally, the graph shows that during stress the production of TTH, or *thyrotrophic hormone*, is also important. As the name indicates, this pituitary substance stimulates the thyroid. The thyroid hormones are among the most potent accelerators of chemical reactions in the body: they stimulate metabolism as a whole.

This then is the general atlas of the stress-reaction as far as I can make it out at the present time. It comprises the most important known pathways through which our bodily reactions are regulated during the general adaptation syndrome. But now we are tempted to ask, "Just what is adaptation?"

The events depicted here are nonspecifically produced. They occur when our muscles have to adapt themselves to hard work, when our nerves must be used to coordinate activities for an exacting new task, when our connective tissue has to fight an invasion by bacteria; they occur under any condition necessitating adjustment. Yet adaptation to different agents certainly poses different problems to different organs. What is the relationship between these distinct adaptive activities and the stereotyped G.A.S.?

14:

The nature of

adaptation

What is adaptation? Adaptation is always a spacial concentration of effort. Implications of the spacial concept of adaptation.

What is adaptation?

Webster's Dictionary defines biologic adaptation as: "modification of an animal or plant (or of its parts or organs) fitting it more perfectly for existence under the conditions of its environment."

In the foreword of *Stress* (Acta, Inc., Montreal, 1950), I wrote, in a somewhat more philosophic vein, and without attempting a definition, that:

Adaptability is probably the most distinctive characteristic of life.
In maintaining the independence and individuality of natural units, none of the great forces of inanimate matter are as successful as that alertness and adaptability to change which we designate as life—and the loss of which is death. Indeed there is perhaps even a certain parallelism between the degree of aliveness and the extent of adaptability in every animal—in every man.

Webster's comments were dictated by pure intellect, whereas mine were perhaps more influenced by my emotional attachment to a phenomenon which I have learned to admire during our lifelong association. But both these descriptions merely try to say what adaptation is for, not what its mechanism consists of.

To find out more about how adaptation occurs, compare the way you perform a task before and after having done it often. You will notice first of all that almost invariably you have gradually learned to do it better as time went by. The degree of adaptation you can acquire varies from case to case, but there are very few things in life which you cannot learn to do at least a little better with practice.

What is the most characteristic difference between the way we do something before and after we have learned to do it well? To me, it is that at first we invariably put many more mechanisms to work on our problem than later. This is so with virtually any task I can think of.

If I have to lift a heavy weight with my right hand, at first I have to pull, not only with the muscles of my arm, but also with my shoulders. I may even have to bend my knees and then stretch them suddenly to give the weight enough momentum. If I lift the weight several times, my heart will have to beat more rapidly in order to get enough blood into the working muscles; my respiration will be accelerated so as to oxygenate this blood sufficiently for the liberation of enough energy for the chemical reactions which take place in the muscles. However, after adequate training, the whole response will become much more localized to the particular muscle-group which is really essential for the performance of the required work. The muscles of the right arm gradually become large and strong, so that the work may be adequately performed by them without having to strain any other part of the body.

Now, take an altogether different situation: suppose I suddenly have to resist great cold. At first I shiver, wave my arms, and run around because only intense muscular activity can increase the internal heat-production rapidly enough to maintain the normal body-temperature under these conditions. But if I spend much time in the cold every day for months, gradually my thyroid will produce more of its metabolism-stimulating hormones to increase internal heat-production even without excess muscular work. At the same time my skin-vessels will learn to contract so as to minimize heat-losses from the surface. Gradually I shall have learned to resist low surrounding temperatures by using only a few of the particular mechanisms which can best be trained to cope with this situation.

The same is true of mental reactions. When we are first confronted with a complex mathematical problem, we attempt to solve it in different ways. We check our results repeatedly to see whether, using various approaches, we will always arrive at the same conclusion. This process may be quite exhausting, but if similar problems come up again and again, eventually we learn always to use the simplest formula which will give us the correct answer with a minimum of effort.

The same gradual simplification by the concentration of effort occurs even in such fundamental tissue-reactions as inflammation. When irritating germs penetrate through the skin into connective tissue, they first cause an acute inflammation with considerable swelling, reddening, and pain. The reaction will tend to spread and to involve a comparatively large adjacent region of tissue; indeed, there may even be fever and a general blood poisoning because the microbes cannot be adequately confined and many of them enter the blood. The characteristic adaptation in this case is the development of a strong connective-tissue barricade which limits the damage to the minimum by restricting the microbes and their poisons to the point of invasion.

Inflammation can also be produced by excessive function in an organ not adapted to intensive activity. For example, excessive work can cause inflammation in and around muscles, due to local irritation by the metabolic products of activity. This is what causes the muscle-stiffness and pain when we perform physical work to which our musculature is not adapted. Inflammation is a sort of nonspecific auxiliary mechanism of adaptation everywhere; it helps to close all doors and to clean up the débris in any overactive compartment of the body.

All this suggests that *an essential feature of adaptation is the delimitation of stress to the smallest area capable of meeting the requirements of a situation.*

Now that we have found a general, that is nonspecific, feature of adaptation, we can explore the relationships between: the general problems facing the body and its fundamental reaction-pattern (the G.A.S.) during adjustment to anything.

Adaptation is always a spacial concentration of effort

In the next drawing the heavy black line on top represent adrenocortical activity during the three stages of the G.A.S. As the alarm reaction develops, corticoid activity rises sharply; during the stage of resistance it falls to a level only slightly above normal; finally, in the stage of exhaustion, it rises again to, or even above, the maximum level reached during the alarm reaction. These are facts which can be verified by actual determinations of corticoids in the blood, or by studying the bodily changes which are characteristic of increased corticoid activity (for instance, disappearance of blood eosinophils, involution of the lymphatic organs, or the generalized loss of body-weight). All these signs are pronounced only during the alarm reaction and the stage of exhaustion.

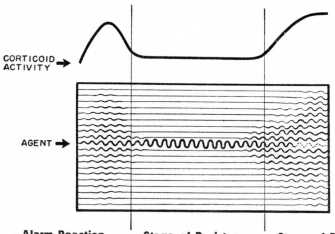

CORTICOID ACTIVITY ➡

AGENT ➡

Alarm Reaction	**Stage of Resistance**	**Stage of Exhaustion**
Auxiliary mechanisms are mobilized to maintain life so that the reaction spreads to large territories. No organ-system is as yet specially developed to cope with the task at hand.	Adaptation is acquired due to optimum development of most appropriate specific channel of defense. Spacial concentration of the reaction makes corticoid production unnecessary	Reaction spreads again due to wear and tear in the most appropriate channel. Corticoid production rises, but can maintain life only until even auxiliary channels are exhausted

In the lower part of the diagram each of the horizontal lines symbolizes the activity of a particular organ or tissue. When an agent acts upon the point indicated by the arrow, it demands maximum adaptive work here, and overactivity will begin at this point. But without training, this one point cannot immediately respond adequately, so that activity must spread to the neighborhood to meet the situation. If the agent is a microbe, not only the cells in its immediate vicinity but even those at some distance from it will become inflamed. Indeed, often no extent of local reaction can prevent some microbes from entering the general circulation; then, to prevent catastrophe, the whole body will have to respond with fever and the production of serologic antibodies against the germs. This is accompanied by a well-marked alarm reaction: adrenal enlargement, lymphatic involution, and all the other characteristics of generalized stress.

But, as irritation at the original point of attack continues, gradually the local adaptive responses can develop sufficiently to cope with the situation. The growth of connective tissue around the microbes will be able to hold them in check, and adaptation becomes limited to the smallest area that must necessarily be involved. Since now only a small tissue-territory is irritated, the number of alarm signals going forward to the pituitary diminishes, and hence adrenocortical activity will no longer be maximally mobilized. The whole reaction has been concentrated to one point.

However, if irritation continues over a very long time, the directly affected cells eventually break down from fatigue, or, if you wish, from exhaustion of all local stores of *adaptation energy*. Then, during the stage of exhaustion, the reaction spreads again because wear and tear have led to the disintegration of the most appropriate channel of defense. Now the reaction must spread again to neighboring areas. In our example, the inflammatory barricade breaks down; the germs invade the surroundings; and eventually, through the blood, they spread to all parts of the body. At this time, when many tissues become involved and again send out their alarm signals, the pituitary and the adrenal cortex are again activated. But, after the auxiliary channels have also become exhausted, recovery is no longer possible and death follows.

In essence, the adaptive hormones of the pituitary-adrenal system appear to be necessary for survival whenever large tissue-regions are under stress. By maintaining life during the alarm reaction, the body gains the time necessary for the development of specific local adaptive phenomena in the directly affected region. During the subsequent stage of resistance, this region can cope with the task without the help of adaptive hormones. Finally, they prolong survival, but only until even the auxiliary mechanisms are worn out; after that there is no further line of defense and death must necessarily ensue.

Implications of the spacial concept of adaptation

It is curious to note such a close interdependence between adaptation and the spacial extension of the body's response to an agent; but the realization of this relationship helped us to form a clearer picture of four hitherto quite inexplicable facts:

1. It had long been established empirically that the more extensive the tissue-damage, the more does it stimulate the production of ACTH and of corticoids. This fact agrees with the hypothesis that within a given time interval, each cell can only discharge a limited number of alarm signals; consequently it is more the extent than the intensity of tissue-damage that stimulates ACTH- and corticoid-production.

2. It had also been shown that an adrenalectomized individual tolerates very intense injury or actual death of a few cells much better than mild injury, or even mere function of many cells. This explains why, for the purpose of self-preservation during stress, the body must produce corticoids in proportion to the anatomic extent of the involved region.

3. The standard response to tissue-injury anywhere in the body is inflammation. Damage or uncustomary function, no matter how produced, can cause inflammation in any part of the body. Thus inflammation is a specific reaction-pattern of nonspecific causation, that is, a manifestation of local stress wherever it occurs. It is of fundamental biologic significance, therefore, that whenever stress spreads to large portions of the body, it automatically evokes a general hormonal stress-reaction which tends to diminish excessive inflammation. When only limited territories are attacked, inflammation is useful; it prevents the spread of the causative agent (for example, of germs or allergens). On the other hand, when disease has already become generalized anyway, it is in the best interest of the body not to put up defensive inflammatory barricades. This is so because: (1) the more the damage has spread the less can be ac-

complished by barricades; (2) inflamed organs do not function well; and (3) inflamed tissue produces toxic substances (enzymes, tissue-decomposition products) which may endanger life when the reaction is very extensive. It is most fortunate therefore that our body possesses a fire-alarm system which automatically puts out the flame of inflammation as soon as its spread threatens life.

4. Finally, we have learned (in Book I) that stress (bloodletting, shock therapies, and so forth) can have a therapeutic value, especially in certain chronic diseases. We have vaguely hinted that it looks as though, during chronic exposure to certain irritants, our adaptive mechanisms would "get into a groove," and that stress would help us to snap out of it. Our last diagram attempts to outline a more precise picture of what actually happens in such cases. Apparently, sometimes when the body uses one organ-system preferentially to cope with a threatening situation, disease can result, either from the disproportionate, excessive development of this particular system or from its eventual breakdown due to wear and tear. Here it is desirable to activate possible collateral channels, thereby giving the preferential one a rest.

In this discussion on the nature of adaptation—as in all our previous considerations—we have tried to point out clearly what is theory and what is fact. It is important not to confuse the two; yet it is not enough to recognize facts; we must also try to formulate ideas about the way the body behaves in health and disease. Only such theoretic concepts can guide us logically to new facts.

I have attempted to define the essence and to dissect the mechanism of successful adaptation. But no biologic reaction is always perfect; the stress-response is no exception. When it fails to cope adequately with a potentially disease-producing situation, the body develops what I have called *diseases of adaptation*. We shall now consider how these arise and how they can be prevented.

Book III:

The diseases of adaptation

Summary

There is an element of adaptation in every disease; but, in some maladies, the direct effects of the disease-producers, in others the body's own defensive adaptive reactions, are more prominent. Only in the latter case do we commonly speak of *diseases of adaptation*. Usually adaptation consists of a balanced blend of defense and submission. Some diseases are due to an excess of defensive, others to an overabundance of submissive, bodily reactions.

It has been possible to simulate a number of renal and cardiovascular diseases in animals by giving them an excess of DOC. This called attention to the possible *role of excessive or insufficient corticoid-production in the development of various diseases* which had never been thought to be related to hormones.

The rest of this section is devoted to a critical discussion of maladaptation as a factor in: *high blood pressure, diseases of the heart and of the blood vessels, diseases of the kidney, eclampsia, rheumatic and rheumatoid arthritis, inflammatory diseases of the skin and eyes, infections, allergic and hypersensitivity diseases, nervous and mental diseases, sexual derangements, digestive diseases, metabolic diseases, cancer, and diseases of resistance in general.*

In discussing these maladies I shall briefly describe the design of the laboratory experiments which helped me to appraise the maladaptation factor in each case. This will permit the correlation of the experimental diseases produced in animals with the corresponding clinical conditions as they occur in man, so that the reader may see for himself *how the laboratory analysis of a malady can guide the physician in his efforts to treat it.*

15:

Diseases of the kidney,

the heart, and the

blood vessels

What is disease? The chickens. Can corticoids produce renal and cardiovascular diseases in mammals? Do the pituitary and the adrenals play a part in the spontaneous renal and cardiovascular diseases of man? When its cause disappears, the disease should also disappear. When the disease is present, the suspected agent should be demonstrable in the body. Metacorticoid hypertension. Eclampsia.

What is disease?

Some diseases have specific causes, the direct actions of certain particular disease-producing agents, such as microbes, poisons, or physical injuries. Many more diseases are not caused by any one thing in particular; they result from the body's own response to some unusual situation.

It is not always immediately obvious that, in the final analysis, our diseases are so often due to our own responses. For instance, if a man is hit over the head with the club of a policeman and suffers permanent brain damage from the injury, it seems rather obvious that his disease was caused by the club. But, if you come to think of it, the blow was not the real first cause; it was but one link in the sequence of a chain-reaction that eventually led to brain injury. What actually happened may have been that the officer asked the man not to loiter, whereupon the latter reacted by violently insulting and assailing the policeman, who in turn hit him over the head with the club. So, in fact, the principal, immediate cause of the man's injury was his own unwarranted, aggressive behavior.

The parts of the body work in a very similar way. We have seen, for instance, that if a dirty splinter of wood gets under your skin, the tissues around it swell up and become inflamed. You develop a boil or an abscess. This is a useful, healthy response, because the tissues forming the wall of this boil represent a barricade which prevents any further spread throughout the body of microbes or poisons that may have been introduced with the splinter. But sometimes the body's reactions are excessive and quite out of proportion to the fundamentally innocuous irritation to which it was exposed. Here, an excessive response, say, in the shape of inflammation, may actually be the main cause of what we experience as disease. Since we had learned that inflammation, in turn, is regulated by adaptive hormones, the question arose whether excessive or deficient hormonal responses to injuries might play a part in the development of various diseases. Could, for instance, the excessive production of a proinflammatory hormone, in response to some mild local irritation, result in the production of a disproportionately intensive inflammation, which hurts more than it helps? Could such an adaptive endocrine response become so intense that the resulting hormone-excess would damage organs in distant parts of the body, far from the original site of injury, in parts which could not have been affected by any direct action of the external disease-producing agent?

The chickens

Frankly, I cannot remember just why I suddenly decided to work with newly-hatched chicks, when the problem of the diseases of adaptation arose. For me it was certainly an unusual thing to do: we did not keep any chickens in the lab; I had never experimented with them before; and I knew nothing about how to raise them. But the oddest thing about it is that I had no conceivable reason for selecting chicks in preference to any of the usual laboratory animals, such as mice, rats, guinea pigs, or rabbits. Yet the choice was certainly lucky. It turned out that the next thing I wanted to do had to be done on newly-hatched chicks; it could have been done on no other animal, and indeed not even on older fowl.

The problem may be stated like this: if the adrenal must produce an excess of corticoids to maintain life during stress, it is quite probable that the resulting hormone-excess in itself may have dangerous consequences. It is a well-known fact that flooding the body with any hormone produces disease. When the thyroid secretes too much of its hormones, metabolism is unduly accelerated. When the pituitary manufactures huge amounts of STH, the result is gigantism. When the adrenal medulla discharges an excess of its adrenalines, the pulse quickens and the blood pressure rises dangerously. It was quite natural to ask, therefore, "What would happen if the adrenal secreted an excess of corticoids?" It obviously does so during stress. But this question could not be answered by just examining a patient in stress; in him it would be impossible to distinguish between the effects of the corticoids and those of stress itself.

There is a curious disease called the *adrenogenital syndrome,* which had long been traced to an overactivity of the adrenal cortex. In this malady there is an excessive, and often abnormal, development of the sex organs, but these morbid changes are due to overproduction of adrenocortical sex hormones. Typical corticoids, such as P-Cs and A-Cs, could not be responsible for this disease because they do not affect sex. We had to discover the syndrome caused by flooding the body with these hormones.

If an electric heater maintains the temperature of a room, we can compensate for excessive cold by using more current. But this is possible only within certain limits. As more and more current is used, there comes a point when the wires burn out; then the whole heating mechanism breaks down, and, significantly, its failure is the direct result of effective heat regulation. This kind of breakdown can occur in most compensatory mechanisms. It seemed unlikely that, in the adjustment to stress, the secretion of corticoids would be an exception.

Naturally, the thing to do was to give enormous amounts of corticoids to normal experimental animals and just see what happened. But, in 1941 when we reached this point in our work, only one corticoid, DOC (one of the P-C hormones) was available in adequate amounts for such experiments, and even it was very scarce and expensive. Besides, most of the common experimental animals are singularly resistant to DOC. If one just injects this hormone into the usual laboratory animals nothing seems to happen; and, of course, at that time nobody knew how to sensitize or condition the body for this substance. Curiously, even now, after some fifteen years of research, I have found no animal which would be more sensitive to DOC (without special conditioning) than the newly hatched chick. This is why it was fortunate that, by sheer accident, I happened to use young chicks for my first experiments.

Since the demonstration of the role played by corticoids in the causation of renal disease has opened interesting new avenues to medical research, it may be amusing to learn how the first relevant experiments were actually carried out in practice.

To start with, I bought 24 three-day-old white Leghorn chicks. After consultation with people who knew something about how to raise pullets, Mr. Nielsen—whom I have already introduced to you (p. 36)—constructed a large wooden box for them in an attic under the roof. He equipped this box with electric bulbs because we had learned that young chicks cannot maintain their body-temperature unless they are kept warm. Soon we also found out, much to our dismay, that they would not eat the usual rat-food, so we got them a special diet, commercially prepared (and sold under the self-explanatory name of Chick-Startina) to start chicks off in life. I mention these details only because it still puzzles me just why I went to all this trouble when there was nothing to indicate that young chicks were the only kind of animals in which our experiment would work.

When we were satisfied that our birds were well taken care of, we divided them into two groups: twelve received daily injections of DOC, and the other twelve acted as untreated controls. During the first ten days I could see no difference between the two groups. Then all the DOC-treated chicks began to drink much more water than the controls, and gradually they developed a kind of dropsy. Their bodies became enormously swollen with fluid-accumulations under the skin and they began to breathe with difficulty, gasping for air, just like certain cardiac patients.

On the twentieth day, we killed both the DOC-treated and the control pullets to examine their internal organs. Upon dissection it was striking that, under the influence of the hormone, large amounts of fluid had also accumulated in their body-cavities and especially within the sac that surrounds the heart (the pericardium). The heart itself was much enlarged and the walls of the blood vessels had become thick and rigid; they looked very much like those of patients suffering from high blood pressure.

The most pronounced changes occurred in the kidneys, which were swollen and had an irregular, discolored surface. Upon histologic examination, they showed lesions which had been described in man more than a hundred years earlier. In 1827 at Guy's Hospital in London, Richard Bright discovered such renal changes in patients with enlargement of the heart and dropsy. Ever since then the condition has been known to physicians as *Bright's disease*. In this malady, the heart becomes big and strong, presumably because it must pump the blood under high pressure, to get it through the narrow and hardened arteries.

Bright had noticed another important sign which he considered characteristic of his disease: the presence of albumin in the urine. In chicks the urine and the intestinal contents are eliminated together through one opening, so that even normally their excretions are rich in albuminous matter which comes from the gut. But, on histologic section it could be clearly seen that in our DOC-treated pullets the fine renal tubules, which carry the urine within the kidney, were also filled with an albuminous precipitate. This was not so in the untreated chicks.

It is difficult to determine the blood pressure in birds accurately, but in several instances we succeeded in showing that under the influence of DOC it rose to very high levels.

Clearly here, in an experimental animal, we had reproduced all the six major features of Bright's disease: (1) characteristic structural changes in the kidneys; (2) enlargement of the heart muscle; (3) thickening and hardening of the arteries; (4) high blood pressure; (5) generalized dropsy; and (6) elimination of albumin into the urine.

Now, before going further, we shall have to say more about kidney diseases. In man there are three common types: nephrosis, nephritis, and nephrosclerosis. Some physicians regard these as essentially distinct maladies, but this is improbable because there are many

transitions between them, and probably they are all closely inter-
related. Nephritis—which corresponds to Bright's disease—usually
develops into nephrosclerosis as time goes by. The former is a
simple inflammation; the latter is a kind of scar-formation due to
the healing of chronic renal inflammation. Nephrosis is considered
to be a degenerative disease. But it is not always possible to distinguish the inflammatory from the degenerative changes, and
nephrosis may develop into nephritis; hence there are no sharp bor-
derlines between these diseases. In any event, the derangement
produced by DOC in our chicks exhibited elements of all three
renal diseases, although it corresponded most closely to nephrosclerosis. I must mention these details to avoid a distortion of my
description by oversimplification; but actually the important point
in this experiment was the demonstration that an equivalent of
clinical kidney disease can be produced by overdosage with a
corticoid hormone.

I published these first observations on the hormonal production
of renal disease during 1942 in the *Canadian Medical Association
Journal*, concluding my article with the sentence: *"Hence it is perhaps not too far-fetched to suspect adrenocortical involvement as a
causative agent in nephrosclerotic hypertension."*

This paper started a great controversy in medical literature. Hypertensive kidney disease is one of the most common fatal maladies
of man; and since nothing was known about its cause, naturally any
clue had to be carefully analyzed. Physicians were particularly reluctant to accept my view, because, in the whole of endocrinology,
there was no precedent of any such inflammatory or degenerative
disease caused by hormones. At that time the textbooks on hormones
were virtually limited to the discussion of the primary diseases of
the endocrines, i.e., maladies which originate within a hormone-
secreting gland. In principle, we distinguish two types of such
diseases: those caused by the destruction of an endocrine gland (for
instance, by cancer or a localized atrophy), and those which result
from a primary overgrowth of an endocrine gland (for instance,
hypertrophy or tumor-formation). These are the derangements
which cause such typical endocrine conditions as diabetes, gigantism, sexual anomalies, and hyperthyroid goiters. The production of

nephrosclerosis by DOC seemed to fall into an altogether different category. No wonder the idea of "adrenocortical participation in nephrosclerotic hypertension" was received with great skepticism.

Can corticoids produce renal and cardiovascular diseases in mammals?

The first question which now arose was whether an experimental Bright's disease could be produced by corticoids only in chicks or also in mammals. The structure of the kidney is similar in man and in other mammals, but in birds it is quite different. Naturally we wanted to repeat our experiments on mammals. In this we failed. When DOC was injected into rats, guinea pigs, dogs, or cats, no obvious changes were noted either in the kidneys or the heart or the blood vessels. It seemed for a while as though we had just accidentally stumbled upon some peculiar hypersensitivity for corticoids, characteristic only of newly-hatched chicks: a mere laboratory curiosity which could have no bearing upon the causation of human diseases.

It was at this time that the idea of some special "conditioning" for corticoids began to take shape. Could we identify the factor which renders chicks particularly sensitive to an excess of corticoids? Would this same factor participate in the development of corticoid-overdosage diseases in man?

Medical experience had shown long ago that patients suffering from Bright's disease cannot stand much salt. Perhaps the kidney of the baby chick resembles the diseased human kindey in having a low salt-tolerance. Would ordinary kitchen salt (sodium chloride) be the factor we were looking for? If we could prove that, with salt, chicks can be further sensitized to the kidney-damaging action of DOC, this would be yet another important fact suggesting a relationship between the experimental and the clinical forms of Bright's disease. Besides, using sodium chloride as a sensitizing procedure, it might even become possible to show—at least under certain conditions—that corticoids can produce renal and cardiovascular disease in mammals.

With this in mind, we proceeded to give newly-hatched chicks dilute solutions of sodium chloride as a drinking fluid; half of them, the controls, received no hormone treatment; the other half were given injections of DOC. It turned out that surprisingly small doses of DOC can produce Bright's disease in birds kept on dilute sodium-chloride solutions which caused no damage in themselves.

We had proved that the experimental DOC disease resembled clinical Bright's disease in that both were aggravated by salt-supplements.

An interesting by-product of this work grew out of the observation that, on more concentrated solutions of sodium chloride, baby chicks develop a kind of Bright's disease, even without any hormone-treatment. This malady is well known to farmers and veterinarians as a spontaneous disease of pullets. It had been given many names—such as *avian Bright's disease, pullet disease* or *blue-comb disease*—but nothing definite was known about its cause. Usually it occurs in epidemics, so that most people believed it to be contagious. Our observations on its causation by salt were subsequently confirmed by veterinarians in various countries. It had been shown that avian Bright's disease tends to occur whenever the food of pullets contains too much sodium. This would explain the epidemic character of the malady, although salt is probably not the sole causative factor. After the importance of sodium chloride was clarified, it has often been possible to get rid of the condition in hatcheries by simply reducing the salt-content of the food and water offered to the chicks.

But let us get back to problems of clinical medicine.

Corticoids can produce renal and cardiovascular diseases in mammals

What we had learned so far suggested that perhaps DOC could produce renal damage even in mammals if they were kept on a high sodium diet. This approach proved to be fruitful. In rats forced to drink 1 per cent sodium chloride, instead of water, DOC did produce nephrosclerosis and hypertension. Yet very large doses of hormone had to be injected for many weeks, and even so the changes were rather mild.

We then argued that the immature pullet may not have sufficient safety margin of renal function to adjust itself well to overdosage with salt and corticoids. If so, perhaps we could further augment the DOC-sensitivity even in mammals by simply taking out one of their kidneys.

In the next experimental series we removed the right kidney in a group of rats which were then forced to drink 1 per cent sodium chloride while receiving DOC. Here the hormone produced extremely marked and rapidly fatal nephrosis and nephrosclerosislike changes in the kidney, enlargement of the heart, hardening and inflammation (arteritis) of the blood vessels, as well as a pronounced rise in blood pressure. Most of these rats died from coronary lesions and cardiac infarcts.

Thus, we finally succeeded in developing an experimental technique of conditioning which consistently permitted the production, by a corticoid hormone, of Bright's disease in a mammalian species.

This was an important turning point in the analysis of these diseases. Within the next few months it could be shown that, after suitable conditioning (removal of one kidney and administration of salt-supplements), DOC also produces similar renal and cardiovascular changes in other mammals, such as the mouse, guinea pig, cat, dog, and even in the monkey, which is the closest relative of man among the laboratory animals. (*See photograph, Plate 2.*)

These observations left no room for doubt; it was quite clear now that, at least under certain circumstances, corticoids could produce inflammatory or degenerative diseases even in mammals, the class of animals to which man himself belongs.

Pituitary hormones can also produce renal and cardiovascular diseases

As I have explained before, corticoids are made by the adrenals under the influence of certain pituitary hormones. It was reasonable to suppose, therefore, that, through their effect upon the adrenals, pituitary extracts would act like DOC. But, contrary to expectations, large amounts of ACTH (the most powerful adrenal-stimulating pituitary hormone) did not do this. Even rats specially sensitized, by removal of one kidney and administration of salt-supplements, failed to develop renal or cardiovascular changes comparable to those we had produced with DOC. Apparently, ACTH stimulates the adrenals to produce large amounts of A-Cs (COL type), but not of P-Cs (DOC type).

On the other hand, pituitary extracts rich in STH did reproduce (in suitably sensitized rats) a syndrome virtually identical with that seen after DOC-treatment. Interestingly, these same extracts were quite ineffective in this respect after adrenalectomy. This finding seems to agree with the view that STH acts upon the kidney and the cardiovascular system by stimulating the production, or by increasing the activity, of DOC-like hormones in adrenal tissue. We are still not certain that this explanation is correct: up to now it has been impossible to show by chemical means that the DOC-content of the blood increases after administration of STH. It would be very difficult to prove this conclusively with present-day chemical techniques, but no matter what the mechanism of the STH-action, one thing is certain: STH can damage the kidney and the cardiovascular system only in the presence of the adrenals.

To summarize the essence of what we have learned from this particular experimental series, we may say that: (1) the pituitary produces substances which can lead to renal and cardiovascular disease; (2) STH (or some substance which is inseparably attached to it) is responsible for this effect; and (3) the production of renal and cardiovascular disease by STH-preparations depends upon the presence of living adrenal tissue in the body.

Do the adrenals play a part in the spontaneous renal and cardiovascular diseases of man?

All this still did not really prove that corticoids (or STH) actually do play a part in the causation of those human diseases which DOC imitates in animals. Besides, our experimentation was not in accordance with an almost routine time-honored pattern for this kind of study; usually, when we want to establish the cause of a disease, we proceed quite differently. If we suspect that some agent (a microbe, poison, or hormone) is the cause of a disease, it must be shown that: (1) when the disease is present the agent is demonstrable in the body; (2) when the agent disappears, the disease disappears. Only after establishing all this, has it been possible, in some cases, to furnish the ultimate proof by actually reproducing the disease in experimental animals through the administration of the causative agent.

For instance, let us take the case of tuberculosis. This disease had first vaguely been ascribed to a variety of causes: bad food, hereditary predisposition, overwork, life in crowded quarters, and so forth. In fact many physicians doubted that tuberculosis always had the same cause. Then, when suspicion fell upon a certain germ as the possible specific cause of tuberculosis, research to prove this theory progressed in accordance with the classical pattern. First, it was shown that the *tubercle bacillus* is present in all patients who suffer from tuberculosis; indeed, it is usually most plentiful in those parts which are most severely affected. Second, it was demonstrated that when the bacilli disappear the disease also disappears. Only after all this did bacteriologists finally succeed in reproducing the disease at will, by injecting guinea pigs with tubercle bacilli. The success of this last crucial experiment was then generally accepted as irrefutable proof of the bacterial theory.

In our studies on Bright's disease, we happened to start with this final step; we first reproduced a simile of the disease with DOC in animals and then progress continued in reverse. As I shall explain presently, the next thing to be shown was that removal of the causative agent (the adrenal) leads to improvement. What is usually the first indication of such a cause-and-effect relationship—namely, that an excess of the suspected (DOC-like) agent is present in the body during the disease—was the last point to be attacked in this study. Before we had accidentally produced the malady in animals with DOC, there was no reason to suspect that corticoids were particularly plentiful in patients who suffer from similar diseases; nor was it known whether withdrawal of DOC-like hormones (by adrenalectomy) would be of curative value here.

Of course, it may seem that, once you have caused a disease with a certain agent, you have proved beyond doubt that the disease is caused by that agent. This type of argument can be misleading. It was quite conceivable, for instance, that the spontaneous renal and cardiovascular diseases of man have nothing to do with corticoids, even if DOC reproduces similar maladies in animals. After all, several roads may lead to the same destination: exercise quickens the heart-rate, but, of course, this does not mean that the rapid pulse of a bedridden, feverish patient is due to excessive exercise. Such an analogy is not quite appropriate, however, because many factors can quicken the pulse, while the particular renal and cardiovascular diseases which we had produced with DOC are rather specific.

In any event, as we shall see, much more evidence has come forth in support of our view that cortical hormones do play a part in the development of certain renal and cardiovascular diseases of man. In discussing these clinical data we must realize that observations on human beings can seldom be made with the precision of animal experiments. The physician's first concern is to help his patient; the acquisition of knowledge about disease is a secondary consideration. This tends to interfere with the interpretation of findings. If we want to know whether the adrenals are indispensable for a biologic reaction in animals, we can just remove these glands—changing nothing else—and see whether or not the response still occurs. In man this is of course not possible. If the biologic reaction is a disease and we are convinced that adrenalectomy would be the best cure, we can remove the adrenals; but the patient must also receive every other treatment that may benefit him, even if this obscures the interpretation of the results.

Despite these inherent limitations of clinical investigation, a great deal of evidence has now accumulated in support of the view that the adrenals participate in the development of various renal and cardiovascular diseases. This evidence is provided by two types of techniques: surgical and chemical. The surgeon can remove the source of the offending hormones (by adrenalectomy or hypophysectomy) and the chemist can demonstrate an excess of them in the blood and urine of patients with kidney or heart disease.

When its cause disappears, the disease should also disappear

To prove this it was necessary to remove the adrenals, which are the source of DOC-like material. Adrenalectomy is a very serious operation. For one thing, a patient who has no adrenals must take pills or injections of corticoids for the rest of his life. If he runs out of corticoids—even if only for a few days—he dies. As long as adequate corticoid-treatment is available, such patients may live an essentially normal and happy life; but it is, of course, very disturbing to know that one is utterly dependent on a drug. There is always the possibility that, on some trip, at some time, corticoids may become quite unavailable; and, for the adrenalectomized patient, that spells death. Yet his situation is not really so much worse than that of a severe diabetic who is equally dependent on insulin. Indeed, if you come to think of it, all of us constantly require food, water, and air, but fortunately very few people are ever stranded in places where any of these vital necessities are unavailable for dangerously long periods.

Besides, often you have no choice. In patients with severe malignant hypertension there comes a point when, under ordinary conditions, death becomes inevitable because no established method of treatment is of any avail. The same is true of certain types of rapidly progressing arterial inflammation. The physician who, in the absence of any precedent, first recommends a hazardous operation in such cases must have a great deal of vision and courage. Yet such decisions must be made whenever medicine attempts to develop a drastic new cure for a dangerous ailment.

Ephraim McDowell made a momentous decision of this kind on December 13, 1809, when he undertook to remove the ovaries of a woman at his private home in Danville, Kentucky. The patient suffered from an ovarian tumor which weighed fifteen pounds; if allowed to go on growing it would undoubtedly have killed her. Yet up to that time no such growth had ever been removed. Perhaps the operation just could not be done. The townspeople were horrified when they learned that their doctor wanted to open a live woman's abdomen and cut out her ovaries. They marched on McDowell's house, ready to hang him, thinking that he must be dangerously insane or criminally irresponsible. But finally mob violence was averted and, against all expectations, the operation succeeded; indeed, the patient lived to be eighty years old, and McDowell had the satisfaction of having initiated an entirely new procedure in surgery.

The basic idea of removing ovarian tumors was a sound one; still, it was largely a matter of chance that this particular patient survived. Anesthesia had not yet been discovered; nothing was known about the need for sterility of instruments; and the Kentucky pioneer's surgical technique was hair-raisingly crude. But the point is that nothing but this operation could have saved that woman in 1809, and—she was saved.

The situation was not nearly as bad when the first total adrenalectomies and hypophysectomies were performed for hypertensive disease. By that time such operations had already been carried out for incurable cancer, yet it took considerable daring and insight to recommend them for hypertension, when the patient's future did not seem to be quite as hopeless. Medicine certainly owes an everlasting debt to those great physicians and surgeons who were not afraid to face the criticism which is always leveled at everything radically new. Some of the first pioneers in this novel approach to the treatment of hypertensive cardiovascular disease were D. M. Green of Los Angeles, J. T. Wortham of Little Rock, G. W. Thorn of Boston, F. D. W. Lukens of Philadelphia, and L. de Gennes of Paris, who showed that at least some otherwise progressive and incurable hypertensive patients could greatly benefit from complete adrenalectomy.

In the *Annals of Internal Medicine* Thorn and his associates, of Harvard Medical School, described a particularly impressive case, to show what can be accomplished by removal of the adrenals in severe hypertension with renal disease. W. Ch., a 34-year-old laborer, was known to have had hypertension for ten years. Three months before his admission to the hospital, this man developed swelling of the lower legs and marked fluid-accumulations in his abdomen. At night he was often troubled by spells during which he could not breathe. Upon medical examination, it turned out that his blood pressure was greatly elevated; his heart was enlarged; and, as a result of cardiac failure, he had developed much dropsy. His difficulties of respiration were caused by the dropsical condition of the lungs. Both adrenals were removed and the patient was maintained mainly on cortisone. After the operation the dropsy disappeared, breathing became normal, and the blood pressure fell essentially within the normal range. This patient, who had been totally incapacitated was able to return to work soon after the removal of his adrenals; and reexamination one year later showed him still "very active and capable of working." From this and similar cases the Harvard group concluded that:

"It would appear, therefore, that bilateral complete adrenalectomy is justified as an experimental approach in man in an effort to determine the possible role of the adrenal cortex in patients with severe hypertensive vascular disease, including those with renal or cardiac impairment.

"In those patients whose blood pressure has fallen in response to adrenalectomy it has been possible to restore the blood pressure toward the original hypertensive levels with desoxycorticosterone [DOC]. . . ."

Another study, made by Doctor R. F. Bowers of Memphis, Tennessee, led to the conclusion that even "bilateral partial adrenalectomy will lower blood pressure in nearly all patients (20 out of 21) to a normal level, for as long as 22 months after the operation, if a small enough piece of adrenal tissue remains."

More recently Professor J. Govaerts of Brussels has demonstrated that complete adrenalectomy can also restore health in patients who suffer from a mutilating type of juvenile arteritis, which histologically resembles that produced in rats by DOC.

Almost at the same time, in Stockholm, Professor H. Olivecrona and Doctor R. Luft successfully performed complete hypophysectomies in man for diabetic hypertension.

Depending upon the character and severity of the disease, the improvement may be quite slight in some cases and extremely striking in others; but the work of all these clinical investigators definitely showed that cardiovascular disease can be treated by removing the adrenals or the pituitary.

To what extent do these findings support our postulate that adrenal and pituitary hormones play a role in the causation of cardiovascular disease?

As I have said, the evaluation of such clinical observations is difficult: no two patients are alike and often additional treatments (prolonged bed rest, special diets, interventions on the nervous system) may be used, which tend to confuse the issue. Also, many of the adrenalectomies were performed not on ordinary but on diabetic hypertensive individuals, merely because here there were two good reasons for removing the source of all corticoids: withdrawal of the A-Cs or *glucocorticoid hormones* (COL type) could be expected to improve the diabetes, and elimination of the P-Cs (DOC type) should diminish the hypertension.

All these are practical points which must be taken into account for the good of the patient, even if they diminish the scientific value of an experimental treatment. In this volume it would be impossible to discuss such details fully, but the principal and best-established facts should be summarized here, at least as far as they shed light upon the participation of corticoids in hypertensive diseases.

Since man cannot live without corticoids, treatment with them had to be given immediately after adrenalectomy in every case. As far as possible the patients were maintained on the COL type of corticoids and were allowed to take only a minimum of salt, because animal experiments had shown that DOC and salt are most conducive to hypertensive cardiovascular lesions. Since under these conditions a rapid improvement occurred in many cases, it must be the removal from the body of the DOC-like P-Cs that counts. This conclusion is further supported by the fact that if such adrenalectomized patients received supplements of DOC or salt, their blood pressure again began to rise dangerously and their blood vessels (most easily observed by direct inspection in the eye) suffered damage.

In other words, these patients behaved essentially like our experimental rats; their disease depended on an adrenal factor of the DOC type. When the adrenals—the source of such hormones—are removed, the disease improves; if COL is then given it is comparatively well tolerated, but DOC and salt rapidly reestablish the hypertensive disease even in the absence of the adrenals.*

Operations, such as adrenalectomy or hypophysectomy, are probably not the final answer to the problem of hypertensive renal and cardiovascular disease, but they point the way to a new rational treatment of these most commonly fatal human maladies. It is to be hoped that, as research progresses, we shall learn more about non-surgical means of inactivating the damaging hormones. This may be accomplished, for instance, by drugs which interfere with the manufacture or activity of pituitary and adrenal hormones. Experiments along these lines are now in progress at our Institute; perhaps in a future edition of this book I shall be able to say more about them. Meanwhile, it is encouraging to know that efforts to cure these ailments need no longer depend wholly on chance; we now have an experimental model of them—the syndrome produced by DOC- or STH-excess in animals—on which the efficacy of possible treatments can be tested.

* Another implication of our work would be to remove the adrenals in patients with incurable nephrosis. If I am right in suspecting a causal relationship between increased aldosterone production and the manifestations of nephrosis, removing the source of aldosterone should be beneficial. Such surgical treatment of nephrosis has not yet been attempted, but it may be worth trying, at least in otherwise hopeless cases.

When the disease is present, the suspected causative agent should be demonstrable in the body

If you suspect that a patient has been poisoned, you only need to demonstrate the poison in his body to prove your point. This is not so with diseases due to DOC-like hormones. The normal body always contains such corticoids and their activity may become excessive, even when they are not produced in excess, because conditioning factors can render them particularly effective. For instance, a derangement in salt-metabolism or a disturbance in renal function can condition the human body for DOC, just as the administration of sodium chloride and the removal of one kidney did in our animal experiments. To understand this problem think of two barrels leaking water. The causative factor may be a hole of exactly identical proportions in both, yet the rate of water-loss may be quite different if, in one barrel, the fluid stands under the conditioning influence of a great internal pressure.

Nevertheless, using the latest, highly sensitive techniques, an actual increase in DOC-like material has now been demonstrated with certainty in several renal and cardiovascular diseases of man.

It has been shown, for instance, that in *nephrosis* (a renal disease accompanied by much dropsy and resembling the initial stages of DOC-intoxication in animals) the urinary excretion of aldosterone (a highly potent DOC-like hormone) is way above normal. It is especially significant that, when the condition of these patients improves, either spontaneously or under the influence of some treatment, aldosterone-elimination in the urine also diminishes. There appears to be a correlation between the severity of nephrosis and the excretion of aldosterone. The same has been demonstrated (by Doctors Luetscher and Venning) for certain types of *cardiac failure* which tend to cause dropsy.

Professor Jerome W. Conn of Ann Arbor made a very remarkable observation last year which has shed light upon this problem. A 34-year-old housewife came to see him because for the past seven years she had suffered from hypertension, kidney trouble, and muscular weakness. She also had various other disturbances, similar to those that can be produced in animals by an excess of DOC: for example, a thirst compelling her to drink so much water that she had to get up several times during the night to void urine. Patients with similar symptoms have repeatedly been observed before, but no physician ever had the astuteness to think of a relationship between their complaints and the experimental syndrome produced with DOC overdosage. Doctor Conn immediately considered the possibility that his patient might have an adrenal hypertrophy or tumor, which would produce an excessive amount of some DOC-like hormone, such as aldosterone. Analysis of the urine showed that this woman did, in fact, eliminate an extraordinarily large amount of aldosterone and, on this evidence, he recommended an operation to inspect the adrenals. The surgeon found, and immediately removed, a large adrenocortical tumor, whereupon the patient recovered her health.

Doctor Conn named this condition *aldosteronism* and concluded from his observation that in the future "patients exhibiting such clinical and laboratory manifestations be subjected to adrenal surgery." Several additional cases have since been observed by other physicians, and there can be little doubt that here the excess production of DOC-like material by the adrenals is the cause of a hypertensive disease.

Until quite recently we have had no satisfactory method for the demonstration of aldosterone and other DOC-like compounds in the fluids and tissues of the body; this is one of the reasons why, up to now, so few investigators have searched for them in patients with ordinary *hypertension*, particularly the malignant type. Certain preliminary observations (by Doctors Venning, Genest, and Heard, of Montreal) suggest that here the production of DOC-like material is also increased. But it would not surprise me if, even with the best methods, it should prove impossible to demonstrate a significant hormone-excess in every patient who suffers from hypertension. First, some cases of hypertension are due to derangements which have nothing to do with corticoids; second—though this may seem paradoxical—when a disease manifests itself its cause is not necessarily present in the body. This has been demonstrated particularly as regards the so-called metacorticoid hypertension.

Metacorticoid hypertension

All the clinicians agree that adrenalectomy for hypertension is most effective when the kidneys are not yet severely damaged by the disease. Apparently an advanced nephrosclerosis can maintain an abnormally high blood pressure even in the absence of the adrenals.

This noteworthy fact checks perfectly with earlier animal experiments performed by two of my former pupils, Professor Sydney Friedman of Vancouver, and Doctor Leal Prado of Saô Paulo, as well as by Doctor D. M. Green, of Los Angeles. These three investigators found—at about the same time and yet quite independently of each other—that, in rats which have become hypertensive as a result of DOC-treatment, the blood pressure returns to normal as long as hormone-administration is discontinued early; on the other hand, if DOC-treatment is stopped only after the kidney has been seriously damaged, the blood pressure continues to rise, even when no more hormone is given.

I called this *metacorticoid* (from Greek *meta*, after) *hypertension*, because here the disease progresses after a transient corticoid overdosage.

Unfortunately, once this stage has been reached, the disease appears to become irreversible; at least our experiments have so far given us no clue to a possible treatment.

Eclampsia

A young woman, who comes from a perfectly healthy family and never had any serious illness in her life, may—when she expects a baby—suddenly come down with one of the most fulminating hypertensive diseases: eclampsia. Often there is nothing to foreshadow this complication and the patient feels perfectly well during the first two thirds of pregnancy. Then, without any warning, she has convulsions, her face becomes congested, she foams at the mouth, and often badly bites her tongue. During these spells she may even die, but as a rule the convulsions are followed by more or less prolonged periods of unconsciousness (coma), from which the patient recovers. These convulsive attacks may become more and more frequent as pregnancy progresses, and then the condition is sometimes mistaken for epilepsy.

It is this sudden onset that earned the disease its name (from, Greek *ek*, out, plus *lampein*, to flash). It has also been called the *disease of theories* because it stimulated so much speculation.

Doctor C. H. Davis's standard three-volume treatise, *Gynecology and Obstetrics,* discusses fifteen theories of eclampsia, only to conclude: "We are wholly ignorant as to the cause of this disease." In any event, the malady belongs to the general group of the toxemias of pregnancy, which also includes the milder *preeclampsia* (minus convulsions or coma), the vomiting of pregnancy, and various types of renal and hypertensive diseases.

Actually eclampsia itself is also a hypertensive disease which affects the kidney and the blood vessels. It is characterized by frequent sudden, intense rises in blood pressure, the excretion of albumin in the urine, and morbid changes in the blood vessels which may lead to hemorrhages in the brain, liver and other organs.

The safest treatment is to accelerate delivery because, as soon as mother and baby are separated, all the symptoms and signs disappear. But if premature termination of the pregnancy is impossible, there is not much that can be done, either for the mother or for the baby. It is instructive, however, to examine what sheer experience has taught physicians about the treatment of this disease. Even before the possible participation of corticoids in the development of eclampsia was suspected, it was found that the best thing to do (apart from combating the convulsions with sedatives and complete rest) was to give much fluid or ammonium chloride, which stimulated the excretion of urine and, particularly, of sodium. It had also become known that, on the other hand, foods rich in sodium chloride tended to aggravate this disease.

The beneficial effect of washing out sodium, the damaging action of sodium-chloride intake, and the character of the morbid changes in the kidney and blood vessels are all singularly reminiscent of the DOC-overdosage syndrome which we had produced in rats. I may add that even convulsive spells, similar to those of eclampsia or epilepsy, had been noted quite frequently in our rats treated with excessive amounts of DOC. All this strongly suggested some relationship between eclampsia and the adrenocortical hormones. But we needed more proof.

Soon additional evidence of such a relationship was brought to light by the interesting studies of my former associate, Georges Masson, who worked on this subject in cooperation with Doctors I. H. Page and A. C. Corcoran, at the Cleveland Clinic. These investigators found that, after pretreatment with DOC, a few injections of a blood-pressure-raising kidney-extract (renal pressor substance) can produce a syndrome which imitates eclampsia even more closely than the one produced by DOC alone.

Particularly illuminating relevant observations have been published by Doctor Russell R. de Alvarez. He found that DOC is definitely contraindicated in women with preeclampsia because it tends to aggravate their disease, somewhat as sodium does. Moreover, it has been demonstrated recently, in several clinics, that women suffering from eclampsia excrete excessive amounts of aldosterone. This is one of the most convincing clinical observations in support of the concept that an increase in DOC-like hormones plays a role in this disease. All these findings still do not prove definitely that the adrenal plays a decisive role in the production of eclampsia, but they do make it rather probable. In any event, we have learned enough by now about this "disease of theories" to know that the role of corticoids deserves to be systematically investigated, and that treatment based on this concept offers definite promise.

It is still largely a matter of debate which of the *diseases of adaptation* are due to an actual overproduction of, or hypersensitivity to, adaptive hormones. But this is a point of secondary importance. The most significant practical outcome of our experiments was to demonstrate that *hormones participate in the development of numerous nonendocrine diseases,* that is, of maladies which are not primarily due to derangements originating in the endocrine glands themselves. Prior to these studies, we had no reason to suspect that such conditions as nephrosis or cardiovascular disease are in any way dependent upon the pituitary-adrenal axis, and that they might be effectively treated on the basis of this dependence.

Now, let us turn our attention to the inflammatory diseases, in which this approach has been even more rewarding.

16:

Inflammatory diseases

The basic problems. The inflammatory-pouch test. Some practical applications of this test The experimental arthritis tests. Rheumatic and rheumatoid diseases of man. Inflammatory diseases of the skin and the eyes. Infectious diseases. Allergic and hypersensitivity diseases.

The basic problems

In our dissection of stress we have devoted an entire chapter to inflammation (p. 99), because this is the most striking aspect of the L.A.S., the local adaptive response of tissue at the site of injury. We have seen that the principal purpose of inflammation is to put a strong barricade of activated, connective tissue around a territory invaded, or at least damaged, by some disease-producer, thereby sharply *demarcating the sick from the healthy.*

If the invader is dangerous and threatens life because the causative agent could spread into the blood and throughout the body, then—and only then—this reaction is useful.

The diseased part may have to be sacrificed, because when the destructive cells and fluids of inflammation surround and quarantine an area to kill the invader, they often also kill the invaded tissues. We have seen that the pus evacuated from a boil usually contains the dead bodies both of the microbes and of the body's own tissue cells. Besides, inflammation causes swelling, pain, and interference with the function of the affected parts. All this is a small price to pay, however, when this reaction is our only means of maintaining health or even life: that is why inflammation is essentially a useful, adaptive response to injury.

But, *if the invader is harmless,* there is no point in reacting at all.

An inoffensive plant-pollen, for instance, does not damage the tissues directly, and it could not invade the body as a whole. If we react to it with allergic inflammation, this is merely a sign of morbid hypersensitivity. Here the inflammation itself is actually what we experience as disease. In such cases we are not being injured, we merely injure ourselves. Here the reactions of our tissues are quite comparable to those mental overreactions (worry, anger) to inoffensive insults, which do not help but merely hurt. Worry and even anger are useful mental responses when we have to take some energetic action to defend ourselves. The trouble is that only too often we do not have enough self-control over our mechanisms of defense, so that we use them too much or too little.

The *principal problems* posed by the inflammatory diseases are: first, to determine how inflammation can be influenced (for instance, by hormones), and then to establish when it should be enhanced and when inhibited. We have already seen that the body can make proinflammatory and anti-inflammatory hormones with which to influence inflammation; and, of course, the physician can use these substances for treatment whenever the body's own response is imperfect. But this is possible only after we have learned just how these hormones work and exactly where such treatment is indicated or contraindicated.

No conscientious physician would like to take the risk of learning all this by random observations on patients. That is why experimental medicine had to step in and devise *similes of human diseases which could serve as experimental models*, so that the elementary lessons might be learned on animals.

Normally the inflammatory response is rather irregular and unpredictable; it does not lend itself to exact, experimental research. You can produce inflammation in animals by simply dropping some irritating material under the eyelid, by rubbing it onto the skin, or by injecting it into internal tissues. But the results are quite unpredictable, because much of the material rubs off the eye or the skin and, if you inject it into deeper tissues, it distributes itself quite irregularly, so that the response can never be predicted. From all we have said about inflammation, it is clear that what we really needed was an experimental model of it in animals, one which could readily be produced and which possessed the following features: (1) it must not permit the causative irritant to escape, other-wise it would be impossible to establish the quantitative relation-ships between irritant and response; (2) it must have a predictable, regular shape and size, so that it can be accurately measured; (3) the two major components of inflammation, the cellular barri-cade and the inflammatory fluid, must not be intermixed (as are the solid and fluid parts of a wet sponge), so that each can be sepa-rately measured, because each has different functions; (4) the bar-ricade must form a sac of even thickness, so that its functional value as a barrier can be measured—for instance, by injecting microbes or corrosive chemicals into its cavity and determining how much the pouch-wall can stand before it perforates.

This is quite an order, and I have spent many years trying to devise such a test without success. I always felt that some kind of mold could do it, as for instance, a glass bead or a small ball of metal which, when inserted into connective tissue, would force it to take up a regular, spherical shape. But it would have to be a very bland and elastic foreign body and one which would eventually dis-appear, so as to leave a cavity for fluid accumulation. All the molds I have tried were hard and caused the surrounding skin to perforate wherever the rat pressed against it; besides, there still remained the problem of removing the mold after the barricade had formed. It seemed a more theoretical than practical idea to use this type of a procedure, until finally a lucky accident showed the way.

The inflammatory-pouch test

In patients suffering from consumption, it is often useful to inject air (or some other gas) into the chest-cavity, so as to collapse a diseased lung and give it a rest to promote healing. Since, on the other hand, any kind of stress is particularly bad for tuberculous patients, I was interested in finding out exactly how stressful the air-injection itself would be. To determine this, I injected air into the chest-cavity in rats, with the intention of then measuring their adrenal-response as an indicator of stress.

It so happened while I was doing this, that a group of Brazilian physicians who visited our Institute, were shown into my lab by one of my assistants. As I turned around to greet them, my needle slipped out of the chest-cavity of the rat I was just injecting and all the air went under the skin; there it formed a perfectly regular, roughly egg-shaped connective-tissue sac. Why not *use air as a mold* with which to force connective tissue to form a sac of predictable size and shape? Air is very elastic and it need not be removed to permit fluid accumulation in the pouch. I then made such air-sacs on purpose, and injected some irritant (usually croton oil) into the cavity, so as to transform the lining connective tissue into an inflammatory barricade.

This proved to be a very practical procedure. As soon as the lining was transformed into inflamed connective tissue, the cavity filled up with inflammatory fluid. After the rat was sacrificed, this fluid could be measured accurately by aspirating it into a graduated syringe, and the connective-tissue barricade could be dissected and weighed separately. In fact, if the rat were shaved, the progress of inflammation could be followed every day by transilluminating the sac with an electric flashlight and measuring the height of the fluid-column. Even function tests for the delimiting value of the barricade can be quite easily performed on this test-object by injecting microbes or corrosive chemicals into the cavity of the sac and determining the concentration which can be tolerated without causing perforation.

To see how this kind of work is done, it is interesting to follow the manner in which certain basic problems in the development and

This is what the pouch looks like on a rat

A

walking about
in daylight

B

or held up straight
for transillumination
in the dark

treatment of inflammatory diseases could be analyzed with this simple test. (*See photograph, Plate 3.*)

Some practical applications of the inflammatory-pouch test

How do the anti-inflammatory hormones work? Immediately after the introduction of ACTH and cortisone into practical medicine, certain clinicians were puzzled by the fact that these substances influenced so many varied diseases. Physicians attempted to explain this by assuming that the anti-inflammatory hormones act like an "asbestos suit," which protects various cells against the "fire of disease," by somehow preventing the disease-producing agents from getting into the cells.

The validity of this assumption could easily be checked by the inflammatory-pouch test because it permitted us to explore the problem under strictly reproducible conditions, in what might be called *a living test tube* of connective tissue. For instance, by placing a chemical irritant, such as croton oil, into the subcutaneous connective-tissue pouch, we could explore its effect upon the lining connective tissue, as well as upon some adjacent structure, such as the skin which covers the sac. This way it was easily demonstrated that, in a normal rat, a given amount of croton oil transforms the lining tissue into an inflammatory barricade which protects the adjacent skin. In a COL-treated rat, on the other hand, the same amount of croton oil causes little or no inflammation; consequently, the irritant spreads into, and destroys, the adjacent skin. Far from acting as an asbestos suit, COL actually prevented the formation of a protective shield (that is, the inflammatory barricade) and thereby aggravated the situation in this test.

It was concluded that, in general, COL and similar anti-inflammatory hormones act nonspecifically because they inhibit the immediate inflammatory defense reaction to various agents. This may be advantageous when the irritant is mild and unlikely to cause much destruction anyway, or it may be detrimental when the irritant is severe and kills surrounding tissues if it is permitted to spread into them.

How do proinflammatory hormones work? Similar tests with DOC or STH showed that these substances actually increase inflammatory-barricade and fluid formation; indeed if they are given concurrently with anti-inflammatory hormones, they neutralize the effects of the latter. In this manner it was possible, within certain limits, to titrate proinflammatory and anti-inflammatory hormones against each other, using inflammatory fluid and connective-tissue formation as indicators of activity.

Of course, whenever we clarify the mechanism through which a biologic agent works, other questions arise. We now must ask, "Through what chemical reactions do these hormones regulate inflammation?" Much work along these lines is in progress. Most probably, the hormones influence certain enzyme reactions within the connective-tissue cell. Probably they can act upon disease in many other ways as well. For instance, hormones have important effects upon nervous activity, and they can influence immune reactions against microbes and other disease-producers. Yet it is of great practical value to know that one of the most fundamental mechanisms through which these hormones affect resistance to disease-producers is by regulating the development of inflammatory barricades.

How is it possible that general stress sometimes cures and sometimes aggravates a local disease condition? Various shock therapies and other nonspecific treatments have clearly shown that general stress can cure certain diseases; yet we also know that so often a latent disease-tendency is transformed into a manifest malady by too much stress and strain. Could we not use the inflammatory-pouch test as a simple model with which to analyze this apparent paradox?

I took two groups of rats, in which an inflammatory pouch was produced under exactly identical conditions, except that in one group I put a weak irritant (dilute croton oil), in the other a strong irritant (more concentrated croton oil) into the air-sac. Shortly afterwards both these groups of animals were exposed to a general stressor in the form of a frustrating experience. Without going into the technical details, let me say that, in such tests, the animals are forcefully immobilized, so that they cannot run around freely; this causes them to struggle and to become very angry. A rat wants to have his own way, just like a human being, and does not like to be prevented from doing what he wants to do. I thought that this kind of frustration and struggle would come about as close to the most common human stress-situations as we can come in rats, and wondered how it would influence local tissue-reactions to irritants.

The results were very illuminating and are illustrated in the sketches below.

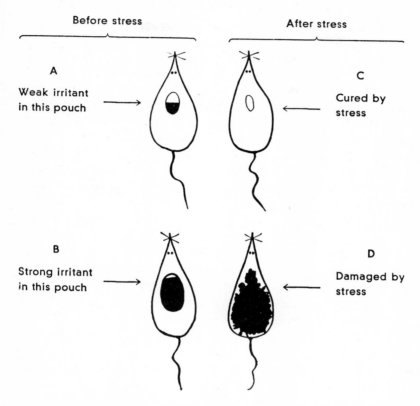

In the rats which received the weak irritant, there was little inflammation and the general stress actually cured the local disease by inhibiting this tissue-response. The irritant was not strong enough to destroy the covering skin in any case, so it did not matter whether the substance was allowed to spread or not. Inflammation was the whole disease here and, by inhibiting it, the rat was cured.

In the animals treated with the strong irritant, there was much more inflammatory-barricade formation and fluid formation; still the adjacent tissues remained healthy, because the inflammatory barricade prevented the strong croton oil from spreading into the surroundings. Under the influence of general stress, however, the skin and all the adjacent tissues were infiltrated and destroyed by the spreading concentrated croton-oil solution. This was the crucial experiment showing that stress can either cure or aggravate a disease, depending upon whether the inflammatory response to a local irritant is necessary or superfluous.

I should add that there can be no doubt about the role of adrenal hormones in this type of general stress-effect. We repeated the whole experiment on rats whose adrenals had previously been removed and found that, in them, general stress had no effect upon the course of inflammation, whether produced by weak or by strong irritants.

It is hardly necessary to insist upon the importance of such observations as a guide to clinical treatment. Without this kind of information we would have been tempted to treat any inflammatory disease with anti-inflammatory hormones. The result would have been disastrous in certain maladies—for instance, in tuberculosis or acute appendicitis—where spreading must be prevented, whatever the cost. Yet, once we understand the mechanism through which these hormones act, even such diseases can benefit from them. For instance, in many cases, it is possible to eliminate strong microbial irritants by suitable antibiotic treatment; after that, removal of the inflammatory barricade is no longer dangerous but actually helps by removing the painful inflammatory tissue which has now become useless.

Is there a critical period for the treatment of inflammation by hormones? We have seen that inflammation is a feature of the L.A.S., which develops in three stages, just as the G.A.S. does (see pp. 87, 108). In other words, the microscopic structure and the function of inflammation vary, even while tissue is constantly exposed to the same irritant. It seemed rather important to determine at what point of its development inflammation is most sensitive to the action of hormones.

Using again the inflammatory-pouch technique, I found that COL-treatment is comparatively ineffective, if given on the day the irritant is introduced into the pouch. It is also quite difficult to influence an already fully developed inflammatory pouch with this hormone. But if COL is given a few days after the irritant has been applied, then inflammation can be suppressed very easily. In other words, there is a definite critical period during which inflamed tissue is especially sensitive to this hormone. Almost exactly identical results were obtained in animals exposed to some general stressor; apparently, the COL secreted by the rat's own adrenals during stress also acts best during the critical period.

Can there be a lack and an excess of COL in different parts of the same individual at the same time? The hormones produced by endocrine glands are discharged into the blood stream and consequently every part of the body is supplied with blood having the same hormone-concentration. Nervous impulses can be led selectively to one region or another, but hormones are distributed equally. At first sight, it would seem quite impossible that, in the same person, one region might have too much and another too little of the same hormone. Classic endocrinology has recognized only diseases caused by an excess or a deficiency of hormones, but the question had never even been raised whether, in the same patient, there might be an excess in one place and a deficiency elsewhere.

The point seemed of fundamental importance, and the just-mentioned experiments with the weak and the strong irritants led me to suspect that this apparently ridiculous question might be well worth a careful investigation. You will remember that COL-treatment had a curative effect in the rats bearing an inflammatory pouch produced with a weak irritant, but that in animals exposed to a strong irritant, it was actually damaging. What would happen if, in the same animal, we exposed one region to a weak and another to a strong irritant? This was the sort of problem that we could easily test with the inflammatory-pouch technique. All we had to do was to prepare two pouches in the same rat and put a weak irritant into one, a strong irritant into the other. The result of such an experiment is shown in the pictures on p. 158.

In both rats shown here, the weak irritant was put in the pouch on the neck and the strong irritant in the one on the back. The animal on the left was not treated with any hormone; that on the right was given subcutaneous injections of COL. Obviously, after being taken up into the blood from the subcutaneous tissue, the COL must have been distributed equally to all parts of the body. Yet, under the particular conditions of this experiment, the amount of COL given was too little for the pouch on the neck (it did not prevent inflammation), and too much for the one on the back (it caused tissue-destruction worse than inflammation).

The weak irritant in the pouch on the neck still produced some (though now less) of the essentially useless inflammation. Had we given more COL, we would have inhibited all signs of disease, be-

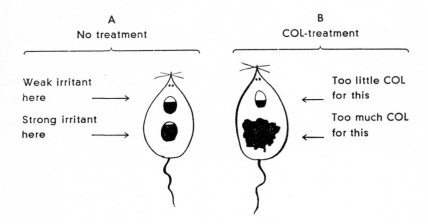

A	B
No treatment	COL-treatment

Weak irritant here ⟶

Strong irritant here ⟶

⟵ Too little COL for this

⟵ Too much COL for this

cause (just as in the rat on top of p. 155) here inflammation was virtually the whole disease and its inhibition would not have led to any serious tissue-injury anyway. On the other hand, the pouch on the back contained a strong irritant, which normally causes much inflammation, but this is useful because, at least, the surrounding tissues remain protected. Even the moderate amount of COL given here suppressed inflammation sufficiently to permit the strong irritant to penetrate into and destroy the surrounding skin. This led to the formation of a large open wound surface, which was worse for the animal than the untreated inflammation.

The important lesson learned from this experiment is that there is no such thing as a definite proper amount of COL for an animal or a person. A certain quantity is appropriate only for a given degree of local stress. To maintain the healthy, steady state (homeostasis) of tissues, the amount of stress hormone must be adjusted to the intensity of the stress. It is definitely possible to have regional excesses and deficiencies of hormones in the same individual, as long as irritation (local stress) in the various parts is uneven.

This again has considerable practical application because, in man also, different regions are often—in fact, usually—exposed to uneven degrees of stress. We are now studying various techniques which permit us to concentrate COL-activity in different parts of the body at will. In accessible parts this is easy: we merely apply the COL locally. We have not yet found any way to direct COL molecules selectively to various internal organs at will, but we can increase regional tissue-sensitivity through the phenomenon of conditioning (p. 95). For instance, certain blood-vessel-constricting drugs sensitize limited regions of the body to the anti-inflammatory effect of COL.

Is there such a thing as a focal infection? According to certain Egyptian tables—which date back to 650 B.C. and were found in the ruins of Nineveh—the great king, Annaper-Essa, suffered from a terrible disease, consisting of intense headaches and pains in the joints. No treatment known at the time was of any avail. Then, upon counsel of his physician, Arad Nassa, the royal patient had his bad teeth extracted and immediately all his troubles miraculously disappeared.

During the seventeenth century, the French surgeon, Jean Louis Petit, pointed out, in his famous *Treatise on Surgical Maladies,* that dental caries can produce all sorts of ailments throughout the body and that these can be treated by removing the infected teeth. As time went by, many physicians noted that infections in the mouth and throat can produce disease in distant organs, so that the discovery of this fact is certainly not new. Still, it was to the great merit of the American physician, Frank Billings that, in his classical paper (1912), "Chronic Focal Infections and Their Etiologic Relations to Arthritis and Nephritis," he first formulated the problem with sufficient precision to bring it to the attention of the medical profession throughout the world. Professor Russell L. Cecil, in his standard *Textbook of Medicine* (W. B. Saunders Co., 1943), defines focal infection as "a localized infection which presumably produces symptoms in other parts of the body and in which there are usually no demonstrable bacteria in the blood stream."

It is still something of a mystery just how focal infection works, but undoubtedly much depends upon the architecture of the inflammatory barricade around the infecting microbes. It *is* well known, for instance, that children who often suffer from very bad sore throats are predisposed to rheumatic fever. This cannot depend wholly upon the microbes in the infected tonsils because, when these same germs are introduced elsewhere in the body, they rarely cause rheumatic fever. Perhaps the architecture of the inflammatory barricade around the germs must be such as to permit only very small numbers of them (or small amounts of their poisons) to enter into the blood stream at one time. This prevents massive invasion of the blood with demonstrable living bacteria and may modify the course of the illness by protracting the effects of the infection. There are many other theories, but we need not waste time on them because none has been definitely substantiated.

About twenty years ago it was fashionable to ascribe almost any ailment of unknown origin to some focal infection. But, to quote Cecil's textbook again: "Many thoughtful physicians . . . who originally accepted the theory of focal infection with enthusiasm, have watched with interest and some trepidation its rapid development in the various fields of medicine and are now wondering if the time has not arrived for the re-evaluation of the theory. Many students today question seriously its validity and some are quite willing to throw it completely overboard. This is particularly true in Europe, where the idea of focal infection has never met with enthusiastic acceptance. But even in America, many practitioners are becoming a little wearied of the theory which has been accepted as if it were an established fact."

You may wonder how there could be so much uncertainty about a condition which has allegedly been known since ancient Egyptian times. The trouble is that the development of focal infection is quite unpredictable. Sometimes a localized infection will be followed by rheumatic heart disease or arthritis and sometimes by nephritis or some other change in organs far removed from the site of infection. Sometimes surgical removal of the infected focus (for instance, the teeth or tonsils) leads to a cure and sometimes it does not. This being the case, it is difficult to prove a causal relationship between a localized infection and disease-manifestations elsewhere in the body.

To prove definitely the existence and study the mechanism of the focal infection syndrome, we would first have to succeed in reproducing the condition regularly in experimental animals. This has never been done. It has been tried many times—ever since the discovery of bacteria—but the results have been just about as inconsistent and unpredictable in animals as is the effect of a sore throat upon the heart or of an infected tooth upon the joints, in human beings.

In the inflammatory pouch we have a test which permits us to regulate, more or less at will, the architecture of the barricade between the infected and the healthy tissues. By introducing different kinds of irritants, with or without microbes, we can force the wall of the sac to be built differently. Can one purposely construct a wall which will result in the consistent production of the focal syndrome in experimental animals?

This proved to be possible. Using certain combinations of irritants and microbes in rats, we finally managed to produce a syndrome characterized, among other things, by an inflammation of the heart valves (endocarditis), very similar to that which occurs in children suffering from rheumatic fever. Under certain circumstances, this was accompanied by inflammation of the kidney (nephritis) and excessive stimulation of the blood-forming organs. After we had learned how to produce this syndrome regularly, we could proceed to an experimental dissection of its mechanism, using essentially the same standard techniques that proved so useful in the analysis of the G.A.S. (removal of endocrine organs, injection of hormones, and so forth). It turned out, for instance, that the proinflammatory and anti-inflammatory hormones can modify the whole focal syndrome and that an excess of salt in the diet, after removal of one kidney, selectively aggravates the nephritis in the remaining kidney. This work is still in progress and it would be premature to discuss it at great length. It is already evident, however, that here we are also dealing with some kind of disease of adaptation (which, in this case, is due to an improper adjustment of the body to invading germs); and now that we have constructed an experimental model of the disease in animals, it can be subjected to a systematic scientific analysis.

The experimental arthritis tests

The inflammatory pouch proved to be very useful in the study of inflammation in general, but, of course, the character of inflammation largely depends upon the organ in which it develops. Chronic inflammation of the joints (arthritis) is one of the most common, crippling, wear-and-tear diseases of man. We still had no adequate procedure for reproducing this condition in animals for the study of its mechanism and for the assay of hormones or drugs which may be used to treat it.

In searching for such a test, I noted that if we inject a drop of some irritant solution (Formalin, croton oil) under the skin of the sole into a hind paw of a rat, there develops a *local experimental arthritis* (in technical language: *topical irritation arthritis*). First there is acute swelling at the site of injection, and then this gradually transforms itself into a chronic arthritis of the many small joints in the paw and, particularly, of the ankle joint. This arthritis, due to local stress, becomes a permanently crippling disease for the rat, because the joints stiffen with hard connective tissue, so that they can no longer be moved. On the other hand, if the rat develops an alarm reaction due to some stressor or if anti-inflammatory hormones (for instance, ACTH, cortisone, or COL) are given at the right time —during the critical period of development—the arthritis can be completely suppressed and here again the proinflammatory hormones (STH, DOC) have an opposite, aggravating effect.

This test proved to be useful, among other things, in the routine screening of new hormone derivatives and other antiarthritic drugs, especially now that so many university laboratories and pharmaceutical companies are making such compounds. New drugs may be worthless or even dangerous and, of course, we must have an experimental assay procedure which permits us to select the best ones without having to try them out on people.

One disadvantage of this test is that an arthritis produced by the local injection of irritants into a joint is not quite comparable to the kind of arthritis that people develop. It was a great step forward, therefore, when Dr. Gaëtan Jasmin—while working for his Ph.D. degree at our Institute in 1955—discovered a more natural type of *multiple experimental arthritis*. Two of my earlier postgraduate students, Drs. A. Horava and A. Robert, had noticed that a peculiar inflammatory fluid was produced by certain experimental tumors, when they were grown in the inflammatory pouch of the rat. Dr. Jasmin found that if one injects a single, cubic centimeter of this tumorfluid into the blood of a rat, within a few days a pronounced inflammation appears in many of the joints, most frequently in the ankles, wrists, elbows, knee joints, and the many little joints between the vertebrae of the spinal column. It is impossible to say whether or not this experimental disease is closely related to the rheumatic or rheumatoid arthritis of man, but they certainly resemble each other in many respects. It was extremely instructive, therefore, to learn that this induced generalized arthritic tendency of the rat also depends upon the function of the pituitary-adrenal defense mechanism. The principal findings were these:

1. In intact rats—which can respond to stress by anti-inflammatory hormone-production—comparatively large amounts of tumor-fluid must be used to produce this arthritis.

2. In adrenalectomized rats maintained exclusively on the pro-inflammatory DOC, small amounts of fluid suffice to produce very pronounced and widespread arthritic changes.

3. In adrenalectomized rats treated only with the anti-inflammatory COL, even the largest doses of tumor-fluid produce little or no arthritis.

4. In adrenalectomized rats treated with both COL and DOC, the anti-inflammatory effect of the former is neutralized by the latter hormone.

In conclusion, it seems that, in the intact rat, the injection of the tumor-fluid produces enough stress to activate the pituitary-adrenal system and the resulting increased secretion of anti-inflammatory hormones largely prevents the production of arthritis. In the absence of the adrenals, this protective response is, of course, impossible. Here the development of arthritis will largely depend upon the kind of hormone injected. DOC sensitizes, COL desensitizes for it. These findings confirm that certain external disease-producing agents will or will not induce arthritis, depending upon the body's hormonal defenses; and, whenever these self-protecting mechanisms are imperfect, we have it in our power to correct them by suitable hormone-treatment.

Here again we have a typical tripartite disease-production, in that the malady depends upon: (1) the tumor fluid (which acts as a selective stressor for joints); (2) the amount of anti-inflammatory hormone; and (3) the amount of proinflammatory hormone in the blood.

More recently, my associate, Dr. Pierre Bois, and I were able to show that some presumably infected inflammatory fluids (for instance, the liquid formed in the inflammatory pouch after local treatment with nonsterile solutions) can also acquire the property of producing multiple arthritis in ankles, wrists, elbows, knee joints, and the spinal column, when injected into the belly-cavity of another rat. This brings up interesting points concerning the relationship between local inflammation in one part of the body and generalized inflammatory reactions in joints everywhere. The bearing of this observation upon the problem of focal infection is now under study.

The photographs (*Plates 4 and 5*) illustrate what I have just said and will help the reader to get a first hand impression of the way these experimental models of disease actually present themselves to the investigator in the laboratory.

Rheumatic and rheumatoid diseases of man

It takes no specialized medical training to realize that what we have said in the preceding passages about the role of hormones in inflammatory diseases is applicable to clinical problems. Rheumatic fever and rheumatoid arthritis, for example, are typical inflammatory maladies; their essence is inflammation in the joints, the heart valves, and other tissues. These diseases are not identical with the experimental conditions which we produced in rats—no spontaneous malady of man is identical with its artificial counterpart in animals —but they are certainly very closely related and presumably governed by the same general laws. The primary cause of rheumatic fever and of rheumatoid arthritis (the factor which would correspond to the croton oil, the Formalin, or the tumor-fluid in our experiments) has still not been definitely identified; but their manifestations, like those of their experimental counterparts, depend largely upon the hormones produced by the patient.

This was perhaps most clearly demonstrated by Professor Philip S. Hench and his associates at the Mayo Clinic in 1949, when ACTH and cortisone became available in sufficiently large amounts to be tested on patients. These investigators found that rheumatic and allied inflammations can be largely suppressed by anti-inflammatory hormones. Their observation opened the way for the clinical use of this type of treatment.

The extent to which such inflammatory diseases depend upon an insufficient mobilization of the body's alarm system is particularly well illustrated by such observations as those made by Drs. Wilhelm Brühl and Hans-Jürgen Jahn, at the Civic Hospital in Korbach, Germany. These physicians wanted to put the concept of stress therapy to practical use in patients suffering from very severe rheumatoid arthritis which did not respond to treatment with the usual anti-inflammatory drugs. They wondered whether the combined effect of naturally produced anti-inflammatory hormones and the conditioning action of stress could not help here. In order to produce stress, they used a modified type of insulin shock which proved very effective in otherwise rather hopeless cases of this type. For instance, they describe the case of a 44-year-old woman, bedridden and crippled by an intense chronic rheumatoid arthritis in the joints of the hands, feet, and knees. After a series of insulin shocks, she was able to get up and walk about for the first time in three years. The German doctors ascribed this success to the production of an alarm reaction, with a discharge of ACTH and anti-inflammatory corticoids by the patient's own endocrine glands. Many similar observations have been published by other physicians who used different kinds of stressors.

All this makes it quite clear that the rheumatic maladies are really typical diseases of adaptation, because if the body's defenses are adequate the disease is suppressed without any intervention by the physician. Here the primary disease-producer (whatever it may be) is certainly not very harmful in itself. When the inflammatory barricade against it is removed by hormones—be they secreted by the glands or administered by the physician—the causative agent (germ, poison) of the rheumatoid diseases does not produce much tissue-destruction. These diseases are essentially due to inadequate adaptive reactions against comparatively innocuous injuries. They are due to maladaptation.

Inflammatory diseases of the skin and the eyes

We can discuss ailments of skin and eyes conjointly here because, generally speaking, they behave quite similarly in relation to stress and the adaptive hormones.

The great majority of all the skin and eye diseases are essentially inflammations, and many of them are caused by agents which would not be particularly harmful if the body did not react to them with unduly violent inflammatory responses. Here again we are apparently dealing with maladaptations, senseless overreactions to cutaneous or ocular injuries. It had long been noted that during periods of intense general stress the predominantly inflammatory diseases of the skin and eyes tended to become better. Various nonspecific therapies have therefore been devised to combat such conditions and, more recently, even more striking improvements have been obtained by the use of anti-inflammatory adaptive hormones (ACTH, cortisone, COL).

Of course, an excess of any hormone has harmful side-effects, and in this respect the adaptive hormones are no exceptions. For instance, a patient heavily overdosed with cortisone tends to become very prone to infections and may develop high blood pressure, insomnia, gastrointestinal disturbances, and so forth. Indeed, often it is impossible to give enough cortisone to cure an inflammatory disease without automatically producing the unpleasant side-effects of hormone overdosage. But, in the cutaneous and ocular diseases, cortisone or COL may be applied locally, through ointments and eye drops, so that a great concentration can be achieved in the diseased area without much getting into the blood. In other words, here this kind of treatment can often be applied without the usual dangers of overdosage.

Infectious diseases

We have already seen that various germs, and particularly those of tuberculosis, can take a foothold in the body more readily than is usual if inflammatory and immunologic defense reactions are impeded by anti-inflammatory hormones. It is important to keep this in mind when prescribing ACTH, cortisone, or COL in the treatment of rheumatic, cutaneous, or ocular diseases because, so often, a hitherto latent nodule of tuberculosis in the lung begins to spread dangerously when, due to these hormones, the inflammatory barricades shrink throughout the body. It is, of course, a very high price to pay for the improvement of a comparatively benign joint, skin, or eye condition if the hormone opens the way for the spread of tuberculosis or some other severe infection. Whenever there is any danger of this, hormone-treatment must be stopped, or at least antibiotics must be given to fight the germs.

That the balance between proinflammatory and anti-inflammatory hormones is of paramount importance, even in tuberculosis, has clearly been shown by experiments performed in our Institute by Dr. Paul Lemonde. The rat is normally resistant to the human type of tuberculosis, but it can be made very sensitive to it by overdosage with cortisone. Dr. Lemonde found that this artificially induced sensitivity to tuberculosis is in turn abolished if, simultaneously with the cortisone, large amounts of the proinflammatory STH are injected. In other words, the natural tuberculosis-resistance of the rat can be abolished by an anti-inflammatory hormone and restored again by a proinflammatory one.

It would be difficult to furnish more eloquent proof of the important role played by adaptive hormones in determining disease-susceptibility. It is an old and well-established fact that stress and strain predispose to tuberculosis. That is why patients suffering from this disease are advised to take long rest cures, in order to recover their resistance against tubercle bacilli. The analysis of the stress-mechanism helped us to understand why this is so. Apparently, the anti-inflammatory hormones, which are produced in excess during stress, remove the protective barricades around the foci of tubercle bacilli and thereby permit them to spread.

Dr. B. Carstensen and his associates in Sweden have reported rather encouraging results with a certain type of STH in tuberculous patients. Unfortunately, most of the STH-preparations now available are not yet sufficiently pure to be suitable for routine clinical use. But, when more purified STH becomes available, it will be interesting to see whether or not a tuberculosis-resistance—such as can be obtained in animals—can also be induced in human patients. Of course, DOC is available right now but, unfortunately (for reasons which are not yet quite clear), it cannot substitute for STH in such animal experiments; nor has it been useful in treating the tuber-culosis of man.

In this passage I have discussed tuberculosis at length, because our own research work was mainly concerned with this infection. But essentially the same could be said about the role of stress and of adaptive hormones in other types of infection. All kinds of infections are met by the body with an inflammatory response which tends to delimit them. Therefore, the hormones regulating inflammation are evidently important in determining the course of various infections. Even the *saprophytes* (microbes which live in our lungs, gastrointestinal system, and on our skin without ever causing any disease) can become dangerous disease-producers when our normal defenses against them are broken down by anti-inflammatory hormones. I have seen, for instance, that in rats treated with large amounts of ACTH, cortisone, or COL, such saprophytes can invade the blood and produce considerable tissue-destruction, finally resulting in death. STH prevents all this.

These findings confirm the role of the hormones in determining just what microbe is a disease-producer. Almost no germ is unconditionally dangerous to man; its disease-producing ability depends upon the body's resistance.

Allergic and hypersensitivity diseases

Immediately after the discovery of the G.A.S., I spent a great deal of time trying to find out just how stressful various medical treatments are. Among other things, in 1937 I injected rats with a variety of drugs and assessed the resulting stress by the adrenal enlargement and by other signs of the G.A.S. In the course of this work one group of rats was injected with egg-white, just to see how much stress this foreign protein would produce. Much to my surprise, egg-white did not act merely as a stressor, but produced a very specific and strange syndrome. Immediately after the injection the rats seemed to be quite all right, but soon afterwards they started to sneeze and sat up on their haunches, scratching their snouts with the forepaws. A few minutes later, their noses and lips became greatly swollen and red, giving the animals a very peculiar appearance. A friend of mine suffered from hay fever at that time, and the resemblance. . . .

Well, in any case, this seemed to be a new experimental disease, due to some innate hypersensitivity of the rat to egg-white.

To follow this up, I then injected other animals (guinea pigs, rabbits, dogs) with egg-white, but they did not respond in this singular fashion. Apparently, just as among people there are some who do and some who do not respond with hay fever to certain plant-pollens, so among animals, the rat is sensitive to egg-white, while most other species are not. This seemed to offer interesting possibilities for the study of what we call *allergic* and *anaphylactic hypersensitivity reactions.* Mind you, egg-white in itself is not particularly damaging, even to the rat, because no special response to it is seen locally, wherever it is injected. In fact, when the substance is distributed to all parts of the body through the blood, it causes swelling and inflammation only in certain hypersensitive parts, such as the nose and the surrounding facial tissue. Usually the paws and the ears also become inflamed, but the rest of the body remains quite unaffected by the egg-white.

Even some twenty years ago, when cortisone and COL were not yet available, it was quite easily proved that this inflammatory reaction also depended somehow upon adrenal hormones. We merely removed the adrenals of rats and then injected the egg-white, to see how the absence of corticoids would affect the reaction. The result was most spectacular. The rats which had no adrenals showed a much more intense reaction, the swollen parts became bluish because of engorgement with venous blood, and within hours all these animals died.

This still did not prove that anti-inflammatory hormones made by the animals' own adrenals could combat such a hypersensitivity response. To establish this I then produced marked alarm reactions in other rats, using a variety of stressor agents: invariably the rats with the large, overactive adrenals tolerated egg-white perfectly well, without showing any hypersensitivity response. This type of anti-inflammatory effect is fundamentally the same as that of insulin shock in patients with rheumatoid arthritis; it is due to the increased secretion of ACTH and COL-like hormones by the endocrine glands.

Of course, now that we have highly potent, purified preparations of ACTH and of anti-inflammatory corticoids, it is much simpler to administer these than to expose a patient to stress and make his own endocrine glands produce the proper adaptive hormones. In fact, it is common knowledge that, in a variety of diseases due to hypersensitivity, treatment with anti-inflammatory hormones proved to be very effective. This was so, for instance, in many cases of hay fever and asthma, as well as in certain types of dermatitis and conjunctivitis, which are due respectively to allergic irritation of the skin and eyes.

Incidentally, this test—just like the experimental arthritis and the inflammatory-pouch tests—has now become a standard technique in screening for effective anti-inflammatory drugs. It is used particularly in testing remedies which may prove useful in the treatment of acute hypersensitivity reactions. The extraordinary sensitivity of the test to anti-inflammatory hormones is illustrated by the photographs (*Plate 6*).

In this chapter I have spoken about the effect of stress and adaptive hormones in inflammatory diseases. Inflammation is the most nonspecific local response to the stress of tissue-injury, and it is understandable that the stress hormones have found their most spectacular applications in this type of malady. But, of course, these hormones also have many other effects, and our report would be quite incomplete if it failed to consider the role of stress in such conditions as mental and sexual derangements, digestive diseases, metabolic diseases, cancer, and resistance in general.

17:

Other diseases

Nervous and mental diseases.
Sexual derangements. Digestive
diseases. Metabolic diseases.
Cancer. Diseases of resistance in
general.

Nervous and mental diseases

It is common knowledge that *maladaptation plays an important part in nervous and mental diseases.* Such expressions as, "This work gives me a headache" or "drives me crazy" are not without real significance. Many types of intense headaches or mental breakdowns are actually caused by work to which we are ill adapted. Heredity can certainly predispose to certain types of mental disease, but there are imperceptible transitions between the normal, the slightly queer, and the frankly insane personality. In people with a given hereditary structure, it is often the stress of adjustments to life under difficult circumstances that causes a change from normal to queer, or from queer to frankly insane. Conversely, we have also seen that a sudden stress (shock therapy) can help a person to snap out of an abnormal behavior pattern.

I am not competent to discuss this from the psychiatrist's point of view, but, as an endocrinologist and as a student of stress, I have been naturally interested in exploring whether or not there are any demonstrable *relationships between abnormal mental reactions and the objectively measurable features of the G.A.S.* Again—as in so many other investigations described in this book—my attention was called to this possibility by the accident of a spoiled experiment.

In 1941 I was working on the effects of various adrenal and ovarian hormones upon the sex organs. For this purpose I injected rats with DOC and with progesterone (an ovarian hormone chemically related to DOC). These injections were given under the skin of the animals in the usual manner and, after a few weeks of treatment, the sex organs were removed for microscopic study. Eventually, I handed this work over to a technician who had just then joined our laboratory, but much to my surprise the next day she reported that all the animals were dead. Since I had given the same amount of the same hormones before without any trouble, I thought she must have made some mistake in preparing her solutions and merely told her to repeat the experiment more carefully. But next day all her rats died again. I could not imagine what might have gone wrong, so I asked the technician to inject another group of rats in my presence. It turned out that, being unacquainted with our techniques, she injected the hormones into the belly (the peritoneal cavity) of the rats. I did not think this would make much difference, but while we discussed the point, all the rats became extremely excited and ran around in the cage as if they were intoxicated. After a time they fell asleep, just as if they had received a strong anesthetic, and eventually all of them died.

Now this was very odd, and I repeated the experiment several times, using smaller doses of hormones. Always there was an initial stage of excitement, followed by deep anesthesia; but after injection with smaller amounts the animals woke up within a couple of hours and were perfectly all right. Here we were dealing with a true hormonal anesthesia, with sleep induced by natural products of our endocrine glands. There remained no doubt that hormones can affect consciousness and that, at least under our experimental conditions, they act very much like an excess of alcohol, ether, and certain narcotics, which tend to cause excitement followed by depression.

Could the corticoids secreted under stress influence mental activity? Could the delirium of fever be related to adrenocortical activity? Could we use such hormones in man as sleeping pills, or for the treatment of mental derangements, or perhaps even for the induction of surgical anesthesia? A multitude of problems was raised by this incidental observation and hundreds of medical publications have since dealt with experiments designed to answer them. Here are a few of the more outstanding facts which have come to light:

1. Various species, including man, can be anesthetized with hormones. My associates and I found that hormonal anesthesia can be produced, not only in the rat, but in every animal species (fishes, birds and all mammals, including the monkey) which we have used for this work up to now. In fact, in 1954 a team of investigators at the Department of Obstetrics and Gynecology of Ohio State University in Columbus (Drs. W. Merryman, R. Boiman, L. Barnes, and I. Rothchild) showed that, in women, sleep can also be produced quite regularly by giving them progesterone. Shortly afterwards, in the *Journal of the American Medical Association,* appeared a paper in which a group of California physicians (F. J. Murphy, N. P. Guadagni, and F. DeBon) reported their findings on people who were successfully anesthetized for surgical operations with a close relative of DOC (known as *hydroxydione*). The advantages of this compound over other anesthetics have been carefully explored in laboratory animals by Drs. G. D. Laubach, S. Y. P'an, and H. W. Rudel. It remains to be seen to what extent such hormone derivatives should be used for ordinary routine anesthesia in surgery, but their effect upon the central nervous system and consciousness, which we had noted in animals, is certainly also evident in man.

2. Adaptive hormones can combat convulsions. In rats in which I had produced epilepsylike convulsions with certain stimulants (Metrazol, pictrotoxin), DOC and related hormones acted as tranquilizers. Dr. D. M. Woodbury and his associates at the University of Utah discovered that if such convulsions are produced with electric current, their intensity could be diminished by DOC and augmented by COL. This was the first indication of an actual antagonism between anti- and proinflammatory hormones as regards a nervous manifestation.

3. Under certain conditions an excess of DOC can produce brain lesions such as are often seen in old people. We have already discussed the blood-vessel damage that is produced in rats by DOC-poisoning (p. 135). When the arteries of the brain are involved, the animals can suffer a stroke or even repeated strokes which eventually destroy large parts of the brain and cause widespread nervous derangements (*Plate* 7). Interestingly, such rats become extremely irritable and aggressive, a change quite characteristic of certain senile mental derangements among people whose brains often show the same kind of destruction.

These findings showed quite conclusively that there are very obvious relationships between mental derangements and the adaptive hormones. The importance of this became even more evident when ACTH and cortisone were introduced into clinical medicine.

4. Adaptive hormones can cause mental changes in man. Many patients who take ACTH or COL first develop a sense of extraordinary well-being and buoyancy, with excitement and insomnia; this is sometimes followed by a depression which may go so far as to create suicidal tendencies. In hereditarily predisposed people, profound mental derangements may result, although fortunately, these are rare and always disappear when the hormone-treatment is interrupted.

At a recent research conference organized by the CIBA Foundation in London, Professor Peter Forsham of San Francisco discussed the effect of ACTH and cortisone upon "heightened perception" and the "dissociation of the ego and the id." He reported, among other things, one observation which illustrates the effect of adaptive hormones upon mentality so eloquently that I would like to quote it in full:

"The dissociation of the ego and the id has many forms. I had an American housewife with dermatomyositis [an inflammation of skin and muscles] who had been taught how to play the piano when she was little, and had continued for the entertainment of the children, but didn't get very far. When she started on large doses of ACTH she was suddenly able to play the most difficult works of Beethoven and Chopin—and the children of the neighbours would gather in the garden to hear her play. Here was a dissociation of the ego and the id that was doing good. But she also became a little psychotic, and so her dosage of ACTH had to be lowered, and with every 10 units of ACTH one sonata disappeared. It all ended up with the same old music poorly performed."

Many problems still remain unsolved in this field. Certain breakdown products of adrenaline can cause hallucinations. Could excessive adrenaline secretion during stress play a part in the production of mental changes, for instance, in patients who become delirious as a result of high fever or after burns?

Normal   Alarmed

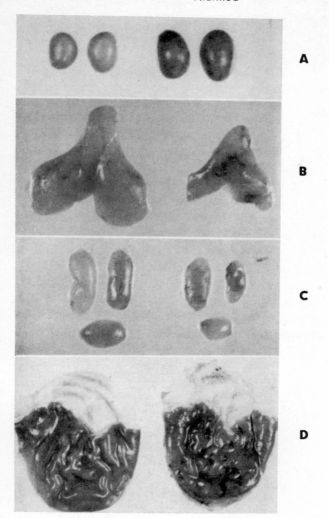

A

B

C

D

Plate 1

The typical triad of the alarm reaction. A. Adrenals. **B.** Thymus. **C.** A group of three lymph nodes. **D.** Inner surface of the stomach. The organs on the left are those of a normal rat, those on the right of one exposed to the frustrating psychologic stress of being forcefully immobilized. Note marked enlargement and dark discoloration of the adrenals (due to congestion and discharge of fatty secretion-granules), the intense shrinkage of the thymus and the lymph nodes, as well as the numerous blood-covered stomach ulcers in the alarmed rat. (*After H. Selye, "The Story of the Adaptation Syndrome," courtesy of Acta, Inc., Montreal.*)

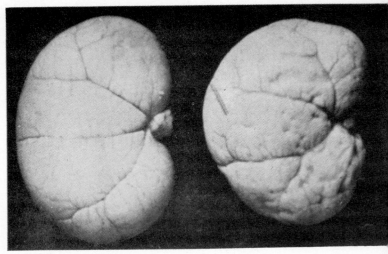

Plate 2 **Nephrosclerosis produced by DOC in a cat.** Compare smooth surface, marked only by the normal blood vessels, in the kidney of the untreated control cat (left), with the granular, shrivelled-up surface of the kidney in the DOC-treated animal. (*After H. Selye, "Textbook of Endocrinology." courtesy of Acta, Inc., Montreal.*)

Plate 3

Dissected inflammatory pouch. This is a pouch produced by injecting air and croton oil under the skin in the rat. This pouch has first been dissected, then—after removal of the fluid—cut open to show both inner and outer surfaces. Note the great regularity of the thickness of its wall. (*After H. Selye, courtesy of the "Journal of the American Medical Association."*)

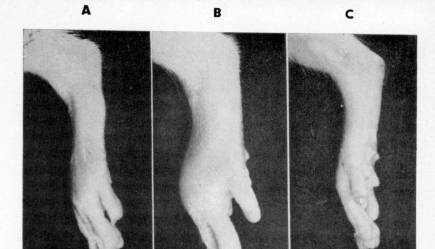

Plate 4 Inhibition of local experimental arthritis by the alarm reaction in the rat. A. Paw of untreated control. In the other two animals, Formalin was injected directly into the paw to produce local irritation. **B.** Full development of inflammation and swelling in an otherwise not treated animal. **C.** Almost complete inhibition of the arthritis by the stress-effect of cold. Other stressors and anti-inflammatory hormones caused a similar inhibition. (*After H. Selye, courtesy of the "British Medical Journal."*)

Plate 5 Multiple experimental arthritis. On the left: untreated normal rat. On the right: rat which received a single injection of inflammatory fluid. Note the bilateral arthritis in the wrist joints. This animal also had similar lesions in the ankle and knee joints. (*After H. Selye and P. Bois, unpublished.*)

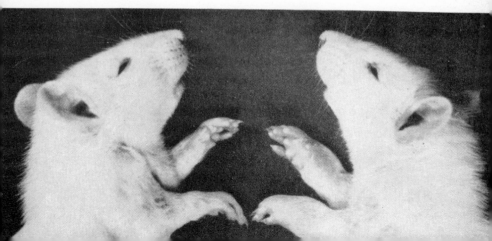

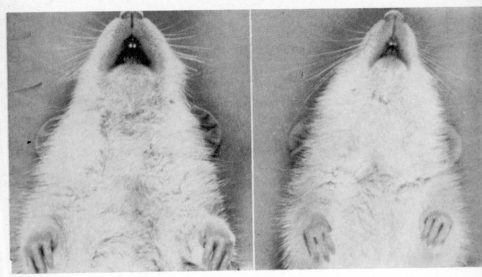

Plate 6 Effect of ACTH upon hypersensitivity type of inflammation in the rat.
Both these animals have received the same amount of egg-white. **A.**
Otherwise untreated rat, showing pronounced swelling and congestion
of the snout and paws. **B.** Animal treated with ACTH. Note complete
absence of hypersensitivity type of inflammation. (*After H. Selye, courtesy of the "Journal of the Canadian Medical Association."*)

Plate 7 Stroke produced by DOC overdosage in a rat. On the left, normal brain
of untreated rat. On the right, swollen and congested brain of DOC-
treated animal. Note large bleeding into brain-substance (dark area).
(*After H. Selye, courtesy of "The Journal of Clinical Endocrinology."*)

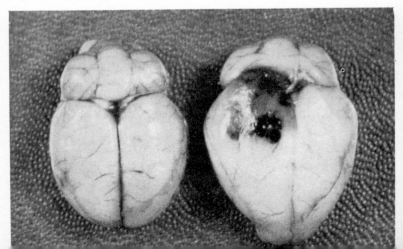

5. Perhaps adaptive hormones may even be used as tranquilizing agents in mental patients. In chronic alcoholics, there sometimes develops a delirium characterized by terrifying hallucinations, great excitement, and trembling. This is known as *delirium tremens*. Preliminary observations of the great French surgeon, H. Laborit, suggest that hydroxydione, the anesthetic DOC-derivative, has a striking beneficial effect upon this condition. Is there a causal relationship between adaptive hormones and certain delirious conditions in mentally deranged people?

The tranquilizing agents (chlorpromazine, reserpine) which are now so effectively employed in psychiatry, resemble in many of their actions the tranquilizing DOC-derivatives. Could hormones be used in the treatment of confused and disturbed mental patients?

6. DOC-like hormones can cause spells of periodic paralysis. There is a rare hereditary disease which runs in families and tends to produce sudden spells of paralysis. It is called *periodic familial paralysis* and—apart from the fact that the predisposition to it is hereditary—nothing has been known about its cause. Interestingly, very similar spells of paralysis occur in patients in whom an adrenal tumor produces an excess of the DOC-like aldosterone (p. 144). It is very probable that DOC-like hormones have something to do with this condition. Many years ago a group of researchers (D. Kuhlmann, C. Ragan, J. W. Ferrebee, D. W. Atchley, and R. F. Loeb) at Columbia University in New York had discovered quite similar paralytic spells in dogs treated with DOC. Later Dr. C. E. Hall and I (n aking similar observations in monkeys) found that in the DOC-treat d animal, attacks can be precipitated and cured at will, by merely giving or withdrawing dietary sodium chloride. In monkeys the paralysis was often accompanied by intense or epilepsylike attacks of convulsions. Obviously here again we are dealing with nervous derangements produced by DOC, and again these disturbances are aggravated by sodium chloride, just as the changes which the same hormone produces in the kidney and in the cardiovascular system. Is there a causal relationship here?

The many question marks in this chapter eloquently show how little we know and how much must still be learned. But the reader of a book on stress could not fail to be interested in getting at least a glimpse of how scientists think about using the stress concept as a guide to the study of the intriguing and mysterious borderline between mind and body.

Sexual derangements

That animals in which intense and prolonged stress is produced by any means suffer from sexual derangements was one of the first observations on the G.A.S. During stress the *sex glands* shrink and become less active in proportion to the enlargement and increased activity of the adrenals. The sex glands are stimulated by gonadotrophic hormones of the pituitary, just as the adrenals are activated by adrenocorticotrophic hormone (ACTH). It seemed probable, therefore, that during stress, when the pituitary has to produce so much ACTH to maintain life it must cut down on the production of other hormones which are less urgently needed in times of emergencies. This change of emphasis was called the *shift in pituitary-hormone production*. Our explanation seemed all the more likely, since other functions which depend upon the pituitary are likewise diminished during stress. For instance, young animals cease to grow and lactating females produce no milk during intense stress. It will be recalled that growth and milk-secretion are also governed by hormones of the pituitary.

Clinical studies have confirmed the fact that people exposed to stress react very much like experimental animals in all these respects. In women the *monthly cycles become irregular* or stop altogether, and during lactation *milk-secretion may become insufficient* for the baby. In men both the *sexual urge and sperm-cell formation are diminished*.

All this again reminds us of the finite nature of man's adaptability or adaptation energy. At times of imminent danger, in the face of extreme stress, the body must use all its reserves just to keep alive; while it does this the less pressing demands of reproduction are necessarily neglected.

In 1931 Dr. R. T. Frank described the *premenstrual syndrome*, a condition which tends to develop in women just before their monthly periods. It is characterized, among other things, by nervous tension and the desire to find relief in foolish actions which are difficult to restrain. Many of Dr. Frank's patients also suffered from migraine headaches and swelling of the face, hands, and feet, with a definite increase in weight due to water-retention. Other signs of the syndrome are: pain in the back and in the breasts, small hemorrhages in the skin, a feeling of stuffiness in the nose, asthma, and (very rarely) epilepsylike seizures. All these symptoms disappear suddenly at the onset of the monthly cycle, but recur again as the next period approaches.

This long overlooked syndrome is actually very common. A statistical study by Drs. W. Bickers and M. Woods revealed that, in one American factory employing 1,500 women, 36 per cent applied for treatment in the premenstrual phase; and Dr. S. L. Israel calculates that symptoms of this kind occur in 40 per cent of otherwise healthy women. The derangement deserves very serious attention also because it is frequently accompanied by a number of disturbing mental changes such as: periods of abnormal hunger, general emotional instability, and, occasionally, a morbid increase in the sexual drive. It is particularly noteworthy that, according to extensive statistical studies, 79 per cent (J. H. Morton and coworkers) to 84 per cent (W. R. Cooke) of all crimes of violence committed by women occur during, or in the week before, their periods.

Despite the frequency and severity of this condition, until recently very little had been done to alleviate it. "This is partly due to the attitude of the patients," say Drs. R. Greene and K. Dalton of London, England, because the syndrome is just accepted by them "as a necessary part of the business of being a woman, so still they pass through one week or discomfort in every month usually without complaining to their doctors but not necessarily without disturbing the tranquility of their homes."

Is there any relationship between premenstrual tension and stress? The great tendency to retain water, the predisposition for various allergic and hypersensitivity reactions, the occasional occurrence of convulsive seizures, vascular disturbances, and rheumaticlike pains are, of course, very reminiscent of the DOC-intoxication syndrome. I might add that our DOC-overdosed monkeys also probably suffered from sick headaches prior to the convulsive fits. At least I think so, because they usually retired to a corner of the cage, holding their heads between their hands; the facial expression was one of intense pain, and their attitudes rather unmistakably suggesting migraine. Autopsy of animals which died during these spells revealed intense congestion and swelling of the brain.

It is also of interest that, among all the drugs with which I have so far tried to combat the DOC syndrome in animals, ammonium chloride proved to be most effective—presumably because this salt washes out sodium and therefore acts just like a salt-free diet. It deprives DOC, the mineralocorticoid, of sodium, the mineral substance through which this hormone normally appears to act. In this manner it helps to decongest and dehydrate the swollen tissues, including the brain. Now, interestingly, in women with the premenstrual syndrome, ammonium chloride (7½–15 grains, about three times a day during a fortnight preceding the period) is often also very effective, especially if the patients are at the same time using as little salt as possible in their food. Furthermore, certain sex hormones, which alter mineral metabolism and which we found to influence the DOC syndrome in animals, affect the premenstrual syndrome of women essentially the same way. All these considerations led the Pakistan journal *Medicus* to state editorially that the "syndrome in our opinion should be designated as 'premenstrual stress,' because it represents a derailment of the general adaptation syndrome."

Be this as it may, there are certainly striking similarities between the manifestations of experimental DOC overdosage in animals, aldosteronism, eclampsia, and premenstrual tension in women. It would seem rewarding, therefore, to explore further the part played by adaptive hormones in this common and important derangement, so that we may perfect our means for treating it.

Digestive diseases

The gastrointestinal tract is particularly sensitive to general stress. Loss of appetite is one of the first symptoms in the great "syndrome of just being sick," and this may be accompanied by vomiting, diarrhea, or constipation. Signs of *irritation and upset of the digestive organs* may occur in any type of emotional stress. This is well known, not only to soldiers who experienced it during the tense expectation of battle, but even to students who pace the floor before my door, waiting—with, I assure you, much less justified but almost equally great tenseness—for their turn in oral examinations.

It is also common knowledge that *gastric and duodenal ulcers* are most likely to occur in people who are somewhat maladjusted to their work and suffer from constant tension and frustration. These chronic peptic (that is, digestive) ulcers are perhaps not quite the same as the acute, bleeding surface defects which developed in the lining of the stomach and duodenum during the alarm reaction in our rats. Still, even such acute ulcers have their equivalents in man. People who have been severely burned often develop bleeding duodenal ulcers within a day or two after the accident. This condition was known in medicine as *Curling's ulcer* long before the discovery of the G.A.S.; but it always remained a mystery just why and through what pathways a skin-burn could so affect the intestinal lining. During World War II, veritable epidemics of "air-raid ulcers" occurred in people living in some of the heavily blitzed cities in Great Britain. Immediately after an intense bombardment, an unusual number of people would appear in hospital, with bleeding gastric or duodenal ulcers which developed virtually overnight. Many of the affected persons had not been physically hurt in any way during the attack but, of course, they suffered the great stress of extreme emotional excitement.

With this background, it was not quite unexpected that, when ACTH and cortisone were introduced into clinical practice, in patients receiving large amounts of these stress hormones—say, for an inflammatory disease—preexistent gastrointestinal ulcers often became worse, and sometimes actually perforated through the gut. Indeed, even any latent tendency to develop such ulcers was prone to turn into manifest disease.

This revived my interest in the *mechanism through which the lining of the stomach defends itself against self-digestion.* Meat is digested in the stomach; why does the gastric juice not digest the lining itself? This problem has occupied many generations of physiologists, but no definite solution was found. The great Russian physiologist Ivan Pavlov (already mentioned in connection with his classic work on conditioned reflexes) thought that perhaps some antienzyme is formed in the lining, which inactivates the digestive enzymes of the stomach. Another view held that any healthy living tissue is immune to attack by gastric juice. This, it was thought, would also explain that the crater (the floor) of a gastric ulcer—

which is denuded of its allegedly antienzyme-containing lining—remains resistant to gastric digestion.

I wondered whether perhaps, here again, the inflammatory-pouch test could help us to understand the situation. It may seem odd to think that an inflammatory pouch produced on the back of a rat, could give information about gastric digestion—but judge for yourself.

I first took some rats and made air-sacs on their backs—in the usual manner, but without introducing an irritant. Immediately after this, I injected 5 cc of fresh gastric juice. The adjacent tissue of the skin was digested within a few hours. This proved that normal living tissue can be attacked by gastric juice.

Then I made a similar air-sac, but injected some croton oil into it, so as to transform the lining into an inflammatory barricade before introducing the gastric juice into the cavity. Now no digestion of adjacent tissue occurred. This proved that the inflammatory tissue itself is an adequate barricade to protect against gastric digestion. Obviously, an inflammatory barricade, such as always paves the crater of gastric ulcers, is in itself adequate protection against digestion, under normal conditions.

Next I repeated exactly the same experiment (introducing the gastric juice into an inflammatory pouch whose lining was transformed into an inflammatory barricade by pretreatment with croton oil), but then exposed the animals to the frustrating immobilization test (see p. 154). Now I witnessed the singular phenomenon of a perforating peptic ulcer on the back of the rat. During stress—presumably due to the secretion of anti-inflammatory hormones—the barricade became so weakened that the gastric juice digested it easily. Apparently in man chronic gastric ulcers, which normally are well under control, also perforate during stress, because an excess of anti-inflammatory stimuli breaks down the resistance of the barricade.

Finally, to prove this theory, I repeated the last-mentioned experiment on adrenalectomized rats. Here the condition was exactly the same as before (an irritated pouch possessing a well-developed inflammatory barricade was exposed to the general stress of frustrating immobilization), but these animals had no adrenals which might have responded by increased anti-inflammatory hormone-secretion.

Here the pouch remained unaffected by the digestive juices even during stress. This was definite proof of adrenal-participation in this type of tissue-breakdown.

A   B   C

Normal tissue is digested by gastric juice.

Inflamed tissue of pouch is normally not digested by gastric juice.

Stress of frustrating forced immobilization causes perforating peptic ulcer on the pouch. Inflammatory fluid escapes.

That essentially the same mechanism is involved in the production of peptic ulcers in man has been clearly shown by various physicians. Particularly instructive findings have been reported by Professor Harold G. Wolff, the well-known neurologist of Cornell University in New York. In a patient with a gastric fistula (an artificial opening through which the stomach can be directly seen), he observed that "during a period of prolonged emotional conflict involving hostility and resentment on the part of the patient," the lining of the stomach became engorged with blood and eventually began to bleed through minute erosions which formed on its surface.

The nerves of the stomach probably also play an important role in the formation of this kind of ulcer during stress; but the part played by adaptive hormones is likewise well established now. Dr. Seymour J. Gray, of the Peter Bent Brigham Hospital in Boston, furnished perhaps the most clear-cut evidence of this. He showed that patients under stress, or treated with anti-inflammatory hormones, excrete increased amounts of peptic digestive hormones in their urine. This would indicate that stress, through the intermediary of adaptive hormones, not only weakens the resistance of the inflammatory barricade but at the same time the attacking influence of the digestive juices is increased because the stress hormones stimulate the production of peptic enzymes.

Of course, there are many other digestive diseases which can be influenced by stress and adaptive hormones. There would be no point in discussing them all here, but at least one more should be mentioned, and that is: *ulcerative colitis*. This—as the name implies —is an inflammatory disease of the colon (a part of the large intestine). It is characterized by bleeding intestinal ulcerations and, in fatal cases, the entire colon is almost invariably involved. The gut is denuded of its lining and death may then result from perforation or some other complication. It is often impossible to determine the cause of this disease, but physicians have always suspected that emotional tension plays an important role in its development. Significantly, this malady is often accompanied by signs of chronic rheumatism and, like the latter, it frequently responds very well to treatment with anti-inflammatory hormones.

Metabolic diseases

Many of the so-called metabolic diseases are also largely diseases of adaptation. We have seen that *loss of weight* is one of the most nonspecific consequences of chronic stress. It is due partly to loss of appetite, but partly also to the fact that a surplus of anti-inflammatory hormones tends to facilitate a kind of "self-combustion." In times of great stress, much caloric energy is needed and since food-intake is usually diminished, it is very important for the preservation of health that the body should burn its own tissues to supply calories for resistance. But, of course, if this goes on for a long time, pathologic emaciation will result.

Conversely, excessive *obesity* may also be a manifestation of stress, especially in people with certain types of frustrating mental experiences. A person who does not get enough satisfaction from work or from his relations with other people may be driven to find consolation in almost anything that may provide comfort. This is just one aspect of the general principle of *"deviation,"* which will be analyzed at length later (p. 267). Some people are driven to food just as others are driven to drink. Many a person eats for lack of anything better to do, or as an excuse for not doing anything better; besides, a stomach full of food also soothes by draining the blood away from a disgruntled and maladapted brain.

Of course, some people have such a strong hereditary predisposition to obesity that they become fat even if they eat very little. Others become obese because of some acquired organic disease in those same brain-centers of adaptation (the hypothalamus), which also regulate pituitary activity. Still, the large majority of fat people overeat because of derailed adaptive reactions. Through this pattern of response they hurt themselves in the same sense as a derailed hormonal adaptive reaction to tissue-injury can predispose to inflammatory disease.

It is important to know that obesity can often be avoided by some self-analysis which may help the patient to stop overeating. Just how to do this will be explained later (p. 260). Here I only want to point out that this is possible and certainly worthwhile, because obesity is not only deforming, it also greatly increases the likelihood of contracting other diseases of adaptation, particularly hypertension and diabetes.

The predisposition to *diabetes* is also inherited, but it depends largely upon the way the body reacts to stress whether or not a latent diabetic tendency will develop into a manifest disease. The outstanding feature of diabetes is an increase in blood sugar, so that eventually much sugar spills over into the urine. Insulin is given to diabetics because this pancreatic hormone diminishes the blood sugar and improves its utilization as fuel for the tissues. This does not mean that diabetes is always due to an insufficiency of insulin formation. Often, it is caused by an excessive production of such adaptive hormones as ACTH, STH, or COL, all of which tend to raise the blood sugar. In fact, it has been possible to treat particularly insulin-resistant diabetics by removing their pituitary or adrenal glands. I have already mentioned the important work of Olivecrona and Luft, who have removed the pituitary in hypertensive diabetic patients and have obtained an amelioration, both of the hypertension and of the diabetes.

Hyperthyroidism is another disease which is often due to stress.

Here, the thyroid gland becomes enlarged (goiter) and is driven to excessive activity by the thyroid-stimulating hormone of the pituitary (p. 117). Sometimes this condition develops immediately after a particularly shocking mental experience; but in man the relationship between hyperthyroidism and stress is not always evident, because—probably due to differences in hereditary constitution —only some people respond that way.

This whole problem was greatly clarified when Dr. J. Kracht of Borstel, Germany, discovered a breed of wild rabbits which regularly develop hyperthyroidism after being frightened, for instance by a barking dog. Here—presumably again due to some hereditary predisposition—the G.A.S. regularly derails, in the sense that the pituitary tends to produce an excessive amount of thyroid-stimulating hormone and correspondingly does not secrete enough ACTH. As a result of this, the thyroid enlarges and the eyes protrude, just as in certain hyperthyroid patients with Graves' disease or exophthalmic goiter. In fact, such rabbits may literally die from fear because of this abnormal endocrine response to stress.

There are also interesting relationships between stress and the *diseases of the liver*. It has been shown by Dr. Paul Lemonde at this Institute that during the alarm reaction the usual liver-function tests reveal a marked hepatic insufficiency. This finding was of particular interest to stress research, because the corticoids are normally metabolized and destroyed in the liver. I first observed this in connection with the hormone-anesthesia studies (p. 173). At that time nothing definite was known about the way corticoids were disposed of in the body, but since the liver had always been regarded as the "central chemical laboratory of the body," it was reasonable to suspect that this organ might play an important role in corticoid-metabolism. To prove this, I injected the same amount of DOC into intact rats and into animals from which I had first surgically removed three-quarters of the liver. It turned out that an amount of DOC which caused little or no anesthesia in the intact animal produced long and profound sleep after most of the liver had been eliminated. Ordinary anesthetics (ether, for instance) do not produce more intense sleep in liver-deficient than in intact rats. It was assumed that DOC-like hormones are normally destroyed by the liver, so that they remain in the blood longer when hepatic function is artificially cut down.

These findings have been confirmed with a variety of techniques in other animals, but it is mainly thanks to the biochemical investigations of Professor L. T. Samuels of Salt Lake City that we learned to appreciate the important part played by the liver in destroying excesses of corticoids in healthy and diseased people. He has shown, for instance that, in certain clinical liver diseases (such as cirrhosis, or morbid scar-formation in the liver), the metabolism of corticoids is often deranged and excesses can be found in the blood and urine.

It is also obvious that, if during the alarm reaction, hepatic function is diminished, the disposal of corticoids must be impeded. This is one mechanism of conditioning through which the body can augment corticoid-activity during stress. By diminishing the normal destruction of these hormones, a given amount secreted by the adrenals can last longer and do more good.

To illustrate the manifold relationships between metabolic and inflammatory diseases, let me mention just one more derangement of metabolism, *gout,* in which inflammation and maladaptation appear to play important roles. This is yet another example of a disease in which both hereditary predisposition and stress are involved. Gout is essentially a derangement of uric-acid metabolism, with the deposition of uric-acid crystals in and around the joints. It tends to run in families, and extremely painful spells of it occur, frequently after some stress, especially in the joints of the big toe. The uric-acid deposits act as local irritants and the pain is due to excessive inflammation around them.

Here again, treatment with anti-inflammatory corticoids has proved to be of great value. It is not yet quite clear why attacks of gout tend to occur immediately after (not during) stress, but most probably, a derailment of hormonal defense reactions is at least partly responsible for this condition.

Cancer

We still know very little about the possible relationship between stress and cancer. This is the way I would sum up what little we have managed to find out:

Many types of cancer develop at sites of chronic tissue-injury. Prolonged exposure of the skin to sunrays or heat may lead to cancer formation at the place of irritation. In an inveterate pipe-smoker, cancer of the lip tends to develop at the place where he holds his pipe. The interesting statistical studies of Dr. F. Gagnon of Quebec City have shown that cancer of the entrance to the womb is virtually never observed among cloistered nuns, although it is quite common in married women, especially after repeated childbirth.

Experimentally, it has been possible to produce extremely malignant cancers by chronic irritation with croton oil in the inflammatory pouch.

These, and many other personal observations, have led Dr. J. Ernest Ayre of the Cancer Institute at Miami, Florida, to conclude, in his editorial in *Obstetrics and Gynecology* (June, 1955), that cancer-production is an abnormal consequence of the local adaptation syndrome to tissue-injury.

On the other hand, *general stress tends to suppress cancerous growth.* The progress of various types of clinical and experimental cancers is often greatly retarded during stress caused by infections, intoxications, and various drugs which cause much nonspecific damage.

It has also been possible to *inhibit the growth of certain cancers by treatment with large doses of anti-inflammatory hormones.* One of the salient actions of these substances is to diminish the response to local injury. Now, if cancer really represents a morbid response to tissue-damage, it is understandable that the hormones which induce tissues to ignore injury should interfere with cancer-production.

ACTH and COL have proved to be particularly effective in slowing down lymphatic cancers and the *leukemias* certain of which are essentially cancers of the white blood cells. Interestingly, during the alarm reaction and after treatment with anti-inflammatory hormones, the growth of lymphatic tissues and of certain white blood cells (lymphocytes, eosinophils) proved to be most intensely inhibited (p. 21).

There are many other observations which suggest *some dependence, at least of certain cancers, upon the adrenals.* The important observations of Professor Charles Huggins of Chicago have made it clear that removal of the adrenals can greatly delay the growth of some cancers, especially those of the male and female sex organs. This would suggest that there are adrenal factors which actually stimulate cancer formation.

It should be clearly understood, however, that all these are isolated observations which merely indicate some relationship between stress, the adaptive hormones, and cancer; these findings are sufficiently suggestive to justify further research from this new point of view, but not yet to formulate any coherent theory.

Diseases of resistance in general

By *general resistance* I mean the ability to remain healthy—or at least alive—during intense stress caused nonspecifically by various agents. The most nonspecific breakdown of resistance is the condition which we call *shock*. A person who has been seriously burned, wounded, poisoned, or otherwise gravely damaged may develop a syndrome in which the blood pressure drops so much that the pulse can hardly be felt, the temperature falls way below normal, and the patient may even become unconscious. This often ends in death, without obvious selective injury to any one of the vital organs. This is what makes shock an eminently nonspecific stress-condition. Accordingly, in such cases autopsy reveals the characteristic triad of the alarm reaction: adrenocortical enlargement, thymicolymphatic atrophy, and bleeding erosions in the gastrointestinal tract. There can be no doubt about this being a disease of adaptation; it is due to a breakdown of the body's defenses in general rather than to the specific action of any one particular disease-producer.

Treatment with corticoids has proved beneficial in certain cases; but it is not always effective, because a lack of corticoids is not the usual cause of the breakdown in shock. Presumably, during extreme stress, in most people, the pituitary-adrenal system performs optimally anyway; only occasionally (for instance, in very severe burns and infections) is it inactivated by exhaustive overstimulation, and it is especially in such cases that corticoid therapy has proved to be effective.

A special kind of what we now call a *disease of adaptation* was described by Thomas Addison in his famous treatise, *On the Constitutional and Local Effects of Diseases of the Suprarenal Capsule [the adrenal]*, almost exactly a hundred years ago (in 1855). Addison worked at Guy's Hospital in London, just as Richard Bright, who discovered Bright's disease a quarter of a century earlier (see p. 132).

Addison's disease is due to a destruction of the adrenals, and one of its most outstanding consequences is an almost total breakdown of resistance. Patients with Addison's disease are not hypersensitive to any one thing in particular, but to virtually any change in and around them. Any infection, intoxication, or exposure to cold, nervous tension, or fatigue can put these people into a state of shock, in which they usually die unless suitable treatment with corticoids is given. Nowadays people whose adrenals are removed (say, for the treatment of cancer or hypertensive disease) become continuously dependent upon treatment with corticoids, because an artificial Addison's disease is produced in them by this operation. In Addison's disease, the thymus and the other lymphatic organs tend to become very large. Both in human patients and in animals, it is the lack of corticoids which prevents the shrinkage of lymphatic tissues during stress. We still do not know, however, whether or not resistance to stress declines because of this irresponsiveness of the lymphatic organs.

A somewhat related, but at this time still very mysterious condition is known as the *thymicolymphatic state*. It usually occurs in apparently healthy boys and girls. Such children may never have shown any indication of disease until, suddenly, after some slight stress (say, a plunge into cold water) they die instantly without any warning. Even autopsy reveals no obvious derangement, except that the adrenal cortex is small and the thymicolymphatic tissues are overdeveloped. It is reasonable to suspect that the low stress-resistance of these children is due to some deficiency in the adrenal cortex, but this has never been proved.

Aging itself—and particularly premature aging—is, in a sense, due to the constant, and eventually exhausting, stresses of life. But since I have already spoken of aging in several other sections of this book (see pp. 66, 111, 273, 276), I mention it here merely for the sake of completeness.

In the last three chapters I have tried to outline how we arrived at the concept of the "diseases of adaptation." To do this I had to correlate my own experiments on animals with clinical observations on the role of stress and of the adaptive hormones in the production and treatment of disease. The observations reported here are not likely to become subjects of contention. They are facts which can easily be verified. But this is not a textbook of medicine and I have made no attempt to give a complete list of all the diseases influenced by stress and by adaptive hormones. Consequently, my selection of data may well be criticized. I have discussed only those maladies in which, to my mind, a derailment of adaptive reactions plays a particularly clear-cut role, and I have listed only the evidence which convinced me of this. But the concepts of stress and of the adaptive hormones are just beginning to show their influence upon the progress of contemporary medicine. It is hardly unexpected, therefore, that many physicians—and among them some highly competent ones —do not agree with certain aspects of my theory. My presentation would lack the impartiality which must always guide medical research if I did not also present the views of those who disagree. Doing so necessarily implies a discussion of conflicting personal opinions—and the cold precision of knowledge ends where opinion begins.

Some of my friends have advised me not to mention dissident opinions in this book, because controversies among scientists would only confuse the general reader and could hardly hold much interest for him. I strongly disagree with this view. Anyone who is sufficiently interested in medical research in general—or in stress in particular—to read this book would, it seems to me, want to make up his own mind about the issues at stake. In any event, he will learn more about what is in doubt if the views of the opposition are not censored. Of course, only specialists can fully appreciate the details, but it is not the details that really count. The thoughtful reader is quite capable of judging the main issues for himself, even if he is not a professional scientist. Therefore, the basic problems should be stated clearly, at least as far as the limitations of non-technical language permit. I propose to try this in the next chapter. Indeed, I shall spare no effort to describe all major causes of contention in an understandable manner, because, to my mind, no one can really grasp the essence of research without trying to comprehend the reasons for disagreement among scientists.

18:

"When scientists

disagree"

On scientific debate: good and bad.
Debates about the stress concept.

On scientific debate

Toward the end of his life, W. B. Cannon—the great American physiologist whose work I have repeatedly mentioned—wrote a semibiographical book about his investigations. He knew from bitter personal experience what it means to be the target of constant, violent attacks by other scientists; this is probably why he wanted to tell the public something about the human element in research. in *The Way of an Investigator* (W. W. Norton & Company, 1945), he reminds us that, after all, science is the product of people, of scientists. Scientists, like all men, possess not only intellectual and technical skills, but also emotions; they can be happy or angry, honored or humiliated, just like anybody else. Some scientists keep their emotions and motives to themselves; others regard them as inherent parts of investigative activity, which should not be suppressed if a research project is to be fully evaluated for the benefit of future investigators.

Cannon devoted an entire chapter of his book to debates about his work. He entitled it, "When Scientists Disagree." It is a remarkably instructive and inspiring chapter, especially for those who knew the author personally; and I could not resist the temptation of using this same caption for the thoughts I would like to put before you here. Not only Cannon's work, but also his way of life, have been a great inspiration to me, and I am certain—were he here today—he would not mind my borrowing his title for the use I want to make of it.

Cannon consoled himself for having been so much attacked with the thought that original scientists have always been the victims of vicious criticisms, and often by highly competent colleagues. He points out, for instance, what happened to one of his distinguished predecessors among the professors of physiology at Harvard. When Oliver Wendell Holmes, Sr., was still a very young physician, he presented evidence that childbed fever "is so far contagious as to be frequently carried from patient to patient by physicians and nurses." Meigs, a prominent and much older Philadelphia obstetrician, contemptuously commented on this foolish suggestion of "some scribbler," and declared that he was not impressed by the opinions of "very young gentlemen." Instead of weighing the evidence judiciously, Meigs righteously declared: "I prefer to attribute cases of childbed fever to accident or Providence, of which I can form a conception, rather than to a contagion, of which I cannot form any clear idea." This must have sounded very cautious and proper at the time; but the fact is that young Holmes was right and Meigs was wrong. Ignaz Philipp Semmelweis, the Hungarian obstetrician who subsequently proved the contagious nature of this disease, saved the lives of countless mothers by prescribing antisepsis in the delivery room. Yet even this great benefactor of humanity was violently attacked and ridiculed by his peers, so much so that he eventually became mentally deranged.

In discussing these problems, Cannon did not refer to himself, but the intimate feelings of the much criticized Father of Homeostasis come through to the reader when he mildly adds: "Any aspersions, any slurs cast upon the skill or ability or the personal uprightness of the man whose work is being corrected are sure to stir resentment."

Cannon was my first critic. I can still vividly remember his reaction when—just after having completed my initial experiments on stress—I talked to him about them. We discussed stress twice: first briefly, when I visited his laboratory in Boston, and again a few years later in more leisurely fashion, in the Faculty Club of McGill University, just after he had delivered a remarkable lecture to our students. I felt quite frustrated at not being able to convince the

Great Old Man of the important role played by the pituitary and the adrenal cortex in my stress syndrome. He gave me excellent reasons why he did not think these glands could help resistance and adaptation in general and even why it would seem unlikely that a general adaptation syndrome could exist. But there was no trace of aggressiveness in his criticisms, no sting that could have blurred my vision to the point of refusing to listen. His comments only sharpened my eye for the limitations in the part played by the pituitary-adrenal axis during stress. They helped me, among other things, by inspiring the experiments which established that certain stress-manifestations could still be produced in the absence of this gland system.

Of course, even the most objective scientist is not infallible. One of the greatest physicists of all times, Michael Faraday, said, "That I may be largely wrong I am free to admit—who can be right altogether in physical science, which is essentially progressive and corrective?" This is, of course, even more true in a less precise science, such as medicine. A detached analytic debate helps to point out and correct errors; but criticism must always remain objective. It should be offered in the friendly tone which behooves colleagues in the same field of learning, who merely want to promote science by mutual constructive advice. Above all, debate must, as far as our human limitations permit, not be directed by considerations of personal prestige. The question is not, "*Who* is right?" but, "*What* is right?" An old Hebrew proverb maintains that "the envy of scholars will increase wisdom" (*Newsweek*, August 15, 1955). Even debate inspired by jealousy can stimulate research; but it is less efficient and certainly less pleasant than cooperation.

Great progress can be made only by ideas which are very different from those generally accepted at the time. Unfortunately, it is not only literally true that the more someone sticks out his neck above the masses, the more he is likely to attract the eyes of snipers. "The new truth," says Jacques Barzun, "invariably sounds crazy, and crazier in proportion to its greatness. It would be idiocy to keep recounting the stories of Copernicus, Galileo, and Pasteur, and forget that the next time the innovator will seem as hopelessly wrong and perverse as these men seemed." (*Teacher in America*, Doubleday Anchor Book, 1955.)

Very few fundamentally new ideas manage to by-pass the heresy stage. Among the really outstanding discoveries, only procedures which have immediate and important practical applications are relatively immune to violent criticisms from the start. This is illustrated by the discovery that penicillin (Fleming, Florey, and Chain), streptomycin (Waksman), and the sulfonamides (Domagk) have marked antibacterial actions, that antihistamines can suppress allergies (Halpern), or that ACTH and cortisone are useful in combating arthritis (Hench and Kendall). Although all these were truly great contributions to knowledge, they have stimulated only minor debates, mostly about limitations of the usefulness and about the damaging side-effects of these remedies.

On the other hand, a new concept in biology, such as Darwin's theory of evolution, is almost certain to provoke what Huxley called a "public war dance."

When Pasteur proclaimed that infectious diseases were due to germs, when Clemens P. Pirquet and Charles R. Richet discovered allergy, the literature was full of biting, hostile remarks, in which those who did not have the originality of creating—or even understanding—new concepts in medicine, tried to compensate by displaying their wit.

In his biography of Freud, Ernest Jones points out that the psychiatrist Walther Spielmeyer had, at first, denounced the use of psychoanalysis as "mental masturbation." Indeed, by 1910 the mere mention of Freud's theories was enough to start Professor Wilhelm Weygandt—then chairman of a medical congress in Hamburg—to banging his fist and shouting, "This is not a topic for discussion at a scientific meeting; it is a matter for the police." (*The Life and Work of Sigmund Freud,* Basic Books, 1955.)

Even the greatest physicians may, especially as they grow older, become quite blind to new concepts. A much quoted example of this was the unqualified rejection, by the great pathologist Rudolf Virchow, of young Robert Koch's theory that the little rods he saw under the microscope were the cause of tuberculosis.

Of course, the more uncontroversial discoveries, the finding of facts immediately applicable to practical medicine, can be made empirically, that is, through observation and experiment, more or less by chance, without using any theory. But this is rare; you cannot count on it. Such discoveries are like winning a fortune on a horse race; no matter how great the practical gain, the accomplishment is immediately finished and offers no promise of future success at the same game. "The history of science demonstrates beyond a doubt that the really revolutionary and significant advances come not from empiricism but from new theories." (James B. Conant, *Modern Science and Modern Man,* Doubleday Anchor Book, 1952.) Some scientists make important, immediately applicable discoveries, using the technique of sheer trial and error, somewhat as the old-fashioned inventors used to work. This becomes increasingly less profitable in modern medicine, for even when the discoverer himself did not have to formulate a theory to arrive at a result, he was almost invariably guided by current concepts previously formulated by others.

So theories are indispensable. They stimulate controversy, but this is all to the good because it brings out the weak points in our concepts, showing where further research is needed. Even a theory that does not fit all the known facts is valuable, as long as it fits them better than any other concept. To quote Conant again: "We can put it down as one of the principles learned from the history of science that a theory is only overthrown by a better theory, never merely by contradictory facts." (*On Understanding Science,* Mentor Book, New American Library, 1953.)

It is not true that "exceptions strengthen the rule," but they do not necessarily invalidate it either. Sometimes facts which at first seem to be quite incompatible with a theory gradually find their natural place in it when more facts come to light. In other cases the theory is sufficiently plastic to be readily adjusted, so as to cover apparently paradoxical, incongruous new observations. As I ventured to say elsewhere, "the best theory is that which necessitates the minimum amount of assumptions to unite a maximum number of facts, since it is most likely to possess the power of assimilating new facts from the unknown without damage to its own structure." (*Second Annual Report on Stress,* Acta, Inc., 1952.)

There is a great difference between a sterile theory and a wrong one. A sterile theory does not lend itself to experimental verification. Any number of these can easily be formulated to explain virtually anything, but they are perfectly useless; they could not possibly help understanding; they lead only to futile verbiage. A wrong theory, on the other hand, can still be highly useful, for, if it is well conceived, it may help to formulate experiments which will necessarily fill important gaps in our knowledge.

During the last century, the great French neurologist, Pierre Marie, discovered that, in certain kinds of giants (called *acromegalics*), the pituitary is completely replaced by cancer. He immediately formulated the theory that the pituitary produces some growth-inhibiting hormone, since destruction of this gland results in overgrowth. This theory was not only wrong, it was exactly the opposite of the truth. Actually, the pituitary produces STH which, as we said, is a growth hormone. Now, the cancers Marie saw did replace the pituitary, but they did not destroy its activity; on the contrary, they consisted exclusively of abnormal pituitary cells which produced an excess of STH. Marie's interpretation could not have been farther from the truth. Yet it was his wrong, but highly fertile, theory which first called attention to an unsuspected, yet very real, relationship between the little gland under the brain and the growth of our tissues in general. The original faulty interpretation was later adjusted by Marie himself to fit the known facts. To do so, he actually had to reverse his first formulation; still, it should be remembered that it was the initial wrong theory—not the corrected modification—which acted as a starting point for research on the endocrine activity of the pituitary. It was this line of research which, when carried forward by such eminent contemporary investigators as H. M. Evans, P. Smith, B. A. Houssay, J. B. Collip, C. H. Li, and A. E. Wilhelmi, eventually led to the isolation of highly purified STH from animal glands.

Science cannot be fully appraised without understanding scientists. The way a man sees a thing depends equally upon the man and the thing. The motives and consequences of scientific debates are of paramount importance to the creative investigator: and hence to his investigation. This is one reason why I thought I should discuss these points at length in this section. Besides, the same considerations also apply to debates about facts and theories in everyday life; in this sense they concern everybody directly. In any case, without this introduction I could not have mustered the energy and courage to present the next section.

Debates about the stress concept

The stress concept is now one of the most widely discussed problems in medicine. Here we can not go into all that has been published about its virtues and limitations; but we can present the main issues. Let us first take the principal arguments which have stood in the way of acceptance of this concept in the past; then we shall turn to the gaps which still remain in the theory and hence represent fruitful fields for further investigation.

What is new in this concept? At first, several investigators actually denied the very existence of the G.A.S.; others thought that these three letters functioned merely as a new catchword for something that had been definitely proved long ago. These two criticisms could not both be right. Since the first no longer has any serious proponents nowadays, we shall consider only the second.

This is not the place to discuss all the biologic reactions which, at one time or another, have been claimed to be identical with the G.A.S. Almost every nation and every specialty of medicine has mustered at least one: the so-called *irritational syndrome,* described by the French bacteriologist Reilly; the *vegetative reorientation* of the German internist Hoff; the defense through *conditioned reflexes,* so ably explored by the eminent Russian physiologist Pavlov; the *defensive neurosis* theory of the Austrian psychiatrist Freud; the hippocratic concept of *pónos,* which dominated ancient Greek medical thought; and Cannon's *emergency reaction.* And these are only a few representative examples. We could add an almost endless list of scattered observations, which have been made so often and by so many people that they were never attributed to any one author in particular. For instance, it had long been common knowledge that animals infected with diphtheria usually have large *adrenals,* that one or another drug can produce *gastric ulcers,* that in children the thymus can undergo *accidental involution* under the influence of this or that agent. Then there are all those *shock therapies* and *"nonspecific therapies"* about which we spoke in Book I. But the G.A.S., the stress syndrome, could not very well be identical with all these individual observations, since they are certainly very different from each other.

Many of these earlier findings are of paramount importance in themselves and, in retrospect, it is easy to see that they are all somehow related to the G.A.S. After what we have said about the ubiquity of stress, it is clear that no human being could have failed to note some of its individual manifestations. The chief value of the G.A.S. concept is precisely to give a *common basis which unifies all these, hitherto apparently unrelated, observations.*

Of course, you could say that the first cave man who saw lightning had already observed what later merely received the catchword *electricity*. The first woman who made her hair crackle by combing it vigorously even knew how to generate electricity at will. Yet, these, as all other early observations on electric phenomena, remained puzzling, disconnected mysteries, because they could not be subjected to quantitative scientific study until Galvani began to define the basic concept which gave them unity.

In any case, the birth date of the G.A.S. is inconsequential in comparison with the value of the concept as we understand it today. So let us turn our attention to the debates about its worth.

Are experimental observations on animals applicable to man? Some reactions of animals just do not occur in man. What we know about respiration in fishes is not readily applicable to problems of human physiology; the fish gets its oxygen from water through its gills, and man breathes air through his lungs. This is perhaps an extreme example, but even certain chemical reactions of the lower mammals are quite different from those of man. For instance, it is impossible to study the effects of vitamin-C deficiency in the rat. The tissues of this animal can make vitamin C themselves, but a human being is dependent upon the dietary ingestion of this foodstuff because his body cannot make it. Each species has its own peculiarities. Yet, the whole of *experimental medicine is based upon the fact that most of the fundamental biologic reactions are essentially the same in man and in other mammals*. In this respect the G.A.S. is no exception.

First, take the *manifestations of stress*. The adrenal changes caused by various stressors are quite similar in man and in the usual laboratory animals. The same is true of other manifestations of stress, for instance, of the characteristic disappearance of blood-eosinophils, the involution of lymphatic tissues, the increased urinary elimination of corticoids, and the inhibition of inflammation. All these changes occur both in laboratory animals and in man during acute stress.

Now take the *actions of adaptive hormones.* In all species, including man, removal of the adrenals greatly decreases resistance to stress, and treatment with corticoids can again restore it toward normal. The anti-inflammatory adrenal hormones (such as cortisone) inhibit inflammation, and the proinflammatory corticoids (such as DOC) and the adrenalines raise the blood pressure. All this has proved to be true in man just as in laboratory animals.

Finally, since the mechanism of the *diseases of adaptation* was worked out in animal experiments, it had been questioned whether or not it would be essentially the same in man. Is it possible actually to prove, for instance, that an inappropriate secretion of pituitary or adrenal hormones can become the decisive factor in the development of diverse diseases due to hitherto unidentified causes? Can we combat any spontaneous disease of man with such a concept as a guide? I believe all this has been answered most eloquently by the work of those clinicians who showed us how to treat so many apparently unrelated maladies of cryptic origin with ACTH, corticoids, hypophysectomy, adrenalectomy, or salt-poor diets.

In view of all these findings, there remains no basis today for the fear that in the field of stress research the results of animal experiments have no bearing upon clinical problems.

Is there really an increase in corticoid-production during stress? After all I have said, you may feel that there could hardly be any doubt about it. Well, the fact is that, even as late as 1954, some competent investigators still doubted the existence of a real increase in corticoid-secretion during the alarm reaction.

This is why: if a patient receives large amounts of cortisone his adrenals involute, because the greater the concentration of corticoids in the blood, the less ACTH is produced by the pituitary. There evidently exists some sort of a *feed-back mechanism,* through which the corticoids automatically depress the secretion of that ACTH which normally stimulates the adrenals to produce corticoids. This arrangement (illustrated on p. 199) is very important to maintain a steady corticoid-concentration in the blood under basal conditions.

It had been claimed a few years ago that—because of this arrangement—a real increase of corticoids in the blood could never develop during stress. This feed-back mechanism would necessarily prevent a rise, just as the thermostat in an air-conditioning system protects a room against overheating, even if the outside temperature rises.

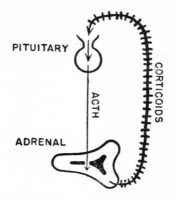

ACTH stimulates the corticoid-secretion of the adrenals; the corticoids inhibit the ACTH-secretion of the pituitary.

Years ago, the well-known American physiologist, Dwight J. Ingle, discovered this self-regulating mechanism through which the adrenals normally protect themselves against overstimulation. Since that time, there has never been any doubt about the existence of such a feed-back arrangement. But, as I found to my surprise in 1940, *during stress this moderator system is largely by-passed.* It turned out that the alarm signals (discharged from the various cells of our tissues during stress) can stimulate ACTH-secretion, even when the concentration of corticoids in the blood reaches the highest attainable levels. This, incidentally, is most fortunate because much more than the normal blood-concentration of corticoids is necessary to maintain life during stress. If the feed-back mechanism were perfect we could never survive a seriously stressful experience. Besides, there are evident signs of corticoid-excess during stress. There is, for instance, an inhibition of inflammation, a tendency for the spreading of infections, an involution of the lymphatic organs, and so forth.

To circumvent this difficulty, those who were still reluctant to accept my concept brought up another possibility. They said that, despite all this, the secretion of corticoids may not be actually increased; perhaps these hormones merely become more effective during stress. Of course, the activity of these hormones can be augmented by certain metabolic changes—the so-called *conditioning factors*—which sensitize our tissues to corticoids. This conditioning undoubtedly does occur in stress, but it cannot explain everything. Surely the adrenal enlargement and the chemically demonstrable increase in the corticoid-content of the blood are sufficient proof that during stress there is also a real increase in adrenocortical activity.

The unitarian theory of adrenocortical function. Although fractions possessing mineralocorticoid activity had been prepared from cattle adrenals some twenty years ago (F. Hartman, E. C. Kendall, T. Reichstein), most of the experts believed, even as late as 1952, that the adrenal does not actually secrete such compounds. It was thought, in line with the "unitarian theory" of adrenocortical function, that only the glucocorticoid type of life-maintaining hormone is actually poured into the blood. The other corticoids which had been extracted from adrenals were assumed to be mere precursors of hormones, stored in the glands but not released into the circulation.

This theory greatly handicapped progress by branding as futile any search for new corticoids in the blood. Yet, unfortunately, it enjoyed great popularity because it was supported by two seemingly weighty arguments: (1) with the techniques available at that time only glucocorticoid activity was demonstrable in the blood; (2) after adrenalectomy the signs of adrenal-insufficiency were thought to be perfectly corrected by COL (a glucocorticoid); the body did not seem to need anything else.

Had these conclusions been correct, they would have invalidated my theory that diseases can be due to excessive mineralocorticoid activity. *In the light of the unitarian theory, DOC mineralocorticoids were considered to be wholly artificial compounds,* and consequently my experiments with this substance were claimed to have no bearing upon clinical problems. For instance, the renal and vascular lesions which I had produced in animals with DOC were attributed to some allergy against this "unnatural compound," or to some infection which I might have introduced accidentally together with the DOC.

Later, my coworkers and I reproduced the same renal and cardiovascular changes by treating animals with pituitary extracts (rich in STH), with a distant relative of DOC (called MAD), or even with stressors (for instance cold). Significantly, all these agents also caused histologic signs of adrenal-stimulation. The opponents of my views immediately took this to mean that the effect of DOC is not specific and has nothing to do with its mineralocorticoid properties. Evidently many things can act like DOC, but there was one important difference only DOC produced disease even when the adrenals were surgically removed. This compound—unlike the other agents (pituitary extract, MAD, cold)—evidently does not act through the adrenals.

We concluded that, *under the influence of various treatments, some DOC-like mineralocorticoids can be produced by the adrenals* of the intact rat; the adrenalectomized animals are saved from disease simply because in them the source of these damaging hormones is removed. No alternative explanation was offered by anyone, but many physicians still did not feel they could go along with my interpretation because it was contrary to the "unitarian theory."

I mention all this to illustrate the many kinds of objections that can, and must, be made before a new concept becomes acceptable. Actually, in the meantime, the unitarian theory completely lost its basis. First, using perfected techniques, *aldosterone,* a typical mineralocorticoid, was detected both in the tissue of the adrenals and in the blood which leaves these glands (S. A. Simpson, J. F. Tait, T. Reichstein). Second, it became evident as time went by that adrenalectomized patients were not as well maintained on cortisone alone as when they were also given small amounts of DOC or aldosterone.

Now, of course, nobody could doubt any longer that *mineralocorticoids are natural hormones* of the adrenals, but it took a great deal of work on the part of a great many scientists to get that far. These investigators persisted in their search despite the discouraging effect of the unitarian theory. Why did they try so assiduously to isolate this aldosterone rather than any one of the many other suspected, but still undiscovered, hormones? The effort would hardly have seemed worthwhile if the goal had been merely to prepare yet another DOC-like compound. On the other hand, any effort to learn more about mineralocorticoids was certainly justified if these hormones really do play a decisive role in the production of the most commonly fatal wear-and-tear diseases of mankind, such as the cardiovascular and renal diseases.

How much DOC is too much? Another reason for doubts about the clinical implications of my work was that I had to use very large amounts of DOC to produce disease manifestations. It was held that such enormous quantities could never be secreted by the adrenals in health or disease.

Well, first of all, *it was disease we produced with DOC so that the dosages used were naturally incompatible with health.* On the other hand, nobody knew how much the adrenals could produce during disease. In view of this, who could tell how much was too much? If I wanted to see whether an excess of this hormone could produce disease, I had to give an excess. The appropriate amount, I thought, was that which would give us an experimental reproduction of some known human malady.

In any case, this objection also lost its basis as new facts came to the fore. It turned out, for example, that the same *disease-manifestations can be induced with much less DOC than I had originally given,* provided the compound is administered not by injection of solutions but by the implantation of solid hormone pellets. From these the hormone is very constantly taken up into the blood and this probably corresponds much more closely to the way the adrenals would continuously secrete it. Injections suddenly flood the body with DOC, but between treatments the hormone-content of the blood is not kept very high.

Apart from this, *the natural mineralocorticoid, aldosterone, proved to be much more potent than DOC,* so that the adrenals would have to produce comparatively little of it to cause a severe overdosage. Finally, it was found a few years ago that patients with demonstrably increased aldosterone-production suffer from kidney damage (nephrosis, nephrosclerosis), just as the theory predicted (see p. 137).

In view of all this, there can hardly be any question today about the ability of the adrenals to secrete large amounts of mineralocorticoids. Furthermore, adrenal-hyperfunction in disease can induce the same kind of cardiovascular and kidney damage in man that DOC produces in animals. Finally, removal of the adrenals can have a curative value in patients suffering from such diseases.

Can there really be an imbalance between anti- and proinflammatory corticoids? In 1949 the extraordinary anti-inflammatory effectiveness of ACTH and cortisone was first demonstrated in patients with rheumatoid arthritis. In view of the animal experiments which had demonstrated the proinflammatory effect of DOC, this new observation supported the idea that an imbalance between two types of corticoids plays a part in the production of inflammatory diseases. When inflammation is excessive, as, for instance, in rheumatoid arthritis, the situation is corrected by treatment with anti-inflammatory corticoids. Conversely, an adverse effect could be expected from such treatment in diseases characterized by a relative inability to put up adequate inflammatory barricades against invaders, as, for instance, in tuberculosis.

To many of us this seemed to be a rather natural—in fact, the only possible—explanation of the facts known at that time. Yet some physicians still felt that the idea of a balance between proinflammatory and anti-inflammatory hormones was pure speculation, designed to reconcile the newly discovered anti-inflammatory effects of ACTH and cortisone with the earlier observations on the proinflammatory actions of DOC.

There can be no doubt now that the two types of hormones can mutually antagonize each other's actions on inflammation. Many observations have shown this, but it will be enough to mention two: (1) the aggravation of various experimental infections with anti-inflammatory hormones (which remove inflammatory barricades), and their amelioration with proinflammatory ones (which strengthen inflammatory barricades; (2) the protection against anaphylactoid inflammation, topical-irritation arthritis, inflammation in the inflammatory pouch, etc., with ACTH and cortisone, and the abolition of this protection by simultaneous treatment with STH or DOC.

Is there such a thing as a disease of adaptation? Here the answer depends on how you define a "disease of adaptation." *No disease is exclusively caused by maladaptation,* but derangements of our adaptive mechanisms do play a decisive role in the development of many diseases.

You might just as well question whether there is such a thing as an "infectious disease." We are constantly exposed to all kinds of germs which could make us sick, but often do not. Why not? Because the entry of the germs into our system is not in itself the disease. All depends on how much the germs can damage us and how much we can damage them. We cannot injure some of the microbes at all, but if they have no way of doing us any harm either, there is no disease. These germs live peacefully in our intestines, lungs, or throats without causing any trouble.

Other microbes could damage us, but before they get the chance, our tissues quarantine them within impenetrable inflammatory barricades, or actually kill them with chemicals known as *immune bodies*. Some people remain in perfect health although they carry germs of typhoid or diphtheria. Such persons can, nevertheless, infect others, who may then die from diphtheria or typhoid because their defenses are weaker. Almost every adult human being has, at one time or another, been infected with tuberculosis, but the germs usually cause no inconvenience because they are walled off by fibrous inflammatory membranes somewhere in the lungs.

Significantly, exposure to an overwhelming stress (such as prolonged starvation, worry, fatigue, or cold) can break down the body's protective mechanisms. This is true both of adaptation which depends on serologic immunity and of that which is due to inflammatory barricades. This is why so many maladies tend to become rampant during wars and famines.

If a microbe is in or around us all the time and yet causes no disease until we are exposed to stress, what is the "cause" of our illness, the microbe or the stress? I think both are—and equally so. In most instances *disease is due neither to the germ as such, nor to our adaptive reactions as such, but to the inadequacy of our reactions against the germ.*

I have used infectious diseases as an example here, but the same could be said about many other diseases. If a company goes bankrupt and the owner develops a gastric ulcer, what is the cause of the disease, the bankruptcy or the owner's inability to adapt himself to his losses? When a joint becomes crippled by constant inflammation and scarring, is it not correct to blame our own bodily reactions (inflammatory responses) for the deformity? You may say that, had there been no defensive inflammation, the causative germ or allergen might have had other and possibly more serious effects. Quite so; but we are not talking about those. The germ or allergen which stimulated inflammation might or might not have caused another disease, had there not been any tissue-reaction against it; but the illness which did in fact develop was an inflammatory disease. Moreover, when inflammation is suppressed with ACTH or corticoids, often—for instance, in allergies and in rheumatoid arthritis—nothing else develops in its stead.

It still remains to be shown to what extent maladaptation participates in each individual disease, since it seems to play a part in all of them, but a decisive part only in some. Another task for future research will be to show how far man can improve upon nature's own adaptive reactions.

Let me point out here parenthetically that Pasteur was sharply criticized by many of his enemies for failing to recognize the importance of the *terrain* (the soil in which disease develops). They said he was too one-sidedly preoccupied with the apparent cause of disease: the microbe itself. There were, in fact, many debates about this between Pasteur and his great contemporary, Claude Bernard; the former insisted on the importance of the disease-producer, the latter on that of the body's own equilibrium. Yet Pasteur's work on immunity induced with serums and vaccines shows that he recognized the importance of the soil. In any event, it is rather significant that Pasteur attached so much importance to this point that on his deathbed he said to Professor A. Rénon who looked after him: *"Bernard avait raison. Le germe n'est rien, c'est le terrain qui est tout."* ("Bernard was right. The microbe is nothing, the soil is everything.")

But today work along these lines has progressed far enough for us to say that, like all the reactions of the human body, those concerned with adaptation are not always perfect and at least some of the resulting diseases of adaptation can be corrected. They can be corrected, for instance, by the administration of hormones, the removal of endocrine glands, or by treatment with drugs which suppress endocrine or nervous activity.

These were the principal problems which had to be settled before accepting the stress concept. Now let us turn to the *weak points in the theory which still exist today*. Such gaps in our knowledge are particularly important; they focus attention upon the limitations of our concept and thereby point to fruitful fields for further research.

What are the alarm signals and how do they act? In Book II I have already presented the observations which led me to suspect that some *alarm signals are discharged by various cells, as a side-effect of both activity and damage.* We have seen that each type of cell has its own specific reaction-forms: the muscle contracts, the eye sees, the connective tissue responds to injury with inflammation. But the sum of these characteristic responses could not be computed directly because they have no common denominator. Yet the visible degree of stress in a man is proportionate to the sum of everything that is going on in him at the time. How could the body calculate the sum of, say, that much contraction plus that much vision plus that much inflammation? All biologic reactions—no matter how different they are from one another—must produce some nonspecific by-product which can be added up and thus serve as an indicator of all the activity that goes on throughout the body.

This, you will note, is pure speculation. Nobody has ever seen or otherwise demonstrated this by-product by direct methods of observation. Nevertheless, it seems to me that the existence of this indicator is just as definitely established by logic as if we had seen it. No one has ever seen electricity either, but the reality of it is demonstrated beyond doubt by its manifestations. The same is true of the alarm signals. We cannot see them directly, but we can readily prove their existence, and even measure their amount, indirectly by their effects. The discharge of ACTH, the enlargement of the adrenals, the involution of the lymphatic organs, the corticoid-hormone-content of the blood, the feeling of fatigue, and many other signs of stress can all be produced by activity or injury in any part of the body. There must be some way of sending messengers from any cell to the organs which are so uniformly affected by all stressors.

To my mind, our ignorance about the nature of these alarm signals is one of the most serious handicaps in the study of stress; but how can we find out more about them? Well, to begin with, we might examine what *pathways* they could use. There are two, and only two, all-embracing coordinating systems which connect all parts of the body with one another: the nervous system and the blood-vessel system. The alarm signals could be carried everywhere *through nerves*, but it is virtually certain that this is not the only route they could take, because organs can send out alarm signals even when their nerves are cut. It is probable that often, if not always, the signals travel *in the blood*. We know that certain compounds, such as proteins, occur in every cell; parts of protein molecules may split off and then act as blood-borne transmittors of the stress-message. Any other product of cell activity might fulfill the same function, but it is equally *possible that the alarm signal is not a substance, but rather the lack of one*. During activity, cells consume a variety of chemicals, and the withdrawal of such compounds from the blood could also act as an alarm signal.

Intensive research along these lines is now under way in many laboratories throughout the world. Several investigators have published observations allegedly proving that one or another substance (proteolytic enzymes, polypeptides, histamine, acetylcholine, or adrenaline-derivatives) is the first mediator of the stress-response. In my opinion, none of these assumptions has as yet been adequately supported by facts.

It is even *possible that no one substance or deficiency has the monopoly of acting as an alarm signal*. A number of messengers may carry the same message. The actual facts which led us to postulate the existence of the alarm signals would be in agreement with this view also. The various cells could send out different messengers, as long as their messages could somehow be tallied by the organs of adaptation (as, for instance, by the pituitary). To explain, let us assume that the acidity of the blood is what counts. We have no reason to think that this is actually the case, but if it were so, any acid compound discharged by cells (or even the consumption by cells of alkalis) would forward the same message; yet the total amount of it could be computed as "acidity."

All these possibilities must be envisaged in designing experiments to identify the nature of the signals which gear the body for defense.

In the complex picture of a disease, what is due to what? If we look at disease from the viewpoint of the stress concept, a number of additional questions arise which cannot yet be definitely answered. Let us take rheumatoid arthritis as an example. We must ask:

1. What is the causative agent of this disease: a germ, an allergen, or nervous tension?

2. Why does a particular agent (say, a germ) to which everybody is exposed produce rheumatoid arthritis in one person and not in another?

3. We have seen that the most striking feature of rheumatoid arthritis is an excess of apparently useless inflammation. Is this due to excessive local irritation of the joint by the direct action of the causative agent? Is it due to an excessive production of proinflammatory or a deficiency in anti-inflammatory corticoids? Is it the consequence of those conditioning factors which sensitize the tissues to the former and desensitize them to the latter hormone? Or do several of these factors play a part here? The disease consists mainly of inflammation, a tissue-response which is easily influenced by a variety of circumstances, so that the problems presented by every case are naturally complex.

4. Why has it not been possible to show any striking derangement in the corticoid-content of the blood and urine in rheumatoid arthritis? Why is inflammation so readily inhibited in this disease by anti-inflammatory hormones and yet not significantly aggravated by proinflammatory corticoids? Why is it that, in nephrosis, an increase in aldosterone-production is associated with water-retention (dropsy) and a certain type of kidney-damage, with no increase in blood pressure, whereas in the so-called "primary aldosteronism," it is associated with another kind of kidney-damage (nephrosclerosis), high blood pressure, and no dropsy?

Of course, in theory it is always possible to get around such apparently incongruous facts. Possibly they could be due to differences in the speed of development or the intensity of the hormonal derangement, or to variable conditioning by other hormones, heredity, or the diet. It is very probable that explanations should be sought somewhere along these lines, but it is well always to keep in mind that these are still unanswered questions.

The important thing is that now these questions can be asked clearly; once this is possible, sooner or later they will be answered.

True, it may take a long time, but this need not discourage us. The concept of the microbial transmission of disease was outlined about a hundred years ago; yet, even in this field, we are still faced with very similar problems today. Despite all the progress made in bacteriology, all we know of some diseases is that they are infectious. Of other maladies we know the causative germ, but have no remedy against it; or we fail to understand why the same germ causes disease in some people but not in others. Yet, as soon as Pasteur formulated the basic problems of infection, this field began to emerge from centuries of darkness. The science of stress is much younger and correspondingly less well worked out than that of bacteriology, but we have already learned a good deal. For instance, we have recognized the role of the endocrine glands and hormones in the causation and treatment of the most varied diseases. With the greatly improved means for scientific research in our century, we have every reason to expect rapid progress along these lines now.

What is adaptation energy? Here we are touching upon what is probably *the* most fundamental gap in our knowledge about stress. I say "fundamental" because adaptability, or if we want to give it this name, "adaptation energy," is a basic feature of life itself. The length of the human life-span appears to be primarily determined by the amount of available adaptation energy. A better understanding of it promises to show us how to improve recovery from any kind of exhaustion and perhaps even to prolong life. Yet all we really know about this mysterious quantity is that constant exposure to any stressor will use it up. That much is certain; we can verify it by experiment. We can observe that anything to which adaptation is possible eventually results in exhaustion, that is, the loss of the power to resist. Just what is lost we do not know, but it could hardly be the caloric energy—which is usually considered to be the fuel of life—because exhaustion occurs even if ample food supplies are available.

To my mind, these are the most important gaps in our knowledge about stress—which means that these are also the most promising fields for further study.

Now let us see if what we have learned about the mechanism of stress and about the diseases of adaptation can serve as a basis for a more unified concept of medicine as a whole.

Book **IV:**

Sketch for a unified theory

Summary

The study of stress has shown how important it is to *distinguish clearly between specific and nonspecific vital responses.* Can they both be embraced by some unified theory?

Specific responses are simple in kind; they affect one or a few elements only. Nonspecific responses affect numerous elements without selectivity. In life, differences in kind (as different tones on a piano) cannot occur at the level of the elements (any one key); *the impression of a qualitative change is created by blending the responses of the unchanging fundamental units.*

But what are the elements of life? *The cell* is only a structural, not a functional unit: yet it can perform different functions at the same time. And *the atoms* which make up our body are not true units of life either. They do not possess any characteristics of life; it is only their interconnections in living bodies that somehow endow them with vitality. When fitted into the pattern of living matter, individual chemical units cannot react to stimulation selectively. Anything which affects one of them also influences a number of other closely connected chemical units.

The *reacton* is defined as "the smallest particle of life" which can still respond selectively to stimulation. In other words, biologic matter cannot be specifically affected in lots smaller than a reacton. In this sense, the reacton concept is not a theory, but a description of observed facts. The limits of the reaction are comparatively vague, but a quantum has no sharp borders either, yet it is an elemental unit of energy.

The significance of the reacton concept is that it opens to experimental analysis that range of units between the cell and the chemical element; at the same time, it bridges the gap between specific and nonspecific vital responses.

All manifestations of life in health and disease are viewed as simple combinations and permutations of individual yes-or-no responses in these ultimate units of life, the reactons.

The impression of virtually any color, shape, or movement can be created on an illuminated panel by turning off and on different combinations of colored light-bulbs, though each is capable only of one kind of response. As far as we can see, the human body represents an essentially similar, though enormously more complex, three-dimensional panel, in which all the manifestations of life can be evoked by activating various combinations and permutations of primary reactive units, the reactons.

I am particularly indebted to a number of scientists, among them: L. v. Bertalanffy, C. H. Best, G. Biörck, C. Cavallero, W. E. Ehrich, Laín A. Einstein, P. Entralgo, U. S. v. Euler, C. Fortier, I. Galdston, D. M. Green, C. S. Hanes, L. Hogben, B. A. Houssay, J. Jensen, W. Kaempffert, C. D. Leake, A. Lipschütz, G. Marañon, F. Martí-Ibañez, A. Mirsky, J. Needham, J. Ortega-y-Gasset, R. Pasqualini, A. Pi-Suñer, L. Prado, T. H. Rindani, P. Romanell, P. J. Rosch, P. Schwartz, A. Szent-Györgyi, D. L. Thomson, E. Tonutti, P. Weiss, and J. H. Woodgers, who were good enough to peruse the original version of Book IV, "Sketch for a Unified Theory," in manuscript form before it appeared (in more technical language) in the *Third Annual Report on Stress*. Many of these investigators made valuable suggestions which have greatly influenced my presentation of this topic in the present volume.

This section is intended only for those who are keenly interested in the nature of normal and morbid life. Like Book II, it is somewhat heavy, but those who would rather skip the details can do so by reading this outline which will provide the necessary continuity.

19:

The search for

unification

The value of unification. Stress and disease. The bridge from the nonspecific to the specific. Time, space, and intensity. What is apparently distinct and in need of unification? Health and disease. Disease itself and its signs or symptoms. Specific and nonspecific phenomena. Qualitative and quantitative differences. Units and complexes.

The value of unification

Whenever a large number of facts accumulates concerning any branch of knowledge, the human mind feels the need for some unifying concept with which to correlate them. Such integration is not only artistically satisfying, by bringing harmony into what appeared to be discord, it is also practically useful. It helps one to see a large field from a single point of view. When surveyed from a great elevation, some details in the landscape become hazy, or even invisible; yet it is only from there that we can see the field as a whole, in order to ascertain where more detailed exploration of the ground would be most helpful for its further development.

Efforts to arrive at a unified concept of disease have been made by physicians ever since the beginning of medical history. Of course, any attempt at a perfect unification would a priori be doomed to failure. The various diseases differ, both in the mechanism of their development and in their visible manifestations: they could never be reduced completely to any one common denominator. Nevertheless, whenever any new, common, structural, or functional characteristic has been detected in all parts of the body, or in all diseases, efforts have been made to single out this attribute (the cellular structure of living things, enzyme-functions, metabolism, and so forth) as a lookout post from which to obtain a coordinated view of biology and medicine as a whole.

If we do not go any further than this—if we do not look upon these unifying constructions of the mind as anything more fundamental than an elevated position from which we can get a synoptic view of disease—such efforts are, to my mind, quite permissible and often of great practical value in guiding research.

We have seen that stress plays an important part in many diseases. Its general (G.A.S.) and regional (L.A.S.) expressions encompass the very essence of what we call disease. It is rather tempting, therefore, to explore the possibility of using the concept of stress as a basis for some degree of unification.

Stress and disease

We have illustrated with many examples, that the most varied manifestations of disease depend upon a tripartite mechanism consisting of: (1) the direct action of the external agent—the apparent disease-producer; (2) internal factors which inhibit this action; and (3), internal factors which facilitate this action. All potential disease-producers cause some degree of stress. Through this they can modify the body's response by altering the internal forces of resistance and of submission. This appears to be the basic pattern of defense when the body itself fights disease through stress. To improve upon nature's self-healing efforts of this type is also the object of the physician who uses stress therapy in the form of shock, tranquilizing agents, adaptive hormones, and so forth.

In essence, stress therapy (whether administered by the body itself or by the physician) is a *tactical treatment,* such as was hitherto practiced almost exclusively in surgery. In surgery it was always customary to use it whenever the disease-producer could not be eliminated. For instance, when an inoperable cancer occludes the gut, the surgeon makes an artificial opening to by-pass the obstruction. This is no cure, but it helps the patient to live in relative harmony with his disease. Here we accomplish by purely mechanical means what stress therapy achieves through biochemical processes.

Stress therapy is not offensive; it is not specifically directed against any one disease-producer (as are specific serums, antibiotics, and other chemotherapeutic agents).

Stress therapy is *not symptomatic, nor strictly substitutional;* it does not act by merely eliminating any one specific symptom (as does aspirin in a headache), or by patching up a defect (as when a loss of skin is repaired with a graft, or a lack of vitamin with a curative amount of it).

Stress therapy is instead *tactically defensive* in that it adjusts active defense (for instance, barricading off a disease-producer with inflammation) and passive submission (as permitting local death of limited cell-groups, or the spread of inoffensive disease-producers) in a manner favorable to the organism as a whole.

Some agents are virtually *unconditional disease-producers* in that their influence upon the tissues of the body is so great that they cause disease, almost irrespective of any conditioning or sensitizing circumstances. (For instance, ionizing rays, great extremes of temperature, intense mechanical injuries or certain microorganisms to which everybody is susceptible.)

Still, most of the agents which can make us sick are, to a greater or lesser extent, *conditionally acting disease-producers*: that is, they cause maladies only under special circumstances of sensitization. Their disease-producing ability may depend upon hereditary factors, the portal through which they enter into the body, the previous weakening of resistance by malnutrition, or cold, and so forth. Here, it is impossible to decide which, among the many factors necessary for the production of disease, is actually the cause and which the conditioning factor: a complete *disease-producing situation* must be realized before the malady can become manifest. For instance, whether a microbe which could produce disease actually does so or not depends largely upon the forces of resistance and submission which will face it after it penetrates the body. It may have free entry into the blood and cause death by blood poisoning, or it may be completely quarantined within a thick barricade of inflammatory tissue which renders it innocuous. In a case like this it is meaningless to discuss whether the microorganism itself or the body's response is the final cause of the outcome. Here the development of illness depends upon a whole constellation of events.

This interpretation was still not wholly satisfactory as a unifying concept of disease, mainly because it failed to encompass the *noninflammatory maladies*. With the characterization of the L.A.S. it became evident, however, that local stress produces not only inflammation but also degeneration and death, or stimulation, enlargement, and multiplication of cells at the site of its action. All these changes can be regulated by proinflammatory and anti-inflammatory hormones, whose actions (as well as the corresponding effects of nervous stimuli) might therefore be viewed more generally as favoring or inhibiting reaction to injury in general. Therefore, the concept must not necessarily be restricted to the purely inflammatory diseases.

The bridge from the nonspecific to the specific

The question remained, however, *whether the manifold specific effects of agents could also be integrated into this concept.* These appear to be qualitatively different, both from each other and from the nonspecific (stress) effects: they did not appear to lend themselves to any unified interpretation. But then we saw that there were imperceptible transitions between the most and the least specific actions, so that the difference is actually not one of kind but merely one of degree. If we could somehow also express specific actions in terms of stress, all disease-manifestations would be reduced to a common denominator. They could result, for instance, from differences in the intensity, sequence of action, anatomic distribution, and the relative proportions of the three basic components of disease: the stressor, the forces of resistance, and the forces of submission.

Time, space, and intensity

Apart from the relative proportions between the three basic factors of disease, the manifestations of individual maladies would then only depend upon *when, where, and how much* this tripartite situation develops: upon (1) *time* (the duration and possibly repetitive nature of stress), (2) *space* (the location of the stress-situation), and (3) *intensity* (the degree of the whole tripartite phenomenon).

During the past few years, I have attempted to formulate the conceptual foundation for this view through the *reacton theory,* which I should like to explain now. But by way of introduction, let me state at once that, to my mind, the link between the manifold specific and nonspecific reactions is that they are all composed of the same kinds of elementary responses.

Although biologic reactions tend to give the impression of oneness, they actually represent mosaics of simple activation and inhibition (stress) in a great variety of preexistent, elementary, subcellular, biologic units: the *reactons.** Each of these is capable of only one kind of response, but, by blending these elementary reactions in different combinations, qualitatively distinct aggregates result.

To illustrate this with an example, let us remember that one can create a virtually unlimited variety of melodies on the keyboard of a piano by merely activating or inhibiting its chords—varying time, site, and intensity of simple touch on preexistent keys—each capable of only one kind of response. We hope to show that reactons, not cells, are the elementary "keys" of living matter, and that all the manifestations of normal and pathologic life depend only on when, where, and how much (or how many of) these biologic elements are stressed.

This concept is closely related to that of the German Gestalt school of psychology. *Gestalt* means literally "form" or "shape," and is used in this sense for a configuration of separate structures or systems (physical, biologic, or psychologic), so integrated into a pattern as to constitute a functional unit. One may therefore conceive of physiologic, biologic, or psychologic events as occurring, not through the mere summation of distinct elements, but through the functioning of the *Gestalt* (shape) as a single unit. The shape of each

---

* This is not the place to go into a detailed discussion of related biologic concepts, but let us at least mention that the word *biophore* (Weismann) has already been used to describe a hypothetic "smallest body of matter capable of life." Allegedly such particles may be successively aggregated into larger groups called: (1) *determinants,* still beyond the limits of microscopic vision and equivalent to genes, and (2) *ids,* identified with the visible chromatin granules in cell nuclei. The biophore is more or less nearly equivalent to the *bioblast* (Altmann), the *pangene* (Hugo De Vries), the *plasome* (Wiesner), and the *biogen* (Verworn). The idea of *reactons* is also related, but much more distantly, to the concept of the *monads* (Giordano Bruno and later, Gottfried Leibnitz).

disease functions as a single unit, although it is made up of innumerable simple reacton-responses.

What is apparently distinct and in need of unification?

In thinking about the fundamental nature of any phenomenon, man invariably tends to analyze it from two essentially distinct viewpoints: its *primary cause* and its *primary constituent elements*.

For instance, if an intelligent member of a primitive tribe were first confronted with an automobile, he would ask, "Who made it?" (that is to say, what is its cause?) and "What is it made of?" (that is, what are its constituent elements?).

This innate quest for the primary is also quite evident during the period of mental awakening in every child. It manifests itself by what might be called the "serial why," which leads to the following type of conversational pattern: "Why is it dark at night?" "Because the sun sets." "Why does the sun set?" "Because the earth turns away from it," and so forth, until the hard-pressed adult succeeds in changing the topic.

Our craving to climb up along such question ladders does not diminish with maturity; but our hope of reaching the top rung fades away with age, for we come to realize that it is just as inherent in human nature to be blind to the primary as it is to look for it. Yet, as soon as man understands that, for him, the ladder of comprehension has no end, he can find comfort in the realization that consequently there is no limit to his possible progress; no matter how advanced his wisdom, he remains capable of yet another step forward.

We have little to say about primary causes in biology, yet experimental work has led us to a point where we feel that a better understanding of the primary elements of disease could be of great assistance in sketching a more unified picture of medicine. But, before attempting any further unification, I should like to outline what strikes me as being especially in need of it.

What are those concepts of medicine whose distinctness is in question? Let us take five pairs of twin concepts as examples, first, because they are rather basic in biology and medicine, and second, because they seem to defy any effort to reduce them to one common denominator.

These five pairs of twin concepts are: (1) health and disease, (2) disease itself and its signs and symptoms, (3) specific and nonspecific phenomena, (4) qualitative and quantitative differences, (5) units and complexes.

Health and disease

Textbooks usually define health as the absence of disease, and vice versa. The two conditions are alleged to be opposites of each other. Is this really so? Are they not rather different only in degree and in the position of vital phenomena within time-space?

Bleeding, inflammation, loss of weight, or a rise in temperature could be mentioned as typical manifestations of disease, in that they supposedly represent deviations from the condition of health which we call the norm. But the monthly cycle of women is accompanied by bleeding and inflammation in the womb, yet the failure of its occurrence is what we would call a disease in a young adult female. If she bled excessively during her period or from any place other than the womb (as happens in a malady called *endometriosis*), that would also be a disease, as would be the beginning of the monthly periods at an abnormal time (for instance, in precocious puberty).

A loss of body-weight or a variation in temperature can likewise be considered as morbid only in relation to some norm of health; but even health and biologic normalcy are not synonymous. A man born with an undeveloped toe, or with a disfiguring scar across his face, is neither normal nor unhealthy. A defect is not a disease.

It may be argued that the examples given (bleeding, inflammation, loss of weight, a rise in temperature), are merely manifestations of disease, and not disease itself. Perhaps we should distinguish between disease and the signs or symptoms of disease.

Disease itself and its signs or symptoms

The dictionaries tell us that *disease* is "a definite morbid process having a characteristic train of symptoms. It may affect the whole body or any of its parts; its cause, pathology, and prognosis may be known or unknown." ° On the other hand, a *symptom* is "any functional evidence of disease," and a *sign* is "any objective evidence of

° Significantly, the latest edition [1956] of *Blakiston's New Gould Medical Dictionary*—the standard modern reference volume in most of the medical schools—defines disease as "the failure of the adaptive mechanisms of an organism to counteract adequately the stimuli or stresses to which is subject, resulting in disturbances in function or structure of any part, organ, or system of the body."

disease." (From Dorland's *American Illustrated Medical Dictionary*.)

These definitions, though quite generally accepted, are hardly satisfactory to the analytic mind. Is the high blood pressure of ordinary ("essential") hypertension a disease or a sign? If it is a disease, it is also its own sign, and if it is a sign, what is it a sign of? The same doubts arise in connection with nephritis or pneumonia. These conditions could be called diseases, but their consequences (for instance, protein-excretion and hypertension with nephritis, fever and loss of breath with pneumonia) might be regarded as their signs. Yet, if the same renal and pulmonary changes happen to develop in the course of, say, scarlet fever, they are no longer considered diseases in themselves, but signs of the latter malady.

Actually we have a generally subconscious but very practical reason which largely justifies this usage. When we speak of *disease* we actually mean that, in the light of available knowledge, there is no hope of ascending any higher in the causality chain of the condition before us. When we speak of a *sign*, we mean that there is hope that we could climb, at least one rung higher, toward the understanding of the primary cause.

In view of this, the difference between disease and its symptoms or signs does not appear to be very fundamental. We are tempted to ask whether some unifying interpretation of these derangements could not help us to arrive at a more basic understanding of morbid processes in general. Of course, when it comes to signs and symptoms, the first preoccupation of the physician is the degree of their specificity: their reliability as indicators of any one disease.

Specific and nonspecific phenomena

The original meaning of the term *specific* is "that which characterizes or constitutes a species." For instance, we speak of the specific difference between the dog and the wolf, which both belong to the genus *Canis*.

The concept of specificity is of particular importance in stress research, since we have defined biologic stress as something nonspecific: the sum of all the wear and tear in the body caused by life at any one time. In this sense, stress is a condition elicited preponderantly by nonspecific agents, that is, those which act on many organs without selectivity. By contrast, a specific agent acts only on one or few parts and therefore provokes selective (specifically formed) effects. Agents causing very selective, that is, specific changes in strictly circumscribed parts are comparatively rare; most stimuli cause rather diffuse (nonspecifically formed) responses in many parts of the body. Therefore the somewhat loose expression *specific agent* generally implies both specificity in the causation and in the form (or composition) of the change it evokes.

Any one part can stand only a limited amount of wear and tear, but if many parts are nonspecifically affected, the total wear and tear adds up. That is why agents affecting many parts without specificity in the form of their effect are the most effective stressors. I have mentioned the thyrotrophic hormone as an example of a specific agent because few, if any, other substances share its ability to stimulate the thyroid gland selectively. Conversely, many of the changes elicited by severe infections, ionizing rays, or intense worry —for instance, fatigue, gastrointestinal upsets, loss of weight—are rather nonspecific, because they can be duplicated by many agents. And still *it would be impossible to give any example of an absolutely specific or absolutely nonspecific agent.*

Here again we get the impression that the two partners of the conceptual pair, specific and nonspecific, are only apparently different in quality, but actually distinct merely in degree, that is, in some quantitative aspect of their composition.

Qualitative and quantitative differences

This brings us to the very crucial problem of distinguishing between qualitative and quantitative differences in general. One would think, for instance, that the actions of a mild and a potent blood-pressure-raising substance would differ only in degree (quantity), and that the diametrically opposed effects of a nervous stimulant (excitant) and a tranquilizing (depressor) drug would differ in quality. But this distinction appears to be self-evident only because of the terms used. Speaking about excitation and depression implies that we view these conditions from an intermediate level, which we recognize to be the norm. If we begin from absolute lack of activity, we can construct an ascending scale, which rises from zero through the increasingly less pronounced degrees of depression all the way to excitation.

It is perhaps not wholly unjustified, therefore, *to ask whether quantitative and qualitative differences are not likewise merely a matter of degree* and of the distribution-pattern of vital phenomena in time and space. One could imagine, for instance, that the impression of virtually any qualitative difference could be created by mere combinations and permutations of induced activity in a limited number of biologic elements, each capable only of a single kind of response.

Think of those gigantic, illuminated advertising panels in Times Square: the impression of virtually any color, shape, and movement can be created on them by mere combinations and permutations of induced "activity" in a limited number of neon lights, each capable only of a single kind of response. Does the human body represent an essentially similar, though enormously more complex, three-dimensional panel, in which all the manifestations of life can be evoked by activating various combinations and permutations of primary reactive units, the reactons?

This brings us to the last and perhaps the most important twin concept which we shall have to analyze before attempting to arrive at some unified interpretation of biologic phenomena: the problem of the fundamental unit of life.

Units and complexes

The difficulty of distinguishing sharply between units and complexes is, of course, by no means peculiar to biology and medicine. We encounter it also in chemistry, physics, algebra, and geometry. We speak of a unit of matter, or of energy; a number can be taken as a unit, and so can a certain element of structure or form. To take a classic example, the atom has long been considered to be the unit of matter. Yet, in view of recent progress, particularly in physics and mathematics, this apparently indivisible building block has been shattered and, from its fragments, has emerged the most general theory of unification which the human mind has yet been able to create. Still, the atom is a unit, not, however, the ultimate, or fundamental, unit of matter.

In biology a species is a unit among living forms, and so is an individual within this species, an organ within this individual, a tissue within this organ, or a cell within this tissue. Traditionally, the cell has been considered to be the primary or fundamental unit of life, and yet it is still a highly complex aggregate.

In the next chapter we shall explore to what extent the stress concept could help us to bridge the gaps between these basic concepts of biology and medicine: health and disease, disease and its symptoms, specific and nonspecific changes, qualitative and quantitative differences, and, most fundamental of all, units and complexes.

I do not know—nor does it really matter—whether or not the basic arguments in support of my views have already been expressed by philosophers. Probably they have. Priority of discovery, in the sense in which it exists in the natural sciences, hardly has a true counterpart in the science of thought itself. Every pattern of argument compatible with the structure of the human brain has probably been formulated at some time, in some language or form, by some author, especially as regards such basic principles as those with which we have to deal. But there is a great difference between a thing that has been seen (or even described) and one that is known to those whom it concerns. The basic procedures of reasoning are equally applicable to all sciences; yet, in order to use them for the creation of new knowledge and understanding in any one domain, they must first be translated into a language which is understood and accepted by the workers in that particular field. To us, biologists and physicians, *generalizations are acceptable only if they are demonstrably substantiated by many measurable individual data.* We instinctively shy away from philosophic arguments, because the mind works much more rapidly than the hand, and as soon as we risk the formulation of some generalizations about our science, we realize that the laboratory cannot keep pace with the imagination.

Ours should be an *experimental philosophy,* since it is only the teachings of objective observation that we can really assimilate. As its natural counterpart, such an experimental philosophy would create a *theoretic medicine,* which, I believe, could become just as enlightening and practically useful to physicians as theoretic physics has been to our colleagues in the sciences which deal with the inanimate world.

To lay the foundations for this will necessarily be a time-taking endeavor, likely to require the concerted efforts of several generations. The following pages can be regarded only as a very tentative attempt to draw a preliminary sketch, based on the limited number of facts which I have been able to verify in the laboratory.

20:

How could the stress concept lead to a more unified interpretation of biology and medicine?

Stress and adaptation. Stress and growth. Stress and specificity. The structural unit of life: the cell. The functional unit of life: the reacton. Analysis and synthesis of cellular disease. Possibilities and limitations of the reacton hypothesis.

Stress and adaptation

Our earlier work on the G.A.S. and particularly the more recent observations on the L.A.S. have brought out clearly the essential difference between what I called *specific resistance* (resistance to an agent induced by pretreatment with the same agent) and *crossed resistance* (resistance to an agent produced by pretreatment with another agent).

The *stage of resistance* (see p. 87) received its name because here, resistance to the particular agent, which produced this stage of the (general or local) adaptation syndrome, is at its peak; yet, at the same time, resistance to most other agents tends to fall below normal. It seems that the adjustment of our tissues to perform one function detracts from their adaptability to new circumstances. These observations convinced me that we must distinguish between two fundamentally different types of adaptation:

1. *Developmental adaptation* (in technical language: homotrophic adaptation), that is, a simple, progressive, adaptive reaction, accomplished by mere enlargement and multiplication of preexisting cell-elements, without qualitative change. This response occurs whenever a tissue is only required to increase its activity as regards a function to which it is already adapted at the onset, as for instance, when a muscle is forced to perform more than the usual amount of mechanical work.

2. *Redevelopmental adaptation* (in technical language: hetero-
trophic adaptation), in which a tissue, organized for one type of
action, is forced to readjust itself completely to an entirely different
kind of activity. This happens, for instance, when bacteria or the
debris of dying cells come in contact with a muscle cell and the
latter must transform itself so as to engulf and destroy these materials (in technical language: metaplasia for phagocytosis). It is interesting that, whenever such redevelopmental adaptation is called
for, cells specifically shaped to perform certain functions first lose
their acquired characteristic attributes. They must first dediffer-
entiate, become simple in structure and similar to very young cells,
before they can acquire new characteristics to adapt them for other
functions. Stress is very powerful in promoting this dedifferentiation
and rejuvenation of cells; it thereby paves the way for a reorganiza-
tion of their individuality. This should be kept in mind when we
discuss (from a more philosophic point of view) the stress-factor
in the origin of individuality (p. 277) and the role of stress as an
equalizer of activities in general (p. 266).

Here I have used as examples structural rearrangements for
adaptation to local stress. But it is evident that the same considerations also apply to functional responses (since these likewise must
have some material—structural, chemical—basis), as well as to adaptive reactions of the body as a whole (which are essentially composed of many coordinated local responses).

All these diverse adaptive reactions are, in the final analysis, due
to exposing different combinations of tissue-elements to stress. There
emerges the impression of some fundamental unifying law. But this
is still only an impression. As the picture stands at this point, perhaps its most disturbing feature is the difficulty of correlating the
"morbid" phenomena of transformative or redevelopmental adaptation (for instance, of a regular muscle cell into an irregular structure
which engulfs foreign particles) with the "physiologic" type of simple tissue development (growth and maturation). The evolution of
our tissues from infancy to adulthood appears to be directed by the
laws of heredity, without any manifest dependence upon stress.

Stress and growth

It is remarkable that the so-called adaptive hormones, or stress hormones, are also important regulators of *general growth*. ACTH and COL are potent growth-inhibitors, and STH is so effective in the opposite sense that it has actually been called the *growth hormone*. It is not unexpected, therefore, that stress itself can affect the growth of the body as a whole. If children are exposed to too much stress, their bodily growth is stunted and this inhibition is, at least in part, due to an excess secretion of ACTH and COL.

But is there any link between stress (or adaptive hormones) and that selective *local growth* of certain parts, which leads to qualitative changes by molding the shape of the body? Of course, inflammation, one of the most striking features of local stress, is accompanied by selective tissue-growth at the site of injury. Some of this is purely developmental (increase in the size and number of cells), but some is redevelopmental (transformation of connective-tissue cells into other types which can engulf bacteria).

In growing rats I found it possible to inhibit selectively the growth of even one ear, one paw, or part of the snout by local treatment with COL. These are true postnatal malformations. The applicability of this principle to the treatment of abnormal overgrowth of organs in children is now under investigation.

Local growth of certain tissues may be selectively influenced by stress (or adaptive hormones) even at a distance from the site of injury. We have seen that, through the anti-inflammatory hormones, local stress applied anywhere in the body can cause involution of distant lymphatic structures or of inflamed tissues, while the pro-inflammatory hormones have opposite effects.

Often the local effects of stress and hormones—either upon inflammation or upon growth—are manifest only under certain conditions. For instance, local malnutrition due to constriction of blood vessels sensitizes to the growth-inhibitory and anti-inflammatory effect of hormones, and dilatation of the vascular system has an inverse effect. It has become a major branch of stress research to explore the mechanism through which these conditioning factors alter regional tissue-responsiveness, and thereby permit selective reactions to hormones which are equally distributed to all parts of the body through the blood.

It is also possible that during local stress certain cells may develop a special affinity (attraction) for growth-regulating adaptive hormones, although the available biochemical techniques have not yet permitted us to establish this point with certainty. All these factors could endow certain tissue-regions with a selective sensitivity for one or the other type of adaptive hormone and, in this manner, permit stress to mold the structure of the body.

Perhaps the most important local stimulant of growth is activity. A muscle cell forced to perform much mechanical work or a glandular cell stimulated to excessive secretory activity will become enlarged. *Could the stress of local hyperactivity itself act as a conditioning factor for growth-regulating adaptive hormones?* We have already shown that the growth hormone causes more growth in a hard-working than in a resting muscle. But selective activity in a limited muscle-group is a rather specific type of reaction and, by calling this *stress*, we may appear to obscure the limits between specific and nonspecific actions—a distinction which is the very basis of our stress theory.

Stress and specificity

We have seen how specific local stimulation of certain parts (the eye through light, the ear through sound, a muscle through its motor nerve) can produce general stress by sending out alarm signals from the stimulated tissues.

We have also seen that selective local stimulation of any part can produce demonstrable manifestations of local stress. For instance, excessive stimulation of a muscle can produce local inflammation. Indeed, the Swedish investigator R. Barany has shown that intense muscular work can even modify the ability of the overworked tissue to undergo inflammation, following the local application of various irritants. There can be no doubt that the specific stimulation of organs is inseparably interwoven with nonspecific, local, and general manifestations of stress.

Another important point is the *relationship between specificity and quality of response*. Nonspecific agents have been defined as stimuli "which affect many targets and are devoid of the ability to act selectively upon any one." By definition the reverse is true of specific agents. Similarly, a nonspecific change is one which can be elicited by many agents, while a specific change can only be produced by one, or at the most, by a very limited number. The two types of agents appear to be quite unrelated and different in quality. Indeed, one has come to consider them as opposites.

Yet even this apparently fundamental difference between the specific and the nonspecific is perhaps more apparent than real. It has been shown, for a great many reactive elements in living organisms (*receptors* or *targets*), that they can respond to irritation in only one manner. This type of reaction is conditioned by their own structure, not by the stimulus which activates them, although they may be more sensitive to some agents than to others. Whether stimulated by heat, mechanical injury, or electricity, a muscle fiber reacts with contraction, an optic-nerve fiber with the sensation of light, a glandular cell with secretion, and so forth. Could it be that the apparent multiplicity of specific reactions is merely due to combinations and permutations of such single reaction-types of which the various biologic elements of the body are capable? If so, all the manifestations of life—from the regional to the general, from the entirely nonspecific to the most highly specific—could be brought down to a common denominator. They would merely represent various groupings of simple, qualitatively unidirectional responses in the diverse biologic units (organs, cells, cell-parts) of the body.

Viewed in this light, the fundamental uniformity of any vital response—growth and adaptation, reaction to regional (local) or to general stressors—begins to emerge in a more definite form. One great problem which remains is to formulate the precise nature of the interrelations between the specific and the nonspecific responses. I believe that the clarification of this has been particularly handicapped by the general acceptance of the theory which assumes that the cell is the ultimate unit of living matter. *Even a single cell can respond in qualitatively different (specific or nonspecific) ways. It would be difficult to understand this without assuming the presence within the cell of smaller units which are still relatively independent of each other in their reactivity.*

The structural unit of life: the cell

In 1667, looking through his primitive microscope, Robert Hooke saw minute compartments in living plant-tissues. These appeared to be empty spaces separated by walls; he therefore called them *cells*. What we now understand to be a cell is actually filled with apparently living matter: a nucleus and some cytoplasm (cell-body).

More than a century and a half after Hooke's discovery, the German biologists Matthias J. Schleiden and Theodor Schwann noted that all living matter, including both plants and animals, was made up virtually of cells alone. This led them to propose (in 1839) the first great truly unifying scientific concept in biology: the *cell theory*. In brief, they assumed that the cell is the fundamental unit of all that is alive—just as, for some time, the atom was considered to be the fundamental, indivisible building block of matter. The stimulating and fertilizing effect of this concept was as great for biology and medicine as that of the atomic theory was for chemistry and physics. Most of our fundamental biologic concepts are based on the cell theory. To mention but one outstanding example, the Father of Morbid Anatomy, Rudolf Virchow, could not have formulated his famous *cellular pathology* without it, since this doctrine holds that every disease is essentially a disease of cells. It is the essence of science to explore causal and spacial relations between units. No wonder that the recognition of a visible unit of life helped the progress of biologic science!

And still, subsequent research revealed many *facts incompatible with the cell theory* of life. Certain slime-molds, for instance, grow to considerable size and, although they contain nuclei, they show no signs of a subdivision into cells. Conversely, the red blood cells of man contain no nucleus. The configuration of viruses is even more remote from the cellular structure. Still, they do appear to be alive. And why should we consider intercellular substances as inanimate?

Despite these and many other facts which are patently incompatible with the cell theory, the latter was so useful that it became too deeply ingrained in the minds of biologists to be displaced by any other concept. Findings which did not fit into it were merely discarded as unimportant exceptions to the rule. After all, the atomic theory, which postulated the inconvertibility of elements into each other, also had its exceptions.

But now we know that the atom *is* divisible and does not represent the fundamental unit of matter. This explains why it is possible to effect qualitative changes in elements—although each of them consists only of one kind of atom—by rearrangement of their true fundamental units. Yet for a long time work along these lines was actually handicapped by the otherwise fruitful atomic theory of matter. Could these same considerations not also apply to the cellular theory of life?

There can be no doubt that certain targets or receptors of biologic stimuli are of subcellular dimensions. *It is inconceivable that the cell should be the fundamental unit of living organisms because, in a single cell, various portions can perform diverse vital functions independently and simultaneously.* For instance, a single cell can concurrently move about, secrete, engulf a foreign particle, digest food, and perceive external stimuli. An agent can undoubtedly influence one part of the cell (for instance, an organelle or cell-part) or one biochemical unit (for instance, an enzyme) selectively.

The functional unit of life: the reacton

The cell is undoubtedly a building block, a structural unit, of life. It has a visible membrane which separates it from its surroundings and emphasizes the distinctness of this element in space. But it is not the elementary unit of biologic function. We have seen that within the cell there are smaller organizations which must also be regarded as units, in that they can still function independently of each other. In analogy with the larger biologic units (such as the *nephrons* of the kidney, the *neurons* of the nervous system), I have called these *reactons*. The reacton is defined as *the smallest biologic target which can still respond selectively to stimulation.* The limits of these units are not visible under the microscope; in fact they may not have any sharp, structural limits. But, irrespective of their position, they can function in unison, since certain agents act selectively on one type of reacton in many cells and intercellular substances throughout the body. Here the functional organization into reacton units is more important than the structural subdivision into cells.

Are reactons "alive"? In the absence of evidence to the contrary, we must at least consider the possibility that they are, because they exhibit the features regarded as characteristic of life, just as the complete cell does. Among other things, reactons can grow and reproduce their own kind. They also have a great tendency to maintain their characteristic individuality, despite changes in the milieu; that is, they are highly adaptable. For instance, much used parts of a cell can enlarge and become more numerous within the cell.

Let me point out clearly that none of my observations would justify the conclusion that these elementary targets are necessarily bodily structures, that is, matter. It is equally possible that the reacton is only a focus of interaction, a functional plan or pattern which governs the organization of matter. A plan possesses, to an exquisite degree, such accepted characteristics of life as the ability to grow, to reproduce its own kind, and to adapt itself to changing requirements. *The living is undoubtedly matter, but life is only one of its characteristics.* The great strength of the cell theory is that one can see the limits of these "building blocks" and demonstrate that virtually all living matter is made up of them. *But this only shows that the cell is a structural unit. It is not necessarily the fundamental primary unit of life.* The organs are units in the body; the tissues are units in the organs; the cells are units in the tissues. Why must we stop our dissection of living matter at this particular level? The possibility of demonstrating clear borders by optic microscopy is hardly an adequate reason. A quantum has no such borders either, yet it is an elemental unit of energy.

Where then should we draw the line? Living matter, just as inanimate matter, consists of chemical elements, but these cannot be regarded as being specially organized for life. They are specific units of matter, but not necessarily of living matter. Only certain combinations of the elements engender the characteristics of life. A specific element of any organization is the smallest part still specially fashioned to fit a certain composite structure. (For a mechanical analogy illustrating this principle, see drawing on p. 235.) Since this is undoubtedly true, *why not recognize, as the fundamental specific elements of life, those smallest organizations which still exhibit selective reactivity to biologic stimuli and manifest the generally accepted criteria of life?*

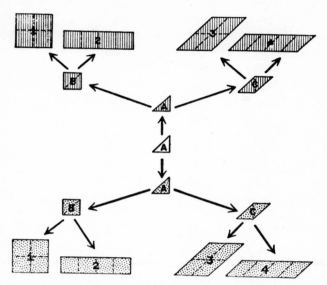

Illustration of the view that specific element is the smallest part still specially fashioned to fit a certain composite structure.

The central white triangle A is a common element of A hatched and A stippled. The latter two differ from the parent structure only in shading, not in form. A whole series of structures can be created with either type of shading, by joining the elements of A and its increasingly more complex aggregates in different ways. Therefore, in either series shown here, A is a specific element of B, as well as of C.

On the other hand, B is a specific element of 1 and 2, but not of 3 and 4, since the latter two could not be constructed from it.

Let us emphasize particularly that A is not a *specific* element of any among the structures 1, 2, 3, or 4, but only of their precursors B and C, since it is only up to this level that the shape of the small triangle (dotted line) is still distinctly implied by the outlines of the whole. In the same sense, the specific element of a species is the individual animal (not the cell), that of a tissue is the cell (not the reacton), and the smallest but still specific element of living matter is the reacton (not the atom).

Let us see now whether this theory of the reactons could help us to understand phenomena which the cell theory does not explain. The theory of the reactons postulates that:

1. *The fundamental specific elements of life are of subcellular dimensions.* They may not have visible limits; they may merely be focal points of interactions between the constituents in living matter (somewhat like the bonds which hold atoms together in inanimate matter). These reactons are defined as the smallest targets capable of selective biologic reactivity.

2. *Each reacton can give only one kind of response.* The nature of this response depends upon the inherent structure of the reacton itself. Hence, at the level of these ultimate units, reaction-patterns cannot yet be separated into the specific and the nonspecific. In other words, the concepts of quality and specificity of response have no meaning at this elementary level.

3. *Specificity of action (causation of effect) depends upon the degree of selective affinity* which an agent exhibits for certain reacton-types.

4. *Specificity of response (form or constitution of effect) depends upon the degree of freedom with which certain reactons can be activated* independently of others.

5. *Intensity of response depends upon the number of reactons activated.* It is still to be determined whether the degree of activation has any importance at this fundamental level, or whether reactons are subject only to the "triggering" type of yes-or-no response, which necessarily leads to the complete discharge of the accumulated action-potential.

6. *Developmental adaptation depends upon simple growth and multiplication of certain previously developed reactons.*

7. *Redevelopmental "transadaptation" depends upon growth and multiplication of certain previously undeveloped reactons, at the expense of inactivity-atrophy in others, which were previously developed.* It is this type of response which we have been accustomed to regard as a "qualitative" change. The schematic drawings on pages 238–240 illustrate these thoughts by a simple mechanical analogy.

At first sight it may be difficult to understand *how mere quantitative responses in a limited number of reactons might give the vir-*

tually unlimited number of qualitatively distinct reaction-patterns of which living matter is capable. Yet this is not without precedent in biology.

For instance, according to the famous Young-Helmholtz theory of color vision, there are only three fundamental color sensations: red, green, and violet. By suitable combinations of these, all other colors can be formed. To explain this, it was assumed that three kinds of nerve-elements exist in the retina of the eye, each of which is specifically responsive to the stimulus of waves of a certain frequency corresponding to a certain color. If the nerve-elements which correspond to red and green were simultaneously set in action, the resulting sensation would be orange or yellow; if mainly the green and violet, the sensation would be blue or indigo, etc. Actually, no such nerve fibers or elements are known, but the theory is equally valid if the stimuli affect three photochemical substance-units. The innumerable melodies which can be derived from the simple keyboard of a piano (although each key can produce only one tone) have already been mentioned as another suitable analogy.

It is not too difficult to imagine that the many reaction-patterns of which any cell is capable could thus be synthesized by simple yes-or-no responses of its constituent reactons. In all these instances, the quality of the true fundamental element (as the pure color or pure tone) is invariable. *Differences in kind cannot occur at the level of the elements; the impression of a qualitative change is created by blending the responses of unchanging fundamental units.*

Analysis and synthesis of cellular disease

The reacton concept suggests experiments to test the feasibility of an analysis and synthesis of cellular disease. For example, it should be possible to analyse and identify, by their characteristic actions upon the cell, common stimulating elements (*actons*) in various complex disease-producers (microbes, drugs, rays), because these will affect one type of reacton preferentially. To explain what I mean, we may take an example from chemistry. The acidity (or the oxidizing power) of various molecules affects cognate receptive groups of various materials in essentially the same manner, and, to a large extent, irrespectively of other characteristics of the acid (or the oxidizing) molecule.

Schematic drawings illustrating the reacton hypothesis as applied to the interpretation of specific and nonspecific actions.

In all the drawings on this and the next page, the individual reactons are schematically represented by round bodies, and the connections between them (interactions) by straight lines. This is similar to the customary representation of atoms and valences in chemical formulas. Although, actually, reactons are arranged three-dimensionally in living matter, they are shown here in a single plane for simplicity's sake. Only reactons representative of special conditions are numbered.

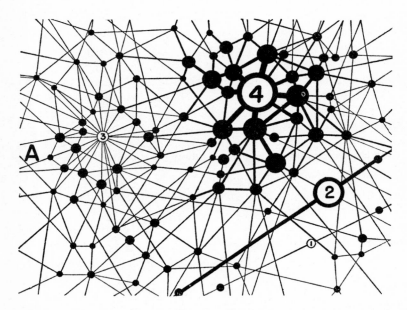

A field containing numerous reactons (dots) in various stages of development. Reactons are associated with each other by interactions of varying importance (straight lines). We might visualize them as the focal knots in a complex network of more or less obligatory or rigid interactions. Evidently pressure exerted upon any focus will displace others as well, and the extent to which local tension can spread will depend upon the number and strength of the connections between the directly affected focus and the rest of the system.

(1) Undeveloped reacton, directly connected with only two others.

(2) Highly developed reacton, directly connected with only two others.

(3) Undeveloped reacton, directly connected with many others

(4) Highly developed reacton connected with many others.

This illustrates that stimulation at a point such as 1 will have a selective specific effect (change to type 2): it will develop the reacton and its two immediate connections. On the other hand, stimulation at a point such as 3 will have a very generalized nonspecific effect, even though the agent acted at one point only (change to type 4).

Sample of seven resting reactons not exposed to any agent. One (No. 3) is most developed and the prominence of the others diminishes as we approach the periphery of the former's activity range. This is intended to be a graphic expression of a situation in which (due to hereditary factors or previous activity), even at rest, one type of reacton is most developed, while the others have evolved only in proportion to the importance of their interactions with the former. (For instance, in a developed muscle, the reactons directly and more or less indirectly related to contractility.)

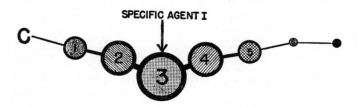

Specific effect with developmental adaptation. Specific agent 1 has acted upon the system represented in the previous drawing stimulating it to perform the function for which it has already been specialized. This leads to simple *work-hypertrophy*, with a proportionate development of all the pertinent reactons and of their interactions. (For instance, in the just mentioned example of the muscle, the repeated specific stimulation through its motor nerve.)

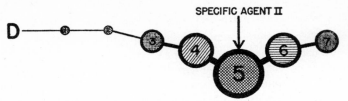

Specific effect with readaptation. Here Specific agent II has called upon the system to perform a function qualitatively different from that for which it had been specialized. Now the chief emphasis is upon a previously not fully developed reacton (No. 5). This leads to a shift, a *transadaptation*, with varying degrees of inactivity-atrophy in previously developed reactons (near the left end of the chain) and a corresponding qualitative change in structure and function. (For instance, selective exposure of a single muscle-group to microbes, with a resulting transformation of the muscle cells into so-called "cleaning cells" or *phagocytes* especially adjusted to engulf foreign particles.)

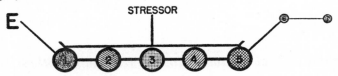

Stress due to a nonspecific action. Here the nature of the stressor is such that it affects all reactons and their interactions. The corresponding dedifferentiation, or equalization, is illustrated by an enlargement of the previously underdeveloped reactons at the expense of involution of the previously most developed reactons. (For instance, exposure of a large tissue-area to heat which directly affects all its cells.)

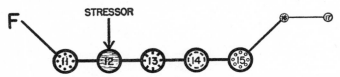

Stress due to a nonspecific reaction. This also affects all reactons (and their bonds) in this field, although the stressor acts selectively on one (No. 12) alone. The reason for the generalization of the stress-effect is the intense dependence of the units (Nos. 11-15) upon each other in this particular field. Therefore, the response of one (No. 12) immediately produces marked repercussions in all others within the system. (For instance, overstimulation of a sensory nerve whose direct effect is highly specific, but the resulting pain produces a widespread stress-response.)

Conversely, it should be possible to synthesize cellular disease by the application, in suitable order and intensity, of several agents containing the requisite combination of elementary disease-producers (actons), even if none of these agents were in itself endowed with the whole desired disease-producing combination. In chemistry this would correspond to the synthesis of NaCl from NaOH and HCl. The inflammatory pouch (p. 151) furnishes a convenient model on which the simplest biologic reactions of this kind can be examined. Preliminary experiments have shown already that, by conjointly introducing several simple irritants—each of which produces different kinds of simple tissue-responses—rather complex vital reaction-forms can be synthesized. Furthermore, just as in chemistry, we can identify elements of matter by the reactions they undergo in contact with various substances in the test tube, so also we can detect elementary units of living matter (reactons) by the simplest cellular reaction-forms which can be provoked in the cells of the "living test tube": the inflammatory pouch.

Possibilities and limitations of the reacton hypothesis

The greatest weakness of the reacton concept is the already-mentioned fact that the *units which it postulates have no sharp limits.* But this is true of most biologic units. It would be equally difficult to delimit with two sharp pencil-lines what we mean by "the trunk" or "the neck." Of course, this fluidity of transition between various constituents of the body is even greater when it comes to functional units. For example, the respiratory system undoubtedly includes the lung, yet this organ also has many other metabolic functions which have nothing to do with respiration; the ribs are necessary for breathing, but they also belong to the skeletal system, and the marrow in them is part of the blood-forming system.

Functional units can only be defined and demarcated by their activities, not by their substance. The same glucose molecule can become part of the respiratory, nervous, or locomotor system, depending upon the function for which it will happen to furnish energy.

A glance at the schematic drawing on p. 238 shows clearly that each reacton is connected with many others. It represents a focal point of activity, whose functional radius overlaps with that of other reactons. This situation could be compared with a complex telephone system, in which there are focal points, the exchanges, and connecting wires. You could point out a building in New York or in Montreal as a focal point of exchange, but the wires between these two cities would belong no more to one than to the other. It would be impossible to analyze the system without recognizing these focal points as units, and yet these would be meaningless without the connecting wires, which in turn make the sharp delimitation of the focal points impossible in a functional sense. It is the great weakness of the cell theory that it recognizes only the exchanges and not the wires of life.

The study of stress has shown us how important it is to distinguish between specific and nonspecific biologic actions. We could not differentiate between simple, specific, and complex, nonspecific, responses of living matter without formulating some idea of the primary elements of activity, the only ones which can be truly simple and specific. That is why we have compared our problem with the task of the chemists, who first had to find the elements of matter before they could distinguish between simple compounds (consisting of one type of atom only) and complex mixtures (consisting of many kinds of atom). We found that the cell is still much too complex to act as a true functional element of life. On the other hand, the atoms and molecules which make up the human body do not yet possess in themselves any characteristic organization for life; it is precisely their interconnections in living bodies that endow them with the features of vitality. The sum of all the elements and molecules in a man does not constitute the man unless they are interconnected and arranged in a certain manner. When so fitted into the pattern of living matter, individual atoms cannot react to stimulation selectively. Anything which affects one of them will also influence a number of other closely connected chemical units. In other words, biologic matter cannot be specifically (selectively) affected in lots smaller than a reacton. In this sense, the reacton concept is not a theory, but a description of observed facts. Only the limits of the reacton are comparatively vague. But this degree of vagueness is an inherent characteristic of any biologic unit; and the significance of the *reacton concept is that it opens to experimental analysis that range of units between the cell and the chemical element.*

21:

Apologia for teleologic thought in biology and medicine

What do we mean by "understanding something"? Purposeful causation. Recapitulation and conclusions.

What do we mean by "understanding something"?

It is evident that our whole unifying concept is based upon teleologic thought: the principle of purposeful causality. It is difficult to understand why, among representatives of the exact sciences, and even among biologists and physicians, there is so much resistance to the use of teleologic arguments. Still, we must admit that many of the most outstanding investigators of our time believe that one can, and should, merely register scientific observations, refraining from all considerations of causality. I cannot follow such arguments. To my mind, the sensations of causality and purpose are inherent in the structure of the human brain. Understanding itself is but the feeling of having securely attached a thing to our treasury of known facts, by solid bonds of obligatory sequences.

Knowledge includes purely descriptive information (the answer to, "What is it like?"), but we can "understand" only the cause of a thing (the answer to, "What brings it about?"). In other words, we can know a thing by its characteristics (a house), or by the instinct of self-evidence ($6 \times 6 = 36$), but we can understand it only operationally (cf. operational definitions, p. 54) in terms of its cause. In conversational English, the two terms are somewhat loosely used. For instance, we say that we "understand" a foreign word, but what we actually mean is that we know its meaning. This is really mere recognition by characteristics, and essentially different from true causal understanding.

This can be illustrated by the following diagram:

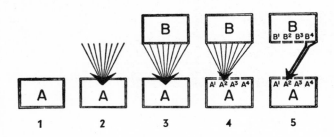

Usual sequence of problems met as we attempt to approximate the understanding of primary causes and primary elements in experimental medicine.

1. We discover a biologic target (say, the adrenal). This gives us knowledge, but not understanding.

2. We notice that the target can vary; it is capable of being changed by agents of as-yet unidentified nature and origin (adrenal enlargement). This gives us more knowledge, but still no real understanding. We ask ourselves, "What is the cause of this change?"

3. We find that the cause is B (some action of the pituitary). This gives us the impression that we understand the cause of the change.

4. But we may find, upon closer investigation, that the apparent change of the whole is really due to an alteration of only one among its elements, A^2 (the adrenal cortex). Actually, B acts on A^2.

5. Then we learn that not the whole of B, but only B^4 is the cause of the change (in our example, not the whole pituitary but only one of its hormones, ACTH). This gives us the sensation of an increasingly better understanding. It is not a coincidence that, as understanding deepens, the sequence of causality becomes increasingly more obligatory. B does not always act on A, but only if it can reach A^2. The response is still more predictable if B^4 itself can be applied in abundance, since other elements of B are ineffective and may be inhibitory. The same argument applies to still more primary causes in the chain of events, when we begin to ask, "What acts on B?"

Purposeful causation

But teleologic (from Greek *telos*, end plus *logia*, science) thought implies more than mere causality. It suggests purposeful causation (i.e., intention) to achieve an end or aim. It is really because of this aspect that so many biologists refuse to accept it. As applied to our topic, the problem is rather clearly put in Professor P. Schwartz's remarkable essay on inflammation. He says:

"One should think that the exalted Law of Nature—to vary a famous saying of Anatole France—recognizes no difference between microbes and man. One cannot consider inflammation as a specific 'cleansing' measure, that is one for the conservation of tissues, any more than one can envisage malignant neoplasia [cancer] as having the 'purpose' or 'duty' to destroy organs: both processes are—just as all manifestations of Nature—*in themselves* aimless and purposeless phenomena."

I can certainly not avoid dealing with this problem here. All my factual observations were made possible by experiments planned on the assumption that stress-responses are purposeful, homeostatic reactions. We must realize that in both the examples just mentioned (inflammation in response to microbes and cancer) there are actually two *teleologic centers*; their interests are opposed but, within each of them, purposeful activity "for its own good" is clearly recognizable. On the one hand is the interest of the patient, on the other that of the microbe or of the cancer. Indeed, the very essence of cancerous growth is the setting up of a center whose own interests are largely opposed to those of its host.

Of course, centers of homeostasis can exist within other such centers and then their interests can no longer be identical in every respect. To take an example, a citizen shares many interests with all his countrymen but, in ascending order, he shares even more with all those who live in the same city, the same district, or the same house. Not only microbes and cancer, but even our own normal tissues constantly compete with each other for nourishment and space. Consequently, every cell, even every reacton within the body represents a teleologic center, whose purposeful reactions must be analyzed in relation to all other centers. Indeed, the terms *teleology* and *purpose* can be meaningful only in relation to an identifiable center. "It is advantageous" means nothing unless we say for whom.

The formation of what we might call *teleologic centers* within the universe appears to be one of the great laws of nature. The stability of the most diverse structures seems to increase up to a certain optimum size or degree of complexity. The acquisition of this stability strikes us as an aim, since everything tends towards it. All structures tend to become unstable after they have reached their optimum complexity; then they "die" by falling apart, so that their elements may initiate another similar cycle. In its product, it is rare to find exactly the same elements arranged in the same manner as in the parent structure, because precisely the same conditions are not likely to prevail twice in succession. This leads to a constant, slow evolution towards increasingly more stable structures.

We see this in the case of small drops of mercury which upon contact tend to aggregate into a larger, more stable drop. This goes on until a certain optimum dimension is reached, then the drop becomes unstable because of its size, and falls apart. We see this when a crystal develops, or an icicle, or an ameba, or a human being. They all grow and then fall apart—though in different ways. There can be simple shattering or disintegration (crystal, icicle), which makes all parts immediately available for totally different constructions. There can be direct and complete division into smaller structures, similar to the parent body (ameba). Here, the falling apart of the old is, in itself, the birth of the comparatively new; there is no "corpse" from which to construct something totally new. And finally, an aggregate can fall apart by a combination of the two mechanisms (man), where a large section of the body disintegrates totally, yielding up its units (the "corpse") for wholly different constructions, while other parts (the germ cells) are preserved for reproducing similar offspring, which are only relatively new.

Everything that has any degree of stability acts as a teleologic center in this sense. For this persistent activity does not need the continued direction of an intelligent external influence with a purpose. Even a man-made object, once finished—an automobile, for instance—will give the impression of continually looking out for its own interests; it will meet hostile influences with "intelligently planned defense reactions." When driven along the highway it will cool its own motor to prevent damage by heat. On bumpy roads it will protect its body against shock with the aid of the springs and—if it has self-sealing tires—it can even be capable of true *wound-healing* after being punctured.

Of course, someone has to make the automobile and someone has to make the maker of the automobile; and this leads us to the point where our teleologically constructed brain can no longer follow, for we cannot understand anything without a cause. Understanding is nervous activity and, in the maze of nerve fibers which make up our brain, every impulse comes from somewhere: its cause.

We sense a Creator mainly because we and our surroundings seem complex, and during his short life-span man sees no really complex structure built up by chance without the purposeful influence of a maker. But could not the organizing effect of a centralizing teleology be our view of the maker? Could it not—in the span of ages—eventually build up awe-inspiring complexities, such as a planet, a tree, or even a man?

Having been built and being capable of building are the most inherent characteristics of our every part. We therefore see everything through an atmosphere of building which tinges all our perceptions, just as a red crystal ball—were it alive and capable of perception—would probably see everything as red, in and outside itself. Teleologic thought does not necessarily have to lean upon an individual, purposeful Creator, nor should it do so, even on religious grounds, since faith does not need the support of understanding. What we must clearly realize in biology is that teleologic analysis is applicable to every unit of creation.

Science cannot and should not attempt to embrace the purpose of the original Creator; but it can and constantly must examine teleologic motives in the objects of creation. Only by doing this can science progress from the mere accumulation of unintelligible facts to what we call *understanding*.

Recapitulation and conclusions

We have seen that, although stress itself cannot be perceived, we can appraise it by the objectively measurable, structural, and chemical changes which it produces in the body. These manifest themselves as the G.A.S. (when stress affects the whole body) and as the L.A.S. (when only a limited region of the body is exposed to stress). Evidently the whole body, as well as its individual organs and tissues, can respond specifically to special stimuli and non-specifically to stress.

These findings have naturally led us to compare the behavior of individual cells under stress and during adaptation to various specific stimuli. It became evident that even *a single cell can respond with many more or less specific, qualitatively different biologic reaction-forms.*

All these studies have sharply highlighted the difference between developmental *adaptation* (simple quantitative progression along evolutionally established lines) and *readaptation* (which involves some regression or disintegration to secure building blocks for subsequent qualitative reconstruction). Since even a single cell has proved capable of readaptation (through a rearrangement of its biologic elements), it could not itself be the fundamental unit of living matter.

Thus we arrived at the hypothesis of the *reactons,* which postulates that *subcellular units can still exhibit the generally accepted characteristics of life.* Of course, it is difficult to define life, because there does not appear to be any sharp line of demarcation between it and the inanimate. Life is perhaps best defined by the degree to which it has developed certain characteristics, particularly those of recreating its own kind (growth, reproduction) out of less highly organized materials and of maintaining its structure tenaciously, despite any environmental changes that would tend to destroy it (adaptation). All these characteristics are recognizable, even in the most elementary subcellular biologic targets, the reactons.

Simple chemical compounds never exhibit these qualities to any great degree. That is why we do not regard them as living. The theory now most generally accepted postulates that the cell is the smallest unit that can still be considered to be alive. Yet many facts are incompatible with this view. Neither microbes, nor viruses, nor even the intercellular substances of man exhibit the characteristic features of cells, yet they appear to be alive in the classic sense of this word. Then too, a single cell can respond in qualitatively different ways to stimuli (perception, locomotion, secretion), and even its constituent parts exhibit the powers of growing (selective growth of portions of an individual cell), of reproducing their own kind (regeneration of cell-parts) and of maintaining their structure, despite external forces which tend to destroy it (new formation of lost secretion-granules, healing). Real elementary units may be large or small, numerous or few (they may show quantitative differences) but, by definition, they cannot be composed of diverse elements (they cannot show qualitative differences).

There is no evidence that new reactons could be formed in any mold other than that of preformed reactons of the same kind. The Latin adage, *Omnis cellula e cellula ejusdem generis* (every cell comes from a cell of the same kind) did not really hold true for the cell: under stress a certain type of cell can transform itself into another one (in technical language this is known as *metaplasia*). It is more consistent with the facts known today to say: *Omne reacton e reactone ejusdem generis* (every reacton comes from a reacton of the same kind).

In the light of this hypothesis we have attempted to formulate some fundamental concepts in biology this way:

Growth = multiplication or enlargement of reactons

Specificity = selective responsiveness of certain kinds of reactons

Developmental adaptation = further activation and growth of previously developed reactons.

Readaptation (or *transadaptation*) = activation and growth of dormant reactons, with relative regression of those which were previously most prominent.

As we see it now, the most fundamental task will be to find strictly objective means with which to test the validity of our principal deduction, namely that: *all vital phenomena depend merely upon quantitative variations in the activation of preexistent elementary targets.*

Book **V:**

Implications and applications

Summary

The most important *applications of the stress concept as regards purely somatic medicine* are derived from the discovery that the body can meet various aggressions with the same adaptive-defensive mechanism. A dissection of this reaction teaches us how to combat disease by strengthening the body's own defenses against stress.

This also has important *psychosomatic implications*. Bodily changes during stress act upon mentality and vice versa. Only by dissecting our troubles can we clearly distinguish the part played by the stressor from that of our own adaptive measures of defense and surrender. We shall see how this helps us to handle ourselves during the stress of everyday life, and in particular, how to tune down when we are wrought up, how to overcome insomnia, and how to get out of certain grooves of stereotyped behavior.

Stress research also has far-reacting *philosophic implications*. We shall see that stress plays a role in such diverse manifestations of life as aging, the development of individuality, the need for self-expression, and the formulation of man's ultimate aims. Stress is usually the outcome of a struggle for the self-preservation (the homeostasis) of parts within a whole. This is true of individual cells within man, of man within society, and of individual species within the whole animate world. After surveying the emotions which govern interpersonal relations (the thirst for approval, the terror of censure, the feelings of love, hate, gratitude, and revenge), we come to the conclusion that the incitement, by our actions, of gratitude in others is most likely to assure our safety within society. Why not seek this consciously as a long-range aim in life? No other philosophy has the exquisite property of necessarily transforming all our natural, egotistic impulses into altruism without curtailing any of their self-protecting value.

But man cannot think only of future safety; he wants more immediate rewards; he has a need for self-expression; he wants to enjoy the pleasures his senses can bring; he wants the satisfaction and equanimity which come from reverently contemplating the great wonders of Creation. In the light of research on stress, my advice would be:

Fight always for the highest attainable aim
But never put up resistance in vain.

There is no ready-made success formula which will suit everybody. We are all different. But, since man is essentially a rational being, the better he knows what makes him tick, the more likely he will be to make a success of life. Man's ultimate aim is to express himself as fully as possible, according to his own lights.

22:

Medical implications

of the stress concept

Stress as a common denominator of biologic activity. Basic tenets for a new type of medicine. What can the patient learn from this?

Stress as a common denominator of biologic activity

In the four preceding sections of this book I wanted to tell you how the concept of stress developed and how it has been applied to problems of normal and abnormal life. I tried to show how this abstract concept helped us to gain knowledge of specific facts: knowledge about the way stress stimulates the pituitary and the adrenal glands to secrete hormones which diminish the wear and tear of stress, knowledge about the diseases that may result when such adaptive responses are faulty, knowledge about how to correct improper adaptive responses by treatment with hormones or by the removal of endocrine glands. Much of this is practical valuable knowledge, but it is not wisdom. Knowledge is the first concern of the scientist, for his principal aim is to find facts; but wisdom is the ultimate intellectual goal of everybody, for wisdom is (as Webster puts it) "the ability to judge soundly and deal sagaciously with facts, especially as they relate to life and conduct." It is about the wisdom to be derived from the study of stress that I should like to speak in this last part of my book.

We have spent quite some time trying to define stress in precise biologic terms; yet, when we finished our laborious analysis of its nature, stress turned out to be something quite simple to understand: it is essentially the *wear and tear* in the body caused by life at any one time.

Whatever we do and whatever is done to us causes wear and tear. Stress is therefore not the specific result of any one among our actions; nor is it a typical response to any one thing acting upon us from without; it is a common feature of all biological activities.

The appraisal of virtually every comparable, common characteristic of matter—for instance, color, weight, and temperature—led us not only to discover new scientific facts and laws, but also to gain a like wisdom about ourselves and the world around us. Man can advance from observation to wisdom in many ways—through instinct, for instance by way of faith, intuition, or art. But, if the gap is to be bridged by science, the subject of observation must first be clearly defined and measurable.

That our bodies gradually wear out during life has always been known, but no one could clearly see or measure stress before, because its visage, the stress syndrome (the G.A.S.) had been covered by the fog of all the specific reactions to the agents which evoke stress. You cannot measure outlines through fog.

My approach was made possible by an *operational definition of stress,* which helped to clear away the confusing specific reactions. It tells you what must be done to produce and recognize stress. If stress is the wear and tear of whatever happens to a living being, you must observe a great many vital reactions and see what happens. Those changes which are specifically induced by only one or another agent must first be rejected; if you then take what is left, that which is nonspecifically induced by many agents, you have unveiled the picture of stress.

This picture expresses itself in the whole body as the G.A.S. Once you know this, you can measure stress objectively in terms of physical and chemical changes characteristic of the G.A.S. For instance, you can measure the enlargement of the adrenals or the shrinkage of the lymphatic tissues in terms of their weights; you can measure with chemical methods the quantities of adaptive hormones produced during stress. In other words, you can objectively assess the magnitude of stress by its measurable effects upon the body. This operational definition also emphasizes that no one measurement can be conclusive in itself. Stress is the whole of the wear and tear—not wear and tear in any one part of the human machine—consequently, the more indices you measure the greater the precision of your appraisal.

Then it was found that the picture of general stress in the body, the G.A.S., has a local counterpart. This is the L.A.S., which can be appraised by exposing many parts of the body selectively to many locally applied agents. The changes which any agent can produce virtually anywhere in the body constitute the syndrome of local stress. Inflammation and degeneration of cells were found to be the chief components of this picture.

Finally it was discovered that the *G.A.S. and the L.A.S. are interdependent*. General stress can influence local stress-reactions, for instance, through hormones (particularly corticoids), which regulate inflammation. Conversely, local stress, if strong enough, can produce general stress and thereby mobilize defensive organs located far from the site of injury. Through chemical messengers (the *alarm signals*) each of the many local stress-reactions, which happen to go on in the various parts of the body at any one time, has a voice in determining the extent of the general counterstress measures to be taken (see p. 85). This procedure of "regulation by majority decision" is very necessary. For instance, a small splinter entering the skin may create great local demands for anti-inflammatory corticoids, but the limited local inflammation caused by this minor irritant may not justify the exposure of the entire body to an excess of corticoids. The central organs of defense must consider the interests of the whole and, of course, to do so judiciously, they have to be constantly informed of the requirements of all parts. It was chiefly the recognition of these close interactions between the G.A.S. and the L.A.S. which made it possible to outline a sketch for a unified theory of medicine (Book IV).

Basic tenets for a new type of medicine

The three most obvious lessons derived from research on stress are: (1) that our *body can meet the most diverse aggressions with the same adaptive-defensive mechanism;* (2) that we can *dissect this mechanism* so as to identify its ingredient parts in objectively measurable physical and chemical terms, such as changes in the structure of organs or in the production of certain hormones; (3) that we need this kind of information to lay the scientific foundations for a new type of treatment, whose essence is to *combat disease by strengthening the body's own defenses against stress.* Once we have learned that in a given situation an excess of a certain hormone is needed to maintain health, we can inject that hormone whenever the body is unable to manufacture enough of it. Conversely, once we have recognized that a disease is due to the exaggerated adaptive activity of some hormone-producing gland, we can remove the offending organ or try to check its activity by drugs.

In other words, we have learned that the body possesses a complex machinery of checks and balances. These are remarkably effective in adjusting ourselves to virtually anything that can happen to us in life. But often this machinery does not work perfectly: sometimes our responses are too weak, so that they do not offer adequate protection; at other times they are too strong, so that we actually hurt ourselves by our own excessive reactions to stress.

In order to adjust or repair a machine we first have to know how it works. This is of course also true of the stress-machinery with which man combats the wear and tear of whatever he does in this world. Therefore the most obvious, tangible outcome of our work was to show that stress can be dissected into its elements, and that the knowledge derived from this analysis helps us to speed up a part which lags behind or to dampen another which goes too far.

Yet, in some diseases, the physician may help by merely increasing or decreasing the total amount of stress in the body, without attempting to act selectively upon any one part of the stress-machinery.

Not only our mental, but even our bodily defense reactions may become stereotyped if we are faced with the same kind of problem again and again. A man can hurt himself by reacting to every proposition according to a set pattern: say, by habitually ridiculing, complaining, agreeing, or disagreeing "on principle." Prejudice is the most common basis for such prejudged, unchangeable mental response-patterns. Everybody is aware of this, but it is less well known that our bodily *defense reactions can also fall into a groove,* for instance, by always responding with the same exaggerated hormonal response, whether it is appropriate to the situation or not.

A child or a hysterical person can snap out of a tantrum if you splash cold water in his face. Even a gramophone needle which gets into a groove and endlessly reiterates the same sounds can snap out of it if you just give it a jerk. Well, the body of a patient can also be shaken out of habitually responding in the same senseless manner if you expose it to the stress of some intense shock therapy, such as, electroshock, Metrazol shock, insulin shock, or injection of toxic foreign proteins (see p. 124).

Another way to deal with essentially the same problems is to provide complete rest, which gives the body time to "forget" stereotyped somatic reactions to stress. Prolonged sleep (e.g., that induced by barbiturates), artificial hibernation, and treatment with such quieting drugs as chlorpromazine and extracts of the Rauwolfia root appear to act largely through this mechanism.

What can the patient learn from this?

All we have said up to now helps to guide treatment on the part of a physician; but therapy with hormones and drugs or surgical removal of endocrine glands are certainly not procedures which the patient could prescribe for himself.

In the chapter on the "Diseases of Adaptation," we also spoke about the important role of the diet in conditioning responses to stress. Generally speaking, undernutrition sensitizes the body for anti-inflammatory corticoids, and overeating augments the effect of proinflammatory hormones. An excess of salt aggravates certain renal and hypertensive diseases, which tend to develop when the proinflammatory corticoids are overabundant; and low-salt regimens have a protective effect in such cases. But even dietary treatment must be controlled by a competent physician. All this book can do in this respect is to *help the patient understand why his physician prescribes a certain regimen*; it could not presume to be an adequate preparation for self-treatment along such purely medical lines.

On the other hand, there are many things I have learned from the study of stress, which the physician cannot use but the patient can. I particularly want to share these lessons with you because they have helped me with many of my own problems and I am sure they can help others as well. I am thinking particularly of the psychosomatic and the philosophic implications of stress, which will be discussed in the next two chapters. I shall speak to laymen as a layman, for I had no formal training either in psychosomatic medicine or in philosophy. Yet it may not be inappropriate for an investigator, who has spent his life exploring any one aspect of life in the laboratory, to pause and contemplate the applicability of his observations to the problems of everyday life. After all—as I said in the introductory passage of this chapter—knowledge is the first concern of the scientist, but wisdom is the ultimate intellectual goal of us all.

Do not take whatever general lessons I have been able to derive from the study of stress more seriously than I do; my technical knowledge is limited to the laboratory. I only ask you to lend me the benevolent ear that the old mariner deserves, when he tries to communicate the wisdom of the sea—not seamanship.

23:

Psychosomatic

Implications

To know thyself. Dissect your troubles. Somatopsychic vs. psychosomatic. On being keyed up. How to tune down. Stress as an equalizer of activities. The stress-quotient. The importance of deviation. Innate vitality must find an outlet. How to sleep.

To know thyself

The ancient Greek philosophers clearly recognized that, in governing human conduct, the most important, but perhaps also the most difficult, thing was "to know thyself." It takes great courage even just to attempt this honestly. As Logan Pearsall Smith says, "How awful to reflect that what people say of us is true!" Yet it is well worth the effort and humiliation, for most of our tensions and frustrations stem from compulsive needs to act the role of someone we are not. Only he who knows himself can profit by the advice of Matthew Arnold:

> Resolve to be thyself: and know that he
> Who finds himself, loses his misery.

It is well established that the mere fact of *knowing what hurts you has an inherent curative value.* Psychoanalysis has demonstrated the soundness of this principle perhaps better than any other branch of medicine. The psychoanalyst helps you to understand how previous experiences—which may have led to subconscious conflicts, sometimes very early in childhood—can continue almost indefinitely to cause mental or even physical disease. But once you realize the mechanism of your mental conflicts, they cease to bother you. Sigmund Freud's efforts to develop a branch of medicine on the basis of this concept were sharply criticized at first, but now hardly anyone doubts that psychoanalysis can help those whose bodily disease-manifestations are due to unexplained mental tensions. Of course, here we are also dealing with diseases of adaptation. Our failure to adjust ourselves correctly to life-situations is at the very root of the disease-producing conflicts. Psychoanalysis cures because it helps us to adapt ourselves to what has happened.

All this is sufficiently well known as regards mental reactions to deserve no further comment. But "to know thyself" includes the body. Most people fail to realize that "to know thy body" also has an inherent curative value. Take a familiar example. Many people have joints which tend to crack at almost every movement; by concentrating upon this unexplained condition, a person can talk or worry himself into a crippling arthritis. If, on the other hand, some understanding physician just explains to him that his cracking sensations are caused by slight, inconsequential irregularities in the joint-surfaces, and have no tendency to become worse, the disease is practically cured—just by the knowledge of its trifling nature.

Almost everybody has had, at some time or other, some insignificant allergic condition of the skin, cardiac palpitations, or intestinal upsets; any of these can cause serious illness through psychosomatic reactions merely because not knowing what is wrong makes us worry. Every physician knows from experience how much can be done for a patient by just taking time to explain the mechanism of his symptoms which thereby lose the frightening element of mystery. To help with this is one of the principal objectives of this book.

Dissect your troubles

We have seen that stress is an essential element of all our actions, in health and in disease. That is why we have analyzed the mechanism of stress so carefully in the preceding sections. Suffice it here to point out once more the principal lesson which we have learned: that most of our troubles have a tripartite origin. The tweezers of stress have three prongs. Whether we suffer from a boil on the skin, a disease of the kidney, or a troubled mind, careful study of the condition will usually reveal it to consist of three major elements:

1. The *stressor,* the external agent which started the trouble, for instance, by acting directly upon the skin, the kidney, or the mind.

2. The *defensive measures,* such as the hormones and nervous

stimuli which encourage the body to defend itself against the stressor as well as it can. In the case of bodily injuries, this may be accomplished by putting up a barricade of inflamed tissue in the path of the invading stressor (the microbe, allergen, and so forth). Mental stressors (orders, challenges, offenses) are met with corresponding complex emotional defensive responses, which can be summed up as the attitude of "not being done in."

3. The *mechanisms for surrender*, such as hormonal and nervous stimuli, which encourage the body not to defend itself. For instance, not to put up barricades of inflamed tissue in the path of invaders, and to ignore emotional stressors.

It is surprising how often a better understanding of this tripartite mechanism of disease-production (and I use the word *disease* here in its widest sense, as anything that disturbs mind or body) can help us to regain our balance, even without having to ask the advice of a physician. We can often eliminate the stressor ourselves, once we have recognized its nature, or we can adjust the proportion between active defensive attitudes and measures of surrender, in the best interest of maintaining our balance.

Somatopsychic vs. psychosomatic

An enormous amount of work has been done by physicians in connection with problems of psychosomatic medicine. In essence, this specialty deals with the bodily (somatic) changes that a mental (psychic) attitude can produce. An ulcer of the stomach or a rise in blood pressure caused by emotional upsets are examples in point.

Almost no systematic research has been done, however, on the opposite of this: the effect of *bodily changes and actions upon mentality*. Of course, I do not mean physical damage to the brain, which could evidently influence the mind, but rather, such facts as that looking fit helps one to *be* fit. A pale, unshaven tramp, who wears dirty rags and is badly in need of a bath, actually does not resist either physical or mental stresses as well as he would after a shave, a bit of sunburn, a good bath, and some crisp new clothes have helped to rehabilitate his external appearance.

None of this is new. Intuitively, and merely on the basis of experience throughout centuries, these facts have long been recognized. That is why, to strengthen morale, armies insist on the spotless appearance of their men. That is also why opposite procedures are used (in some countries) for breaking down the physical and mental resistance of prisoners.

I was first introduced to these truths at the age of six, by my grandmother, when she found me desperately crying, I no longer recall about what. She looked at me with that particularly benevolent and protective look that I still remember and said, "Anytime you feel that low, just try to smile with your face, and you'll see . . . soon your whole being will be smiling." I tried it. It works.

There is nothing new here. But then, confession had been practised long before Freud; relativity was known before Einstein, and evolution before Darwin. Man did not need Pavlov's investigations on conditioned reflexes to find out that a dog can be trained to come when you whistle, or a horse to stop when you say "whoa!" Yet history shows that only the scientific analysis of these subjects by these particular men gave the concepts of psychoanalysis, the relativity of all our notions, the evolution of man's body from lower forms, and the conditioned reflexes, that philosophic impact which they now exercise upon contemporary thinking.

The existence of physical and mental strain, the manifold interactions between somatic and psychic reactions, as well as the importance of defensive-adaptive responses had all been more or less clearly recognized since time immemorial. But stress did not become meaningful to me until I found that it could be dissected by modern research methods and that individual, tangible components of the stress-response could be identified in chemical and physical terms. This is what helped me to use the concept of stress, not only for the solution of purely medical problems, but also as a guide to the natural solution of many problems presented by everyday life.

Let us take a few examples of such practical applications.

On being keyed up

Everybody is familiar with the feeling of being keyed up from nervous tension; this process is quite comparable to raising the key of a violin by tightening the strings. We say that our muscles limber up during exercise and that we are thrilled by great emotional experiences; all this prepares us for better peak-accomplishments. On the other hand, there is the tingling sensation, the jitteriness, when we are too much keyed up. This impairs our work and even prevents us from getting a rest.

Just what happens to us when we are alerted? Being keyed up is a very real sensation which must have a physicochemical basis. It has not yet been fully analyzed, but we know that at times of tension our adrenals produce an excess, both of adrenalines and of corticoids. We also know that taking either adrenalines or corticoids can reproduce a very similar sensation of being keyed up and excitable. For example, a person who is given large doses of cortisone in order to treat some allergic or rheumatoid condition often finds it difficult to sleep. He may even become abnormally euphoric, that is, carried away by an unreasonable sense of well-being and buoyancy, which is not unlike that caused by being slightly drunk. Later a sense of deep depression may follow.

We first saw this condition in experimental animals which had been given large doses of corticoids. Here, an initial state of great excitation—corresponding to the euphoria of patients—was followed by depression which might even proceed to complete anesthesia.

It had long been known that not only mental excitement (for instance, that communicated by a rioting mob or by an individual act of violence) but even physical stressors (such as a burn or an infectious fever) could cause an initial excitement which was followed by a secondary phase of depression. It is interesting to learn that identifiable chemical compounds, the hormones produced during the acute alarm-reaction phase of the G.A.S., possess this property of first keying up for action and then causing a depression. Both these effects may be of great practical value to the body: it is necessary to be keyed up for peak-accomplishments, but it is equally important to be keyed down by the secondary phase of depression, which prevents us from carrying on too long at top speed.

What can we do about this? Hormones are probably not the only regulators of our emotional level. Besides, we do not yet know enough about their workings to justify any attempt at regulating our emotional key by taking hormones.

Still, it is instructive to know that stress stimulates our glands to make hormones which can induce a kind of drunkenness. Without knowing this, no one would ever think of checking his conduct as carefully during stress as he does at a cocktail party. Yet he should.

The fact is that *a man can be intoxicated with his own stress hormones*. I venture to say that this sort of drunkenness has caused much more harm to society than the other kind.

We are on our guard against external intoxicants, but hormones are parts of our bodies; it takes more wisdom to recognize and overcome the foe who fights from within. In all our actions throughout the day we must consciously look for signs of being keyed up too much—and we must learn to stop in time. To watch our critical stress-level is just as important as to watch our critical quota of cocktails. More so. Intoxication by stress is sometimes unavoidable and usually insidious. You can quit alcohol and, even if you do take some, at least you can count the glasses; but it is impossible to avoid stress as long as you live and your conscious thoughts cannot gauge its alarm-signals accurately. Curiously, the pituitary is a much better judge of stress than the intellect.

How to tune down

It is not easy to tune down when you have reached your stress-quota. Many more people are the helpless slaves of their own stressful activities than of alcohol. Besides, simple rest is no cure-all. Activity and rest must be judiciously balanced, and *every person has his own characteristic requirements for rest and activity*. To lie motionless in bed all day is no relaxation for an active man. With advancing years, most people require increasingly more rest, but the process of aging does not progress at the same speed in everybody. Many a valuable man, who could still have given numerous years of useful work to society, has been made physically ill and prematurely senile by the enforcement of retirement at an age when his requirements and abilities for activity were still high. This psychosomatic illness is so common that it has been given a name: *retirement disease*.

All work and no play is certainly harmful for anyone at any age; but then, what is work and what is play? Fishing is relaxing play for the business executive, but it is hard work for the professional fisherman. The former can go fishing to relax, but the latter will have to do something else, or simply take a rest, in order to relax.

What has research on stress taught us about the way *to reach a healthy balance between rest and work*? Are there objective physiologic facts which could guide our conduct in this respect? I emphatically believe that there are, but, in order to grasp their lesson, we must turn back to what we have learned about the most general tissue-reactions to stress: cellular fatigue and inflammation. This may seem odd; you may feel that there is no conceivable relationship between the behavior of our cells (for instance, in inflammation) and our conduct in everyday life. I do not agree. All the reactions of our body are governed by general biologic laws and the simplest way to understand these is to examine how they affect the simplest tissue-reactions.

Stress as an equalizer of activities

It seems to be one of the most fundamental laws regulating the activities of complex living beings that no one part of the body must be disproportionately overworked for a long time. Stress seems to be the great equalizer of activities within the body; *it helps to prevent one-sided overexertion.*

To carry a heavy suitcase for a long time without fatigue, you have to shift it from one hand to the other occasionally. Here, local stress, manifested as muscular fatigue, is the equalizer; it acts by way of the nervous system which experiences the feeling of fatigue and thereby suggests the change-over.

In other instances, general stress may arrange the proper equalization of local activities through the intermediary of the adaptive hormones. Suppose a person has a severe infection in his left knee joint. An arthritis develops with all the characteristic manifestations of inflammation. A strong inflammatory barricade is constructed around the joint to delimit the trouble; then, various cells and enzymes will enter the joint-cavity in order to destroy the causative germs. Now, suppose both knees are infected. There develops an inflammation on both sides, but its degree will be less severe. Why? Because local stress of the inflamed territory sends out alarm-signals, through the pituitary, to stimulate the production by the adrenals of anti-inflammatory corticoids.

This arrangement is also a useful defense mechanism, because there is a limit to how much inflammation the body can tolerate. If only a small region is injured, a strong inflammatory reaction will be the best response, since inflammation has a local protective value;

but if several parts of the body are simultaneously injured, the patient may not be able to stand maximal inflammatory reactions everywhere. Thus it is often in the best interests of the body as a whole to sacrifice some of its parts by cutting down local defensive activities.

This situation is quite comparable to that of a country which, when attacked on one front only, can send all its armies to the endangered region, but not when several frontiers are simultaneously invaded.

Now, since stress is a common attribute of all biologic activities, these considerations apply not only to inflammation, but to all types of biologic work. For instance, the intensity of inflammation in a knee joint may be diminished, not only by inflammation in other regions, but also by excessive muscular work, nervous activity, or anything else that requires effort. This is so because any part under stress sends out alarm-signals to coordinate resistance. For the same reason, any intense reaction in one part can influence (and, to some extent, equalize) all kinds of biologic activities in other parts of the same body.

The stress-quotient

These facts, which have been established by laboratory experiments on rats, also hold remarkably true when applied to the daily problems of man, including even his purely mental activities. In analyzing our stress-status, we must always think, not only of the total amount of stress in the body, but also of its proportionate distribution between various parts. To put this into the simplest terms, we might say that the stress-quotient to be watched is:

$$\frac{\text{local stress in any one part}}{\text{total stress in the body}}$$

If there is proportionately too much stress in any one part, you need diversion. If there is too much stress in the body as a whole, you must rest.

The importance of deviation

Deviation is the act of turning something (for instance, a biologic mechanism) aside from its course. It is not necessarily a pleasant and relaxing diversion. We have seen, for instance, how severe shock (electroshock, drug shock) can—through its general stress-effect upon all parts—deviate the body's somatic or psychic defense reactions from a habitual stereotyped course.

When the concentration of effort in any one part of our body or mind is not very intense and chronic, as we all know from experience, milder types of deviation are often quite effective (sports, dancing, music, reading, travel, whisky, chewing-gum). These do not have to act primarily through the stress-mechanism and the pituitary-adrenal axis, but they always cause a decentralization of our efforts, which often helps to restore a lopsided stress-quotient toward normal.

Deviation is particularly important in combating purely mental stress. Everyone knows how much harm can be caused by worry. The textbooks of psychosomatic medicine are full of case reports describing the production of gastric ulcers, hypertension, arthritis, and many other diseases by chronic worry about moral and economic problems. *Nothing is accomplished by telling such people not to worry.* They cannot help it. Here again, the best remedy is deviation, or general stress. By highlighting some other problem, through deviation, or by activating the whole body, by general stress, the source of worry automatically becomes less important in proportion.

This fact can be consciously used in practice. Of course, for a person who is to undergo a very dangerous surgical operation, or who finds himself on the verge of economic disaster, it is impossible to stop worrying just by deciding not to—especially if he is the worrying kind. *You must find something to put in the place of the worrying thoughts to chase them away.* This is deviation. If such a person undertakes some strenuous task which needs all his attention, he may still not forget his worries, but they will certainly fade. Nothing erases unpleasant thoughts more effectively than conscious concentration on pleasant ones. Many people do this subconsciously, but unless you know about the mechanism of diversion, it is difficult to do it well. Some neurotics compulsively concentrate on the most extraordinary and harmful things in the course of subconscious efforts to divert themselves from sexual frustrations. Psychoanalysts call this *sublimation*, which is defined as "the act of directing the energy of an impulse from its primitive aim to one that is culturally or ethically higher." I would not know about that; but it is deviation.

Incidentally, another practically important aspect of deviation is the development of a competition between memory and learning power. It seems that to some extent *newly learned facts occupy the place of previously learned or subsequently learnable ones.* Consequently there is a limit to how much you can burden your memory; and trying to remember too many things is certainly one of the major sources of psychologic stress. I make a conscious effort to forget immediately all that is unimportant and to jot down data of possible value (even at the price of having to prepare complex files). Thus I manage to keep my memory free for facts which are truly essential to me. I think this technique can help anyone to accomplish the greatest simplicity compatible with the degree of complexity of his intellectual life.

Innate vitality must find an outlet

I have described elsewhere in this book the animal experiments which showed that every living being has a certain innate amount of *adaptation energy* or vitality. This can be used slowly for a long and uneventful life, or rapidly during a shorter and more stressful, but often also, more colorful and enjoyable existence. Let me add now that the choice is not entirely ours. Even the optimum tempo at which we are to consume life is largely inherited from our predecessors. Yet, what is in us must out; otherwise we may explode at the wrong places or become hopelessly hemmed in by frustrations. *The great art is to express our vitality through the particular channels and at the particular speed which nature foresaw for us.*

This is never very easy, but here again, intelligent self-analysis helps. We have seen, for instance, how deviation, not complete rest, may be the best solution for a person who feels generally slowed down, although he has temporarily overworked only one channel of self-expression. In some such cases, rather paradoxically, even general stress (for instance, shock therapy, strenuous work) can help by equalizing and decentralizing activities which have habitually become concentrated in one part of our being.

There are various ways of self-expression. The one which I have found most consistent with biologic laws and most effective in practice will be described later in Chapter 24 in the section on the "philosophy of gratitude."

But if we are just doing too much—though even not too much of any one thing—the problem is one of excessive general stress. This can be met only by rest. It cannot be handled either by deviation or by more stress. Here the great remedy is to learn how to enjoy laziness and how to sleep. I have often tried to enjoy laziness, but I have never succeeded. I suppose it is just not in my nature. I am afraid, if you want to learn this art, you will have to read another author. But, for a long time, I have suffered from insomnia, and I did learn how to sleep, so perhaps I might say a few words about this now.

How to sleep

The stress of a day of hard work can make you sleep like a log or it can keep you awake all night. This sounds contradictory, but if you come to analyze the work that helps you to sleep and the work that keeps you awake, there is a difference. *A stressful activity which has come to a definite stop prepares you for rest and sleep; but one which sets up self-maintaining tensions keeps you awake.* The fatigue of work well accomplished gets you ready for sleep but, during the night, you must protect yourself against being awakened by stress. Everybody knows the value of protection against noise, light, variations in temperature, or the difficulties of digesting a heavy meal taken before retirement. We need not speak about such protective measures here. But what can you do to regulate psychologic stress so it will not keep you awake?

If you suffer from insomnia, there is no point in telling yourself, "Forget everything and relax; sleep will come by itself." It does not.

Sheep-counting, warm milk, hot baths, and so forth, are also of little value, since they only help those who have faith in them. The fact is that by the time you retire it is too late for anything except the sleeping pill. *It is during the whole day that you must prepare your dreams;* for, if you are subject to insomnia, whatever you do during the day, your next night's sleep depends largely on how you do it.

The recipe for this preparation can be deduced from the preceding passages:

Do not let yourself get carried away and keyed up more than is necessary to acquire the momentum for the best performance of what you want to do in the interest of self-expression. If you get keyed up too much, especially during the later hours of the day, your stress-reaction may carry over into the night.

Keep in mind that the hormones produced during acute stress are meant to alarm you and key you up for peak-accomplishments. They tend to combat sleep and to promote alertness during short periods of exertion; they are not meant to be used all day long. If too much of these hormones is circulating in your blood, they will keep you awake, just as a tablet of ephedrine would. (Incidentally, ephedrine is chemically related to adrenaline.) Your insomnia has a chemical basis, which cannot easily be talked away after it has developed; and at night in bed it is too late to prevent it from developing.

Try not to overwork any one part of your body or mind disproportionately by repeating the same actions to exhaustion. Be especially careful to avoid the senseless repetition of the same task when you are already exhausted. A moment of objective self-analysis will suffice to convince you that the same work could be done much more easily after a night's sleep, or even after only a few hours of doing something else (deviation). If you get yourself deep in a rut, you may not be able to stop, and mentally you will keep on repeating your routine throughout the night.

Nature likes variety. Remember this, not only in planning your day, but in planning your life. Our civilization tends to force people into highly specialized occupations which may become monotonously repetitive. Remember that stress is the great equalizer of biologic activities and if you use the same parts of your body or mind over and over again, the only means nature has to force you out of the groove is: stress.

Remember also that insomnia is a powerful stressor in itself. If a sleepless night follows a day of overexertion, next day your usual work will have to be done while you are sleepy. The stress of it may mean another sleepless night and the development of a vicious circle which is difficult to break. Fortunately, this complication will rarely develop if you follow my prescription; but if it does, the best way out is to sleep during the day if you can, or to take a mild sleeping powder at night.

To summarize: protect yourself against stress at night, not only by cutting out too much light, noise, cold, or heat, but particularly by never allowing yourself to be under the kind of stress during the day that may automatically go on throughout the night. This self-perpetuating kind of stress may be the result of a heavy meal, whisky, emotional upsets, and many other things. Watch for them. So, remember: stress keeps you awake while it lasts, but prepares you for sleep later.

24:

Philosophic implications

The wear and tear of life

For our scientific research in the laboratory we needed an operational definition of stress, that is, one which showed us what to do in order to see stress. It is only by the intensity of its manifestations —the adrenal enlargement, the increased corticoid concentration in the blood, the loss of weight, and so forth—that we can recognize the presence and gauge the intensity of stress. The fact that you cannot see it directly, as such, does not make stress less real. After all, as Robert Louis Stevenson put it:

> Who has seen the wind?
> Neither you nor I
> But when the trees bow down their heads
> The wind is passing by.

For the present discussion, however, our shorter, Aristotelian definition—which merely classifies stress as one aspect of wear and tear —is more satisfactory. We can look upon stress as the "rate of wear and tear in the body." When so defined, the close relationship between aging and stress becomes particularly evident. Stress is the sum of all the wear and tear caused by any kind of vital reaction throughout the body at any one time. That is why it can act as a common denominator of all the biologic changes which go on in the body; it is a kind of "speedometer of life."

Now, in discussing my experiments, I have often had occasion to point out that aging, at least, true physiologic aging, is not determined by the time elapsed since birth, but by the total amount of wear and tear to which the body has been exposed. There is, indeed, a great *difference between physiologic and chronologic age.* One man may be much more senile in body and mind, and much closer to the grave, at forty than another person at sixty. True age depends largely on the rate of wear and tear, on the speed of self-consumption; for life is essentially a process which gradually spends the given amount of adaptation energy that we inherited from our parents. Vitality is like a special kind of bank account which you can use up by withdrawals but cannot increase by deposits. Your only control over this most precious fortune is the rate at which you make your withdrawals. The solution is evidently not to stop withdrawing, for this would be death. Nor is it to withdraw just enough for survival, for this would permit only a vegetative life, worse than death. The intelligent thing to do is to withdraw generously, but never expend wastefully.

Many people believe that, after they have exposed themselves to very stressful activities, a rest can restore them to where they were before. This is false. Experiments on animals have clearly shown that each exposure leaves an indelible scar, in that it uses up reserves of adaptability which cannot be replaced. It is true that immediately after some harassing experience, rest can restore us almost to the original level of fitness by eliminating acute fatigue. But the emphasis is on the word *almost.* Since we constantly go through periods of stress and rest during life, just a little deficit of adaptation energy every day adds up—it adds up to what we call *aging.*

Apparently, there are *two kinds of adaptation energy*: the superficial kind, which is ready to use, and the deeper kind, which acts as a sort of frozen reserve. When superficial adaptation energy is exhausted during exertion, it can slowly be restored from a deeper store during rest. This gives a certain plasticity to our resistance. It also protects us from wasting adaptation energy too lavishly in certain foolish moments, because acute fatigue automatically stops us. It is the restoration of the superficial adaptation energy from the deep reserves that tricks us into believing that the loss has been made good. Actually, it has only been covered from reserves—and at the cost of depleting reserves. We might compare this feeling of having suffered no loss to the careless optimism of a spendthrift who keeps forgetting that whenever he restores the vanishing supply of dollars in his wallet by withdrawing from the invisible stocks of his bank account, the loss has not really been made good: there was merely a transfer of money from a less accessible to a more accessible form.

I think, in this respect, the lesson of animal experimentation has a great practical bearing upon the way we should live; it helps us to translate knowledge into wisdom.

The lesson is a particularly timely one. Due to the great advances made by classic medicine during the last half century, premature death caused by specific disease-producers (microbes, malnutrition, etc.) has declined at a phenomenal rate. As a result of this, the *average human life-span* increased in the United States from 48 years in 1900 to 69.8 years in 1956. But since everybody still has to die sometime, more and more people are killed by disease-producers which cannot be eliminated by the methods of classic medicine. An ever-increasing proportion of the human population dies from the so-called wear-and-tear diseases, or degenerative diseases, which are primarily due to stress.

In other words, the more man learns about ways to combat external causes of death (germs, cold, hunger), the more likely is he to die from his own voluntary, suicidal actions. I am not competent to speak about wars—though these are also signs of maladaptation—but perhaps my experiments can teach us something about the way to conduct our personal lives in keeping with natural laws. Life is a continuous series of adaptations to our surroundings and, as far as we know, our reserve of adaptation energy is an inherited finite amount, which cannot be regenerated. On the other hand, I am sure we could still enormously lengthen the average human life-span by living in better harmony with natural laws.

To die of old age

What makes me so certain that the natural human life-span is far in excess of the actual one is this:

Among all my autopsies (and I have performed quite a few), I have never seen a man who died of old age. In fact, *I do not think anyone has ever died of old age yet*. To permit this would be the ideal accomplishment of medical research (if we disregard the unlikely event of someone discovering how to regenerate adaptation energy). To die of old age would mean that all the organs of the body would be worn out proportionately, merely by having been used too long. This is never the case. We invariably die because one vital part has worn out too early in proportion to the rest of the body. Life, the biologic chain that holds our parts together, is only as strong as its weakest vital link. When this breaks—no matter which vital link it be—our parts can no longer be held together as a single living being.

You will note I did not say "our parts die," because this is not necessarily so. In tissue cultures, isolated cells of a man can go on living for a long time after he, as a whole, has died. It is only the complex organization of all our cells into a single individual that necessarily dies when one vital part breaks down. An old man may die because one worn-out, hardened artery breaks in his brain, or because his kidneys can no longer wash out the metabolic wastes from his blood, or because his heart muscle is damaged by excessive work. But *there is always one part which wears out first and wrecks the whole human machinery*, merely because the other parts cannot function without it.

This is the price we pay for the evolution of the human body from a simple cell into a highly complex organization. *Unicellular animals never need to die*. They just divide, and the parts live on.

The lesson seems to be that, as far as man can regulate his life by voluntary actions, he should seek to equalize stress throughout his being, by what we have called *deviation*, the frequent shifting-over of work from one part to the other. The human body—like the tires on a car, or the rug on a floor—wears longest when it wears evenly. We can do ourselves a great deal of good in this respect by just yielding to our natural cravings for variety in everyday life. We must not forget that the more we vary our actions the less any one part suffers from attrition.

We have seen in a previous passage through what mechanisms stress itself can act as an equalizer of biologic activities (see p. 266); but it is equally true that stress, perhaps precisely due to its equalizing effect, gives an excellent chance to develop innate potential talents, no matter where they may be slumbering in the mind or body. In fact, *it is only in the heat of stress that individuality can be perfectly molded.*

The origin of individuality

In 1859, when Charles Darwin published *The Origin of Species,* he promised that in his book "light would be thrown on the origin of man and his history." This volume marked a new epoch both in scientific and in religious thought, because it described observations suggesting that the animal species had developed "by means of natural selection or the preservation of favored races in the struggle for life." In many respects, there is a curious resemblance between the means employed by nature in evolving species and individuals. Limitations of food and space restrict the development of species to the strongest ones. Similar limitations of nutrition and anatomy, within each individual, force stress to develop, through preferential usage, those organs and aptitudes which are best suited to maintain life.

The features of a species reflect the cumulative memories of past generations; individuality results from the gradual engraving upon this inherited background of personal memories (including "biochemical memories") as they are acquired during a single life-span. In the course of the development of a species, every member of each successive generation must relive—as an embryo before entering this world—the entire history of its ancestors from the primeval ameba up to the contemporary newborn stage. Then, after birth, each individual, indeed every organ in his body, again goes through innumerable adaptive reactions, to develop those personal characteristics which distinguish him from all other individuals. *Just as among the races, so among the organs and aptitudes of each person only the favored survive in the struggle for existence.* We have seen that within the individual this is accomplished largely through the stress-mechanism.

When too much is going on in any one place within the body, that part is temporarily put out of action, by tissue-breakdown, acute inflammation, or mere fatigue—which comprise essentially the alarm phase of the local adaptation syndrome. This forces other parts to take over, and thereby gives them a chance to develop as far as they can.

But even without there being excessive activity in any one part, too much may be going on in the body as a whole. Then, the central coordinators of adaptation (the nervous system and the endocrine glands) are informed of this by the sum of the alarm-signals arriving from all parts at any one time. When general stress is excessive the whole organism needs a rest; it cannot afford a struggle anywhere. This provides an opportunity to try again and again, even after repeated failures, until the best distribution of organ-development is reached and the individual is fully molded in harmony with his inherited potentialities and the demands made upon him by his surroundings. Of course, congenital aptitudes form the base-line of adaptability. They depend upon evolution and inheritance from ancestors and parents, but the manifest features of a person are largely the result of the stresses to which this adaptability is then exposed during the individual's own lifetime.

If we are to learn something by observing stress in nature, if we are to derive some lesson that could guide our conduct in our daily life, we must again ask ourselves, "What can we do about all this?" The development of fatigue or inflammation in an overworked organ, the production of ACTH and corticoids during stress, are obviously beyond voluntary control. So is our genetic make-up. There is something compulsive, something strictly obligatory, even in our "voluntary activities." It is all very well to say that our vitality (our adaptation energy) should be used wisely, at a certain rate, and for certain tasks, but all this is theory. In practice, when it comes to guiding human conduct, it seems that we must all bow to the great law which says that what is in us must express itself; in fact it must express itself at a speed and in directions predetermined by our own inherited structure. This is largely true, but not quite—and on the little untruth in this dictum rests my whole philosophy of life.

The need for self-expression

After a pilot has left the ground in a plane—unless he wants to kill himself—he cannot stop his motor before he gets back to earth again. He must complete his mission back to earth. Yet there is very much he can do, through voluntary choice of conduct, to get as far as possible with a given airplane and fuel supply under given climatic conditions. For instance, he can fly at a speed and on a course best suited to his machine under the prevailing weather conditions. The two great limiting factors over which, once in flight, he has no control are: the fuel supply and the wear and tear that the weakest vital part of his plane can tolerate.

When a human being is born—unless he wants to kill himself—he cannot stop, either, before he has completed his mission on earth. Yet he too can do much, through voluntary choice of conduct, to get as far as possible with a given bodily structure and supply of adaptation energy, under given social conditions. For instance, he can live and express his personality at a tempo and in a manner best suited to his inherited talents, under the prevailing social conditions. The two great limiting factors—which are set once a man is born —are: his supply of adaptation energy and the wear and tear that the weakest vital part of his body can tolerate.

So, actually, we can accomplish a great deal by living wisely in accordance with natural laws. We can determine our optimum speed of living, by trying various speeds and finding out which one is most agreeable. We can determine our course by the same empirical method, keeping in mind, however, that occasional deviations have a virtue of their own: they equalize the wear and tear throughout the body, and thereby give overworked parts time to cool down.

In my analogy you will find two weak points which are particularly instructive because they highlight the difference between an inanimate and a living machine.

First, the real fuel of life is not the combustible (food) we take, but adaptability, because the living machine can make considerable repairs and adjustments en route, as long as it has adaptation energy. With this it can assimilate caloric energy from its surroundings. Consequently, resting an overworked part in the body helps not only by "cooling it down" but also by permitting it to make major repairs and even improvements in its structure.

Second (I say "second" as a physician, but would have said "first" as a human being), the object of man is not to keep going as long as possible. This is rather charmingly expressed by the motto on the masthead of the *Journal of Gerontology*, a medical journal devoted to the study of old age: "To add life to years, not just years to life."

Man certainly does not get the feeling of happiness, of having completed his mission on earth, just by staying alive very long. On the contrary, a long life without the feeling of fulfillment is very tedious. And yet, when (and if) they analyze their lives, most people get the feeling of merely muddling through, of drifting aimlessly, from one day to another. Just staying alive, no matter how comfortably and securely, is no adequate outlet for man's vital adaptation energy. Comfort and security make it easier for us to enjoy the great things in life, but they are not, in themselves, great and enjoyable aims.

What are man's ultimate aims?

Philosophers, psychologists, and mystics have argued about this since time immemorial. We have heard many noble and many vulgar answers: to please God, to obtain power, love, or sexual satisfaction, to receive recognition and approval from others or from ourselves, to achieve creative expression—or simply, happiness. All these answers ring true to some people and none of them to all. Looking at this list gives me the same feeling I had when, as a young medical student in Prague, I first examined patients suffering from various diseases: there must be some common denominator here.

It is a very fundamental human need, for instance, to work for some reward, and to judge and enjoy our success in proportion to the magnitude of the compensations we can accumulate. They may be dollars or medals or any other possession. They may even be fellow human beings who become our slaves—because of our dollars or medals or other possessions. They may be good deeds for which

God will repay us. But one thing is certain: they *must be additive.* How else could we count our gains? How else could we know whether or not we have accomplished enough to be satisfied?

I found my answer to these problems in what we may call *the philosophy of gratitude.* It helped me to form my personal attitude toward stress in life. It may help you. But then, I realize, too, that it may not, for you might not see things my way. Here I am outside my element, the laboratory, where a proved fact is binding for everyone. Here, I have ventured into pure philosophy: a very dangerous thing for a medical scientist to do, and a thing for which I shall no doubt be severely rebuked by some of my more reserved and reticent colleagues! But, you see, it is part of my philosophy that I must express myself, so I cannot help it. It was indeed very stressful to spend all my adult life in the laboratory, working on stress; it was perhaps even more stressful to express my thoughts in the form of this book. But well do I know that not to express all this would have been much more stressful still.

Is the need for self-expression the common denominator of man's ultimate aims? Do we always look for rewards because we need some cumulative indicator which tells us to what extent we have accomplished self-expression? If this were so, it would explain why purely sensual satisfaction—the enjoyment of any among the pleasures of the flesh—has never been a truly satisfactory long-range aim for man. No matter how acute the happiness they give, the pleasures of the flesh are ephemeral; they cannot be accumulated in the form of any kind of riches. They cannot give us the sense of a mission well accomplished, of having earned some type of wealth which assures our security.

The philosophic lesson

In the preceding passages we spoke of the role played by stress in the evolution of individuality, of the need for self-expression, and the urge to work for rewards. We saw that to be worthy ultimate aims, these rewards must be endowed with some permanency that makes it possible to accumulate them into a kind of personal possession which gives us a sense of security and, therefore, peace of mind. Let us see now whether, from the study of nature, we may derive some general philosophic lesson, some natural rules of conduct, in the permanent fight between altruistic and egotistic tendencies, which account for most of the stress in interpersonal relations.

It is strange that what I value most, as my personal reward for the time spent on dissecting the stress-mechanism, is not a medical but a philosophic lesson. And yet this lesson is not even very new; vaguely, most people, have always felt it. The scientific analysis of how the body reacts to stress has only helped to translate, into terms of intellect, what the instinctive wisdom of the emotions had always dimly appreciated. Still, in an age so largely governed by intellect as ours, it is gratifying to learn that what religions and philosophies have taught as doctrines to guide our conduct is based on scientifically understandable biologic truths. It is not easy to put this lesson into words, but I shall try.

The evolution of intercellular altruism

The most characteristic feature of life is egotism; it is also its most ancient and essential property. As soon as the first amebalike cell was created in the primeval ocean it had to shift for itself or die. Unlike all the inanimate substances around it, it was not indifferent to its own fate; it lived and it wanted to go on living. To achieve its aim this cell did not have to compete with other living beings, for it alone was alive and the inanimate did not "mind" being exploited.

But another characteristic of life is to multiply and to develop: soon there were two cells, then millions, each looking out for itself first—and often necessarily at the expense of the others. This led to clashes in which the strongest cells won out.

Then, sometime, somewhere, a few cells stuck together and formed a colony with a community of interests, a sort of *collective egotism*. At this moment altruism was born. With regard to other living beings, the community still behaved like an egotist; but it was in the interest of each cell within this colony that the other members also had to strive, because the strength of the whole depended upon all its parts. From any one cell's point of view, altruism toward other cells of the same colony became a form of egotism.

The biologic efficiency of this collective life proved to be so great that, in the course of the struggle for survival, cells found it useful not only to stay together but to rely ever more upon each other.

Eventually large numbers of them learned even to share a single life; they came to form *a single living being*. Man himself is such a multicellular organism. The cells of his body are so strictly inter-dependent that they could not survive in separation. Some of them have become indispensable to feed the whole body, others to move it, yet others to coordinate its manifold activities; but, in acquiring this high specialization for their respective tasks, the parts have given up their capacity for independent existence. The choice be-tween egotism and altruism does not arise between the cells of a single multicellular body; within its confines, there is no motive for competitive fight.

When any kind of foreign living body enters into our tissues, there is considerable wear and tear: that is, local stress, due to a clash of interests between the invader and the invaded. This is evi-denced by an essentially inflammatory defensive response. Only our own organs (for instance, nerves, blood vessels) can penetrate our tissues without causing much stress. Here, no protective barricade is built to fend off the invader; in fact, he is welcome: even the dense tissue of bone melts away under the soft pressure of an invad-ing blood vessel which brings it nourishment.

It took countless generations before single cells evolved the art of peaceful interdependence to avoid internal stress. (Even now a revolt can break out occasionally in a part which forgets the prin-ciple of collective altruism. This is what we call *cancer*. It kills the whole as well as itself by its own unrestrained expansion.)

In short, we may look upon the evolution of complex living beings as essentially a process permitting many cells to develop in har-mony, with a minimum of stress between them, so as best to serve the interests of the whole community.

The evolution of interpersonal altruism

Now let us consider relationships between various multicellular living beings, for instance, between men. Here there has also evolved an interdependence between individuals who have special-ized for diverse tasks. Some raise food, others provide transporta-tion, and others administer and coordinate the activities of the com-munity. But, at present, teamwork between them is still far less satisfactory and far more conducive to stress than between the various organs of one person. Whatever harmony or discord there is in our social relations owes its existence to a single organ: the nervous system. It governs all our major decisions and attitudes toward each other through one type among its many products: the emotions. (Some unobservant people also attribute a major importance to logic in social relations, but they are mistaken; as far as I can see, here logic hardly plays any role at all.

A biologist's view of gratitude and revenge

We may perhaps go even further: it seems to me that, among all the emotions, there is one which, more than any other, accounts for the absence or presence of stress in human relations: that is the feeling of gratitude—with its negative counterpart, the need for revenge. (Ingratitude is not the reverse, but merely, the lack of gratitude.) It is curious how closely the mechanism which deals with stress within the body of one man resembles that which meets the stress of social relations between men.

In this book I have cited many examples showing that a brief period of exposure to stress may result in a lasting gain or loss. This is amenable to scientific study because it can be appraised by measurable indices of physiologic resistance. When the whole body is temporarily exposed to stress, the result may be either a lasting increase in general resistance, or damage, shock. Similarly, when part of the body is thus exposed, the result may be either increased local resistance (inurement, inflammation), or tissue-breakdown (degeneration or even death of cells). In all these instances, it depends largely upon the body's response whether or not exposure results in a gain or in a loss. We have also seen that this response is directed by a system of opposing forces (proinflammatory and anti-inflammatory hormones; adrenaline- and acetylcholine-producing nerve impulses), which meet the stressor from within.

The final outcome always has a triple root, a tripartite causation whose elements are: (1) the stressor, (2) the factors promoting resistance, and (3) the factors favoring submission.

This is the stereotyped somatic pattern of the response to stress within the body. It seems to me that the psychic stress, due to relations between men, is regulated by a strikingly similar tripartite mechanism: there is a clashing of interests, which acts as a stressor from without, and there are balancing impulses for resistance and submission, which meet the stressor from within. The final outcome is not determined only (perhaps not even mainly) by the stressor itself; it depends upon all three elements of the situation. The lasting manifestations of interpersonal stress—just as those of stress arising within any one individual—can be a gain or a loss, depending upon circumstances. The principal difference is that, in interpersonal stress, the lasting asset manifests itself as a feeling of gratitude, and the liability as an urge for revenge.

The lasting bodily changes (in structure or chemical composition) which underlie effective adaptation or the collapse of it are aftereffects of stress: they represent tissue-memories which affect our future somatic behavior during similar stressful situations. They can be stored. But such somatic changes can only govern our attitude toward subsequent stressors within our body. The aftermaths of stress which most forcefully guide our future interpersonal relations are emotions, such as feelings of gratitude or revenge, which direct social conduct.

I think in the final analysis that *gratitude and revenge are the most important factors governing our actions in everyday life*; upon them also chiefly depend our peace of mind, our feelings of security or insecurity, of fulfillment or frustration, in short, the extent to which we can make a success of life. But words do not always mean the same thing to everybody and perhaps, before going further, I should explain the sense in which I use the terms *gratitude* and *revenge*.

Gratitude is the awakening in another person of the wish that I should prosper, because of what I have done for him. It is perhaps the most characteristically human way of assuring security (homeostasis). It takes away the motive for a clash between selfish and selfless tendencies, because, by inspiring the feeling of gratitude, I have induced another person to share with me my natural wish for my own well-being.

I have said that egotism is the most characteristic, the most ancient, and the most essential property of life. Still, it is ugly. Why are we repulsed by it? Why do we try to deny its existence in ourselves if it is natural and unavoidable? I think selfishness, in others as well as in ourselves, disgusts us mainly because it is dangerous.

We are afraid of it. We know it will invariably lead to stress-situations because egotism is the seed of fight and revenge.

Now, *revenge* is the awakening in another person of the wish that I should not prosper, because of what I have done to him. It is the most important threat to security (homeostasis). But it also has its roots in a natural defense reaction. It is a savage distortion of the natural wish to teach others not to hurt us. When we punish a child for doing something bad, our action comes very close to revenge, even if it is guided by parental love. Punishment is an object lesson which teaches proper future conduct by retaliation. Unfortunately, in practice, it is very difficult to draw the line between teaching by punishment for a constructive purpose and senseless, purely vindictive retaliation as an aim in itself, a morbid satisfaction of the urge for self-expression. Professional teachers must be especially careful to make this distinction in all their dealings with students.

This brings us to the general problem of working for a *reward*. Both gratitude and revenge are feelings concerned with reward; they are themselves, in a sense, remunerations: the former for good, the latter for bad actions. But the important point is that both of these types of reward have common, fundamental qualities which might fit them to act as ultimate aims.

We need not give much thought to revenge; it is nothing but a grotesque malformation of our urge to teach; a kind of "disease of the teaching instinct." It has no virtue whatever, and can only hurt both the giver and the receiver of its fruits. The seeds of any fruit can only reproduce the tree they come from. Revenge generates more revenge; gratitude tends to incite still more gratitude. No sane person would consciously select the savage satisfactions of the vendetta as an ultimate aim in life. But "Gratitude is the sign of noble souls" (Æsop) and there are

> Two kinds of gratitude: the sudden kind
> We feel for what we give.
> We feel for what we take, the larger kind.
> EDWIN ARLINGTON ROBINSON

To me, the most striking thing about inspiring gratitude is that it possesses—more than any other value—all those characteristics which we seek in some long-range aim based on the laws of nature:

1. It can act as a common denominator for the most diverse ways

of self-expression; each person can strive to inspire gratitude in others, according to his own talents, for instance, through charity, art, or science.

2. The effects of gratitude are lasting; they can be accumulated.

3. Neither wealth, nor force, nor any other instrument of power can ever be more reliable in assuring our security and peace of mind than the knowledge of having inspired gratitude in a great many people. This surely is a worthy long-range aim for man. But is it really an ultimate aim?

The philosophy of gratitude

Could, and should, consciously planned striving for gratitude become the basis of a practical philosophy—a way of life? Working for any kind of reward seems rather unworthy of becoming the ultimate aim of our existence. Most people would not like to admit, even to themselves, that they do what they do just in order to make other people grateful.

When you ask an artist why he paints, an author why he writes, a soldier why he risks his life in battle, they may give you all kinds of answers (some idealistic, some mercenary) but they would laugh at the suggestion that what they really want is gratitude.

The scientist who sacrifices his private life in favor of exacting laboratory work may admit that he does it only "for fun" or out of a purely altruistic wish "to be of service"; and, if he is more reserved, he may recite the ready-made slogan of "science for science's own sake." But he would be very much surprised, and indeed ashamed, if you succeeded in convincing him that he actually works to earn the gratitude of his fellow men. Most scientists would consider this a very selfish, if not naive, justification for their efforts. And yet, if you come to think of it, which is more selfish and more naive: working "for fun" and such intangibles as "science's own sake," or for the inspiration in others of well-earned gratitude?

My suggestion seems even more preposterous when you think of people who do things which could not be of any material or spiritual help to anybody. Do they also work for gratitude? Take the gunman, whose life is nothing but a chain of brutal robberies and murders. And what of the kind hearted, deeply religious man, who gives anonymously to the poor, precisely because—by not asking for gratitude—he wants to please God?

Yet, if you look a little closer, in the final analysis are not all these varied forms of self-expression subconsciously planned to earn gratitude and approval from one source or another? There is the gratitude of those who are inspired by a great painting or a great idea, the thankfulness of men who have been saved from catastrophe by the valor of soldiers or the genius of scientists? And does not even the most debased thug commit his brutal crimes because all his earlier attempts to express himself in a manner which would earn gratitude have failed? Is it not actually as a result of his frustrating despair that he eventually looks for whatever substitute can be bought, from loose women or underlings, by squandering his loot on them? And does not the saintly giver remain anonymous because he prefers the grateful approval of a divine being to the gratitude of men?

The thirst for approval

Why is everybody so anxious to deny that he works for recognition? In my walk of life, I have met a great many scientists, among them some of the most prominent scholars of our century; but I doubt if any one of them would have thought that public recognition of his achievements—by a title, a medal, a prize, or an honorary degree—played a decisive role in motivating his enthusiasm for research. When a prize brings both honor and cash, many scientists would even be more inclined to admit being pleased about the money ("one must live") than about the public recognition ("I am not sensitive to flattery"). Why do even the greatest minds stoop to such falsehoods? For, without being conscious lies, these ratiocinations are undoubtedly false. Most of the really talented scientists are not at all money-minded; nor do they condone greed for wealth either in themselves or in others. On the other hand, all the scientists I know sufficiently well to judge (and I include myself in this group) are extremely anxious to have their work recognized and approved by others. Is it not below the dignity of an objective scientific mind to permit such a distortion of his true motives? Besides, what is there to be ashamed of?

To give meaning and direction to life, we must have some long-range aim, something in the distance that we can work for. That is why a natural, ultimate aim must have two great characteristics: it must be something we can work *for* (otherwise it would give no outlet to self-expression), and its fruits must be sufficiently permanent to accumulate as life goes by (otherwise it could not be a long-range aim). To please God, to live for the Fatherland, or the family, or any other worthwhile and permanent institution, have long and effectively served man in his search for long-range aims. Even the most ardently desired objective, if it be short-lived, could only furnish a motive for the moment, but never a directive for the future. It is rather self-evident that such an objective will not be present in the future. Why should we be ashamed to plan our lives so as to earn approval and gratitude?

On exhibiting modesty

In discussing man's natural thirst for approval, we should not forget to say a word about modesty. Some people develop such a morbid craving for applause that they spend most of their time trying to attract attention to their own accomplishments. This is not only an ineffectual but also a most repulsive effort to assure one's standing in society. The only related form of conduct which, at least to me, is even more repugnant is the premeditated display of modesty. True modesty remains quietly hidden inside; it is never so immodest as to exhibit itself in public. Really great men are too honest to simulate modesty as a social asset and too humble to exhibit their heartfelt modesty in public. Though proud of their work, they are careful not to exaggerate its importance; they are far too interested in its substance to divert attention to their own contribution by making an obtrusive show of modesty.

The terror of censure

As much as we thirst for approval we dread censure. The common statement, "I don't care what anybody says" is almost invariably untrue. Probably I should not have said "almost," because I do not know of a single person who does not care what anybody says. Is this pretense necessary? If a person is quite certain he is right (which is rarely the case among intelligent people), he should stick to his guns no matter how much he is criticized. Many strong peo-

ple can do this. But no one is indifferent to censure. Why pretend
not to care about criticism? Those who are honest with themselves
know very well that they would rather be approved than criticized
—even when they are quite certain to be right in either case.

Now, perhaps among all human attributes the one most harshly
and justly criticized is egotism. And yet, as I said in previous passages, selfishness is the most fundamental characteristic of living
matter. We cannot avoid being egotists.

These are considerations which lead me to conclude that to incite
gratitude in others is perhaps the most natural basis for a long-range
aim of man. It can be hoarded throughout life and accumulated
into a tremendous wealth, which more reliably than any other assures our security and peace of mind in this world. Thereby it
permits us to enjoy all that is great and enjoyable in life. It is an
egotistic aim; that is why it is so fundamentally natural. It can be
pursued through whatever talents one may have; that is why it
permits self-expression to anyone, irrespective of his background.
It can be cumulated as long as you live, and even your offspring
will benefit by it; that is why it can act as a proper long-range aim.
And—best of all—this is one type of selfishness for which you certainly need not dread censure: no one will blame you for hoarding
avariciously the gratitude of your fellow men.

The philosophy of gratitude is based on deep-rooted, general
laws of nature, which subconsciously direct man's actions in any
age and clime; that is why it cannot clash with the moral teachings
of any natural religion or school of ethics. It only highlights their
biologic basis. And I know of *no other philosophy which necessarily
transforms all our egotistic impulses into altruism without curtailing
any of their self-protecting values.*

So much about the philosophy of gratitude as a guide to conduct
which avoids stress in interpersonal relations and thereby gives man
more freedom to enjoy life's wonders. But what is really enjoyable
in life and its wonders?

To enjoy life's wonders

Gratitude, whether you receive it or give it, is in itself very enjoyable. But there are many pleasing things which do not seem to be
logically related to the incitement of gratitude. The passive receipt

of rewards, for instance. The enjoyment of food and drink, of a beautiful sunny day, of a magnificent painting, or the purely sensual pleasures of sex, are certainly not sought to inspire gratitude in others. But let us not forget that the actual receipt of rewards—no matter how great the delight it can give us—is also quite unsuitable as an ultimate aim in life. Why? Simply because it is too ephemeral. It can be ardently sought to enrich a moment; but we cannot accumulate these sensations into a treasure assuring our security and peace of mind in the future. Still, striving toward gratitude is so deeply rooted in man's nature that we feel the instinctive urge somehow to connect even these values with thankfulness: to say grace before dinner, to ennoble sex with grateful love, to feel indebted to the maker of every enjoyable thing—be it a poem, a health-restoring drug, or a sunny day—has its roots in this feeling.

We have said these passive pleasures are disqualified from being ultimate aims; but they still can be very important aims. To a certain extent, some of them even have a measure of stabilizing (homeostatic) effect, and at least their afterglow can be stocked and accumulated. The passive enjoyment of great art or of the great wonders of nature do help us to achieve a degree of equanimity; and while, to the mere onlooker, they give no means for self-expression, they do help to provide self-sufficiency. In this sense, a great capacity to derive pleasure out of feelings can steady our interpersonal relations, because it makes us less dependent upon society. But, in analyzing the relationship between passive and active attitudes toward pleasure—between means and ends, between work and reward, between satisfying the impulse to express ourselves and our feeling of having accomplished this—we must give special attention to the afterglow of pleasure, which can be stocked. Its benefits are cumulative because the better we learn to enjoy greatness—be it in art or in nature—the more we profit from contemplating it. To learn how to enjoy this kind of greatness can be a very exacting task, and, since it involves activity, it is in itself an outlet for self-expression. This can be learned, and it is well worth learning.

Besides the wish to earn the gratitude of others, through the medical applications of the stress concept, it was the purely selfish desire to enjoy nature better, by learning to understand one of its fundamental mechanisms, that acted as the strongest motive for my investigations. In fact, one of the principal inducements to write this book was the wish to share with others the serene and elevating satisfaction which comes from understanding the inherent, harmonious beauty of nature.

No sensitive person can look at the sky on a cloudless night without asking himself where the stars came from, where they go, and what keeps the universe in order. The same questions arise when we look at the internal universe within the human body, or even just at that pair of sensitive and searching human eyes which constantly strives to bridge the gap between these two universes.

The capacity to contemplate, at least with some degree of understanding, the harmonious elegance in nature's manifestations, is one of the most satisfactory experiences of which man is capable. To attain even a small measure of it is a noble and gratifying aim in itself, quite apart from any material advantages it may offer. But actually it does also help us in our everyday life, very much in the same way as a deep religious faith or a well-balanced philosophic outlook can help us. Looking at something infinitely greater than our conscious selves makes all our daily troubles appear to shrink by comparison. There is an equanimity and a peace of mind which can be achieved only through contact with the sublime.

The fairest thing we can experience [said Einstein] is the mysterious. It is the fundamental emotion which stands at the cradle of true art and true science. He who knows it not and can no longer wonder, no longer feel amazement, is as good as dead, a snuffed-out candle.

You do not have to be a professional scientist to experience the great melodious creations of nature, any more than you have to be a composer to enjoy music. The most harmonious and mysterious creations are those of nature; and to my mind, it is the highest cultural aim of the professional scientist to interpret them so that others may share in their enjoyment.

As children we all had what it takes to enjoy wonderful and mysterious things. When a child points out something unusual which he has never seen before—a colorful butterfly, an elephant, or a sea shell—just watch his eyes as he cries out with enthusiasm, "Look, Daddy!" and you will know what I mean.

We all had this priceless talent for pure enjoyment when we were young, but as time goes by, most of us—not all—lose this gift. We lose it because, gradually, we have seen most of the things that we are likely to encounter in everyday life and custom stales variety. The petty routine of daily problems also tends to blunt our sensitivity to the detached enjoyment of greatness and wonder. But the true artist, the true scientist, never lose this faculty; it is the essence of their being to look for strange, new things. It would be a pity if, out of reticence, they kept their treasures to themselves. It is a pity that nowadays most people are so anxiously bent on being practical, to get ahead in life, that they no longer find time to make sure where they really want to go. After a while, the prosperous businessman, the efficient administrator, the up-and-coming young lawyer begin to get that lost feeling of aimlessly drifting from day to day—toward retirement. So many people work hard and intelligently for some immediate objective which promises leisure to enjoy life to-morrow; but tomorrow never becomes today. There is always another objective which promises even more leisure in exchange for just a little more work. Hence very few people in the usual walks of life retain the ability really to enjoy themselves: that wonderful gift which they all possessed as children. But it hurts to be conscious of this defect, so adults dope themselves with more work (or alcohol) to divert attention from their loss.

The inspired painter, poet, composer, astronomer, or biologist never grows up in this respect; he does not tend to get the feeling of aimlessly drifting, no matter how poor or old he may be. He retains the childlike ability to enjoy the impractical by-products of his activity. Pleasures are always impractical, they can lead us to no reward. They *are* the reward. It is a commonplace to say that money is no ultimate aim, but few people seem to live as though they understood this. The labors of the artist who succeeds in expressing some hidden aspect of his soul in painting, or of the physician who learns how a hitherto inexplicable disease develops, may have practical advantages for him—benefits which can be expressed in dollars —but this is not the kind of reward that can make his life a real success. The great financier must also seek his final compensation elsewhere. To find it he must stop thinking about the success of his enterprises, at least long enough to think of his own success. *He must first find a way of life which can assure him the equanimity necessary for enjoyment, and then he must learn to distinguish between what can give him pleasure and what are only means to buy pleasure.* The most acquisitive person is so busy reinvesting that he never learns how to cash in. "Realistic people" who pursue "practical aims" are rarely as realistic and practical, in the long run of life, as the dreamers who pursue only their dreams.

A way of life

Can the scientific study of stress help us to formulate a precise program of conduct? Can it teach us the wisdom to live a rich and meaningful life which satisfies our needs for self-expression and yet is not marred or cut short by the stresses of senseless struggles?

I have seen a great many books and articles of late, which tell you "how to . . .": how to achieve peace of mind, how to enjoy life, how to become a millionaire or a centenarian, and how to be a success in general. Can one really give definite and generally applicable directions on how to accomplish such complex aims? I could tell a stranger how to get to the station, without having to walk along with him to show the way, but I doubt that by using words only, I could really explain even such a comparatively simple thing as how to drive a car. The best I could do is to show how the car is made (at least as far as I understand its mechanism) and how *I* drive it. Usually, this kind of explanation is quite sufficient, because one learns things involving personal conduct by adding one's own experience to that of others. This is even more true when it comes to complex behavioral problems which must be solved differently by every person in agreement with his own particular personality traits. I believe that the mere fact of understanding the general rules about the way stress acts upon mind and body, with a few remarks about the way this has been used as a basis for one man's personal philosophy, can help others, better than fixed rules, to formulate their own solutions.

Perhaps the best thing to do, therefore, is to summarize here as precisely as possible the rules of conduct which I have found most practical in my own particular case, repeat briefly how I arrived at them from my research on stress, and then let the reader decide for himself what he should accept and how he should use it.

I found it helpful to subdivide my aspirations into three kinds: short-range aims, long-range aims, and the ultimate aim. So, even if this means some recapitulation, let us now arrange them this way.

Short-range aims

Man's short-range aims are designed for immediate gratification. They have comparatively little influence upon our well-being in the distant future. Most of these are readily accessible enjoyments, in that they require no prolonged preparation by learning or planning; you simply allow something pleasant to act upon you. The *pleasures of the flesh* brought to us by our senses are the best example of this type. Some short-range aims are not wholly passive; they imply some activity in the form of self-expression, as for instance, creative activities and the various games. But, in all these, work and reward are virtually simultaneous. In other words, to achieve short-range aims, you merely let things act upon you which give you a pleasant feeling and you do things you like to do.

That these pleasures can give happiness is self-evident. But man's mind is capable of much *more lasting and profound passive satisfactions*. These are not so readily accessible, because they presuppose a carefully developed, acquired taste. They really form a transition between short- and long-range aims. We must plan these; they are not fully developed by our heredity. They are, therefore, more optional and it is well to establish which ones are worth working for. Not everybody has an ear for music, an eye for painting, or a mind for the enjoyment of nature. Each person must seek the kind of pleasure he is fit to enjoy. The task of determining our special predispositions in this respect deserves to be taken very seriously. "To know thyself" from this point of view can do much more to bring happiness than such conventional ideals as money or position.

Personally, I have derived my greatest satisfaction from the mere contemplation of natural laws. But I want to make it very clear that these satisfactions are no farther removed from the general public than are those offered by art. Of course, the more you know about nature, the more she can give you; but there is no essential difference between the pleasure a child can get from watching a butterfly and that of the professional biologist who studies the microscopic structure of a cell. The great thing about these passive pleasures is that they are not practical. They are pure. I think that people in all practical walks of life should keep in mind that, deep in their hearts, they also need the pure enjoyment of impractical pleasures to live a balanced life.

Let me explain. Anybody who likes music can enjoy at least a simple folk song; no special schooling is needed for this. But a person who has a real understanding for the art of combining tones can appreciate really great music much better than the casual amateur. The same is true of literature and of painting. Many people who want to enjoy the finer things in life spend a great deal of time studying the structure and techniques of art or literature, precisely with this in mind—even if they have never wanted to become professionals. Anyone can enjoy the universe by looking at the stars or life by looking at flowers and animals. But there is no reason why one should have to be a professional biologist or a physician to penetrate deeper into the enjoyment of living things. The profound pleasure of studying nature comes from our understanding—however superficially—the lawfulness which governs it. The image of this understanding, the reflection of nature in our mind, somehow fits us more harmoniously into the world within and around us. *The source of our pleasure is the intimacy of this contact with nature;* and it is rewarding to cultivate our acquaintance with her and thus make this communion ever more intimate. Of course no scholar can fully understand even that little section of nature which he has selected for special study. Yet the more he learns about it the more he can get out of it. The difference between the rewards of the most eminent expert and those of the complete ignoramus is not one of kind but only one of degree.

This second kind of aim—the appreciation of art, the admiration of nature—has another advantage over the simple pleasures of the flesh: its afterglow lasts longer. The more you learn to appreciate detail the more you get in return. There are cumulative benefits to be derived from this which come quite close to what we shall have to say about the long-range aims. Most simple pleasures of the flesh tend to become stale as time goes by, but these more complex satisfactions of the mind become increasingly more gratifying as they are cultivated. To paraphrase the Bard: Age cannot wither them, nor custom stale their infinite variety.

Now, just a few words about the *relationship between short-range aims and stress*. When I spoke of the general stress-response, the G.A.S., I described experiments which showed that whatever we do, and whatever happens to us, tends to evolve in three phases. Activity in any part of the body or mind apparently also tends to go through three stages. Our adaptation energy is a finite, hereditarily determined amount of vitality which must necessarily be spent. Hence the inherent urge for man to express himself so as to achieve fulfillment and completion. In general, we must go through with what our bodily and mental structure is built to undertake and, in particular, we feel the urge to finish whatever task we start. Frustration and indecision are only types of incompletion.

Even what we call *failure* is not, as one might think, the most general, all-comprising class of biologic defeat; it is only one sub-division of incompletion. Failure implies merely the inability to complete a voluntary endeavor, but incompletion includes also the purely passive suffering, which may involve neither the mental humiliation of defeat in an undertaking nor physical pain. When you must listen throughout the night to the monotonous sound of drops falling at regular intervals from a faulty faucet, it is the pure incompletion of the theme that hurts; and this hurt can be so great that it has actually been used as a form of severe torture. What we call *deviation* is only a way to simulate completion when true fulfillment is unattainable. Actually, it fools us, but even so, it helps.

I mention all this to underline the importance of completing the three phases of the stress-response in all our activities and all our passive sensations. To me this is the biologic basis of man's need to express himself and to fulfill his mission. In all our activities, we proceed through surprise (alarm reaction), to mastery (stage of resistance), to fatigue (stage of exhaustion), and hence either to rest (with a repetition of the cycle in the same or some other part of our being) or, eventually, to death. Man is constructed for this cycle. He should direct his life accordingly, neglecting no phase of it, and giving each manifestation of life the emphasis which fits his personal requirements.

The great practical lesson is to realize the deep-rooted biologic necessity for completion, the fulfillment of all our smallest needs and greatest aspirations, in harmony with our hereditary make-up.

Long-range aims

Man's long-range aims are designed to permit future gratification. They have comparatively little influence upon our well-being in the present; in fact, they are often in conflict with it. But whether he puts his faith in God or in creation, man realizes that his ultimate aim must outlast the moment and must usually be earned at the price of some momentary sacrifices. To achieve our long-range aims we have to act and we must learn how to choose between various optional modes of action. The difficulty here is to formulate these aims precisely and to develop a code of conduct to guide us in the perpetual dilemmas created by the competition between immediate and future happiness. The long-range aims are essentially social—or, at least, impersonal—in that their object is to create a favorable milieu for future happiness. They should lead us through a meaningful, happy, active, and long life, steering us clear of the unpleasant and unnecessary stresses of fights, frustrations, and insecurities.

Some people hope to find such aims in the acquisition of wealth, power, and social position; others in religion or philosophy. Yet others have instinctively realized that they are unable to solve this problem. They just give up and drift from day to day, trying to divert their attention from the future by some such sedative as compulsive promiscuity, frantic work, or simply alcohol.

That none of these things can assure lasting happiness is self-evident. Of course, there are many better guides to it: love, kindness, or simply the desire to do some good. These are often very successful; but it seems to me that they all have common roots in *man's innate, though often subconscious, desire to earn gratitude and to avoid being the target for revenge.* Why then should we not make this quite consciously our principal long-range social aim in life? Of course, it is an egotistic aim; but then, as we have seen, egotism is an essential characteristic of life. In a sense, selfishness is the original sin, not only of man, but of all living beings. Why pretend that we can do without it? We cannot, and trying this just leads to frustration and self-incrimination. But if we follow the philosophy of gratitude, we necessarily make all our selfish impulses also altruistic without curtailing any of their egotistic, self-protecting values.

From a scientific point of view, this strikes me as the most highly ethical among all possible natural guides to conduct. No one will blame us for hoarding the gratitude of our fellow men. This long-range aim is inextricably rooted in the natural laws governing man's actions. This is perhaps most clearly demonstrated by the fact that, rather than competing with the ethical codes laid down by other philosophies and by religions, it actually finds support in one essential aspect common to them all.

After what we have said, the relationship between long-range aims and stress is so evident that it hardly justifies more than a fleeting comment. Mental tensions, frustrations, the sense of insecurity, and aimlessness are among the most important stressors. As psychosomatic studies have shown, they are also very common causes of physical disease. This is especially important, now that knowledge about microbes, vitamin deficiencies, and other specific disease-producers has given us such effective weapons to combat the maladies which, even at the beginning of this century, were still the major scourges of mankind. How often are migraine headache, gastric and duodenal ulcer, coronary thrombosis, arthritis, hypertension, insanity, suicide, or just hopeless unhappiness actually caused by the failure to find a satisfactory guide for conduct?

But neither short-range nor long-range aims are actually the ultimate aim of man: the objective which should furnish a basis for all our actions. We instinctively feel that one final aim should somehow coordinate and give unity to all our strivings.

The ultimate aim

As I see it, man's ultimate aim is *to express himself as fully as possible, according to his own lights.* Whether he seeks this by establishing harmony and communion with his Maker or with nature, he can do so only by finding that balance between long- and short-range aims, between sowing and harvesting, which best fits his own individuality.

The goal is certainly not to avoid stress. Stress is part of life. It is a natural by-product of all our activities; there is no more justification for avoiding stress than for shunning food, exercise, or love. But, in order to express yourself fully, you must first find your optimum stress-level, and then, use your adaptation energy at a rate and in a direction adjusted to the innate structure of your mind and body.

The study of stress has shown that complete rest is not good, either for the body as a whole, or even for any organ within the body. Stress, applied in moderation, is necessary for life. Besides, enforced inactivity may be very harmful and cause more stress than normal activity.

I have always been against the advice of physicians who would send a high-strung, extremely active business executive to a long, enforced exile in some health resort, with the view of relieving him from stress by absolute inactivity. Naturally ambitious and active men often become much more tense when they feel frustrated by not being allowed to pursue their usual activities; if they cannot express themselves through actions, they spend the time worrying about what might be going on in their business during their absence.

At the risk of sounding facetious, let me present a little motto which I developed while analyzing stress in my experimental animals, in my colleagues, my friends, and myself. It may sound trivial and purely abstract, but it is based on solid biologic laws and—at least in my case—it works. Whatever happens during the day to threaten my equanimity or throw some doubt upon the value of my actions, I just think of this little jingle:

> Fight always for the highest attainable aim
> But never put up resistance in vain.

Everyone should *fight* for whatever seems really worthwhile to him. On the other hand, he should aim only for *things attainable* to him, for otherwise he will merely become frustrated. Finally, *resistance* should be put up whenever there is reasonable expectation of its succeeding, but never if we know it would be *in vain*.

It is not easy to live by this motto; it takes much practice and almost constant self-analysis. Any time during the day, in discussions, at work and at play, when I begin to feel keyed up, I consciously stop to analyze the situation. I ask myself: "Is this really the best thing I could do now, and is it worth the trouble of putting up resistance against counterarguments, boredom, or fatigue?" If the answer is no, I just stop; or whenever this cannot be done gracefully I simply "float" and let things go on as they will, with a minimum of active participation (e.g., during most committee meetings, solemn academic ceremonies, and unavoidable interviews with crackpots).

Probably few people would be inclined to contest the soundness of this motto. The trick is to follow it! But that is where my assistance must stop. That is where you come in. This may sound like an anticlimactic ending, but it really should not. We all must live our own lives. No self-respecting person wants to go from cradle to grave sheepishly following the directives of another man.

Success formula?

One of the main points of this whole discussion is that *there is no ready-made success formula which would suit everybody*. We are all different. The only thing we have in common is our obedience to certain fundamental biologic laws which govern all men. I think the best the professional investigator of stress can do is to explain the mechanism of stress as far as he can understand it; then, to outline the way he thinks this knowledge could be applied to problems of daily life; and, finally, as a kind of laboratory demonstration, to describe the way he himself can apply it successfully to his own problems.

It was the dissection of stress and the analysis of its structure which helped me most with my own problems; and I do not think there is any other way to learn something that, of necessity, must be done differently by every person.

What is the use, for example, of dissecting a sentence and explaining its structure? In actual speech you would never have the time to apply the rules of syntax and grammar by conscious intellectual processes. Still, people who know something about syntax and grammar use better language, thanks to this knowledge. You cannot teach a man how to express himself because it is the first rule of the game that his speech must reflect his personality, not yours. Moreover, few of the rules of syntax and grammar are absolute; the most unpolished slang is often more effective and picturesque than the King's English. All formal teaching can do is to explain the basic elements of language, so as to make them available for translation from conscious intellectual appraisal—which is impersonal, slow, and cold—into instinct—which is personal, quick, and warm.

I intended to do, and could do, no more in these pages than to present the syntax and grammar of stress, illustrating its application to the philosophy of life by one example: my own. A single case does not prove much; but, against my laboratory background, one actual experiment proves a great deal more than volumes of pure speculation. In such an experiment the indices of success are purely subjective; therefore, I could not repeat the test on others and still vouch for the veracity of my findings. All I can say is that the philosophy of stress has helped me enormously in achieving equanimity and a personally satisfactory program for the way I want to go through life. I rather think if you tried it, it might help you too.

But, after all, I am no philosopher and certainly not a prophet! So, let me finish this book by giving an outline of what I think are the most important avenues opened up by stress research in its *strictly medical applications,* the new directions that we should follow in the study of disease: the road ahead.

25:

The road ahead

Now that we have a blueprint of the body's own nonspecific general methods to combat disease, it is largely a matter of time and money to fill in the gaps. For this *organized research teamwork* is necessary. Although this is expensive, the cost will be trivial in comparison with the relief of human suffering that can be expected from it.

One major avenue for future research will be the scientific analysis of *adaptation energy*. We have seen (pp. 65, 87) that the stress syndrome develops in three stages, eventually leading to the depletion of adaptability or adaptation energy. This final exhaustion by stress is strikingly similar to senility; it is a kind of accelerated, premature aging. By learning more about the body's adaptation energy, the *life-span* could probably be greatly prolonged and health during old age improved. The diseases of old age become constantly more important as more and more people live to be old, thanks to medical progress. According to the estimates of the Twentieth Century Fund, there were 14 million people aged 65 or more in the United States in 1956, three times as many as in 1920. Their number, and hence, the national importance of their problems, continues to increase rapidly.

Adaptation energy seems to be something of which everybody has a given amount at birth, an inherited capital to which we cannot add, but which we can use, more or less thriftily, in fighting the stress of life. Still, we have not fully excluded the possibility that adaptation energy could be regenerated to some extent, and perhaps even transmitted from one living being to another, somewhat like a serum. If its amount is unchangeable, we may learn more about how to conserve it. If it can be transmitted, we may explore means of extracting the carrier of this vital energy—for instance, from the tissues of young animals—and trying to transmit it to the old and aging.

Another fascinating field for future research is the study of stress in relation to *cancer*. It is well known that a large variety of cancers do not grow well in animals or people subjected to severe stress. In fact, some types of cancer have undergone considerable (though incomplete) regression under the influence of ACTH, cortisone, and other hormones. To what extent could we, by learning more about the mechanism of such regressions, help in the fight against this, the most terrible among human ailments?

Many of these possibilities are still very remote, but so was treatment with the antibiotics from molds or the hormonal treatment of rheumatoid arthritis, not so many years ago. It may be well for the general public to realize that definite research plans for this type of study do now exist, and are handicapped mainly by the lack of adequate support.

Perhaps the most fascinating aspect of medical *research on stress* is its *fundamentally permanent value* to man. Even the most important drugs (chemicals which have curative value, but are not normally produced by the body) are of importance to us only for a certain time. Sooner or later, they are replaced by still more effective remedies and then they become uninteresting.

Take the arsenic derivative, Salvarsan, that Paul Ehrlich—the Father of Chemotherapy—introduced around 1910 for the treatment of syphilis. Until then this venereal disease was one of the greatest scourges of mankind. That a significant number of cures could be obtained with certain arsenicals had been justly hailed as one of the most important medical discoveries of all times. Yet now, after less than half a century, this treatment has lost its importance because penicillin has proved to be even more effective. And consequently syphilis has virtually vanished. The same fate awaits any of our potent antibiotics whenever still more effective ones shall be found.

The study of stress differs essentially from research with artificial drugs because it deals with *the defensive mechanisms of our own body*. The immediate results of this budding new science are not yet as dramatic in their practical applications as are those of many drugs, but what we learn about nature's own self-protecting mechanisms can never lose its importance. Such defensive measures as the production of adaptive hormones by glands are built into the very texture of the body; we inherited them from our parents and transmit them to our children, who, in turn, must hand them on to their offspring, as long as the human race shall exist. *The significance of this kind of research is not limited to fighting this or that disease. It has a bearing upon all diseases and indeed upon all human activities,* because it furnishes knowledge about the essence of THE STRESS OF LIFE.

Glossary

A more detailed discussion of the concepts mentioned in this glossary will be found in the text at the pages indicated in parentheses.

abscess. A localized collection of pus within a capsule of connective tissue, as for instance, a boil.

ACTH. Abbreviation for the adrenocorticotrophic hormone.

adaptation energy. The energy necessary to acquire and maintain adaptation, apart from caloric requirements. (See pp. 65, 66, 274, 275.)

adaptive hormones. Hormones produced for adaptation to stress. (See p. 85.)

adrenaline. One of the hormones of the adrenal medulla. (See p. 91.)

adrenals. Endocrine glands which lie (one on each side) just above the kidneys. They have a triangular, or Y-shaped, form on cross section, and consist of a whitish outer cortex, or bark, and a dark-brown medulla, or marrow. (See p. 20.)

adrenocorticotrophic hormone (ACTH). A pituitary hormone which stimulates the growth and function of the adrenal cortex. (See p. 86.)

alarm reaction (A.R.). The first stage of the adaptation syndrome. In the G.A.S. it affects the body as a whole; in the L.A.S. it is limited to a part. Correspondingly, we speak of a general and of a local alarm reaction. (See pp. 31–33.)

aldosterone. One of the proinflammatory corticoids. (See p. 202.)

antagonist. An agent which acts against another agent.

antibiotics. Antibacterial substances, most of which are prepared from molds or fungi (e.g., penicillin, streptomycin).

anti-inflammatory corticoids. Adrenocortical hormones which inhibit inflammation, for example, cortisone or cortisol. They have a marked effect upon glucose metabolism and are therefore also known as *glucocorticoids.* (See p. 92.)

atrophy. Shrinkage of an organ. See *involution.*

cell. A relatively autonomous, circumscribed, small mass of living material, visible under the microscope. The tissues of all living beings consist mainly of cells.

COL Abbreviation for cortisol.

CON Abbreviation for cortisone.

conditioning factors. Substances or circumstances which influence the response to an agent, for instance, a hormone. (See p. 95.)

connective tissue. A tissue consisting of cells and fine fibers; it is a kind of living cement which connects and reinforces all other tissues. Inflammation develops mainly in connective tissue. (See p. 101.)

corticoids. Hormones of the adrenal cortex. It is customary to subdivide them into the anti-inflammatory glucocorticoids and the proinflammatory mineralocorticoids. (See pp. 92, 93.)

cortisol (COL). One of the anti-inflammatory corticoids. (See p. 92.)

cortisone (CON). One of the anti-inflammatory corticoids. (See p. 92.)

crossed resistance. Resistance to one agent produced by pretreatment with another agent. (See p. 227.)

desoxycorticosterone (DOC). One of the proinflammatory corticoids. (See p. 93.)

developmental adaptation. A simple progressive adaptive reaction, accomplished by mere enlargement and multiplication of preexisting cell-elements, without qualitative change. In technical language: homotropic adaptation. (See p. 227.)

diagnosis. Recognition; for instance, the recognition of a disease.

diseases of adaptation. Maladies which are principally due to imperfections of the G.A.S., as for instance, to an excessive or insufficient amount, or an improper mixture, of adaptive hormones. (See p. 66.)

DOC Abbreviation for desoxycorticosterone.

duodenum. The first part of the small intestine, which comes immediately after the stomach.

endocrines. Ductless glands which secrete their products, the hormones, directly into the blood. (See p. 77.)

enzyme. A naturally occurring substance, formed by living cells, which accelerates certain chemical reactions (formerly called *ferment*).

eosinophils. Certain white blood cells which can readily be stained by the dye eosin. (See p. 21.) They play an important part in allergy.

extract. A preparation obtained by mixing tissue, e.g., liver, ovary, etc., or constituents of a drug, with solvents (water, alcohol, etc.) and then separating the soluble from the insoluble material. (See p. 20.)

focal infection. Infection (in a more or less circumscribed region) which causes disease manifestations in distant parts of the body through mechanisms other than the mere spreading of bacteria or their poisons. (See p. 159.)

Formalin. An irritating aqueous solution of formaldehyde. (See p. 23.)

G.A.S. Abbreviation for general adaptation syndrome.

general adaptation syndrome. The manifestations of stress in the whole body, as they develop in time. The general adaptation syndrome evolves in three distinct stages: alarm reaction, stage of resistance, stage of exhaustion. (See pp. 31, 64.)

glucocorticoids. See *anti-inflammatory corticoids.*

growth hormone. The somatotrophic hormone.

heterotropic adaptation. See *redevelopmental adaptation.*

histology. The study of the minute microscopic structure of tissues.

homeostasis. The body's tendency to maintain a steady state despite external changes; physiologic stability. (See p. 11.)

homotropic adaptation. See *developmental adaptation*.

hormones. Chemical substances released into the blood by the endocrine glands to stimulate and coordinate distant organs. Bodily growth, metabolism, resistance to stress, and sexual functions are largely regulated by hormones. (See p. 20.)

inflammation. The typical reaction of tissue (particularly of connective tissue) to injury. Its main purpose is to barricade off and to destroy the injurious agent by which it was elicited. (See p. 99.)

insulin. The antidiabetic hormone produced by the pancreas.

involution. Natural shrinkage or decline of an organ. See *atrophy*.

L.A.S. Abbreviation for local adaptation syndrome.

local adaptation syndrome. The manifestations of stress in a limited part of the body as they develop in time. The local adaptation syndrome evolves in three stages, characterized mainly by inflammation, degeneration, or death of cell-groups in the directly affected part. (See pp. 31–33.)

lymphatic tissues. Tissues containing mainly lymphocytes, for example, the thymus, the lymph nodes. (See p. 20.)

lymph nodes. Nodular organs, consisting of lymphatic tissue, in the groin, under the armpits, along the neck, and in various parts of the body. (See p. 21.)

lymphocytes. The smallest white blood cells. They make up the lymphatic tissue, but can also circulate freely in the blood. (See p. 21.)

MAD Abbreviation for methylandrostenediol.

metabolism. The transformation of foodstuff into tissue and energy which occurs in the body.

methylandrostenediol (MAD). An artificial virilizing hormone. (See p. 201.)

milieu intérieur. The internal environment of the body; the soil in which all biologic reactions develop. (See p. 11.)

mineralocorticoids. See *proinflammatory corticoids*.

nephritis. Inflammation of the kidney. (See p. 132.)

nephrosclerosis. A kidney disease often causing hypertension. (See p. 132.)

nephrosis. A kidney disease which leads to dropsy and loss of protein through the urine. (See p. 132.)

nonspecific. A *nonspecifically formed* change is one which affects all or most parts of a system without selectivity. It is the opposite of a specifically formed change, which affects only one or, at least, few units within a system. A *nonspecifically caused* change is one which can be produced by many or all agents. (See p. 56.)

nonspecific therapy. Treatment which is beneficial in various kinds of diseases.

noradrenaline. One of the hormones of the adrenal medulla. (See p. 91.)

ovaries. The female sex glands. (See p. 19.)

pancreas. An endocrine gland which produces insulin.

pathology. The study of disease.

pathos. Greek for suffering, disease. (See p. 11.)

peptic. Aiding digestion (as in peptic juice), or caused by digestion (as in peptic ulcer). (See p. 179.)

pituitary. A little endocrine gland embedded in the bones of the skull just below the brain; also known as *hypophysis.* (See pp. 22, 86.)

placenta. The vascular organ with which the embryo is attached to the mother's womb; the afterbirth. (See p. 19.)

pónos. Greek for toil, stress. (See p. 11.)

pressor substances. Hormones or hormonelike products which raise the blood pressure. (See p. 110.)

proinflammatory corticoids. Adrenocortical hormones which stimulate inflammation, as for example, aldosterone, desoxycorticosterone. They have a marked effect upon mineral metabolism, and are therefore also known as *mineralocorticoids.* (See p. 93.)

psychoanalysis. The method of analyzing an abnormal mental state by having the patient review his past emotional experiences and relating them to his present mental life. The technique furnishes hints for psychotherapeutic procedures.

reaction. In biology, the response of the body, or of one of its parts, to stimulation.

reacton. The smallest possible biologic target. It is the primary subcellular unit in living matter, which still exhibits the property of responding selectively to stimulation. (See p. 233.)

redevelopmental adaptation. Adaptation in which a tissue, organized for one type of action, is forced to readjust itself completely to an entirely different kind of activity. In technical language: heterotropic adaptation. (See p. 228.)

renal pressor substances (RPS). Endocrine substances produced by the kidney to raise the blood pressure. (See p. 110.)

rheumatic fever. An acute and often recurring disease, most common in children and young adults. It is characterized by fever with inflammation of the joints and the heart valves. It often follows upon focal infection in the tonsils. (See p. 164.)

rheumatism. A vague term which includes rheumatic fever, rheumatoid arthritis, and several allied conditions. (See p. 164.)

rheumatoid arthritis. A more or less chronic disease, characterized by an inflammation of the joints, with swelling, pain, stiffness, and deformity. There are several variants in which one or the other among these manifestations predominates. (See p. 164.)

RPS   Abbreviation for renal pressor substances.

shock therapy.   Treatment with shocks elicited by drugs or electricity.

somatic.   Pertaining to the body.

somatotrophic hormone (STH).   A pituitary substance which stimulates the growth of the body in general and of inflamed connective tissue in particular. Also known as *growth hormone*. (See p. 108.)

specific.   A *specifically formed* change is one which affects only a single, or at least, few units within a system, with great selectivity. A *specifically caused* change is one which can be produced only by a single, or at least, by few agents. The term *specific* has no meaning unless we indicate whether it refers to the change itself or to its causation. (See p. 56.)

specific resistance.   Resistance to an agent induced by pretreatment with the same agent. (See p. 227.)

stage of exhaustion.   The final stage of the adaptation syndrome. It may be general or local, depending upon whether the whole body or only a region has been exposed to stress. (See pp. 31–33.)

stage of resistance.   The second stage of the adaptation syndrome. It may be general or local, depending upon whether the whole body or only a region has been exposed to stress. (See pp. 31–33.)

STH   Abbreviation for somatotrophic hormone.

stimulus.   In biology, anything that elicits a reaction in the body or in one of its parts.

stress.   The *state manifested by the specific syndrome which consists of all the nonspecifically induced changes within a biologic system.* Thus stress has its own characteristic form, but no particular specific cause. A detailed analysis of this fundamental definition will be found on p. 53. However, for general orientation, it suffices to keep in mind that by *stress* the physician means the common results of exposure to anything. For example, the bodily changes produced, whether a person is exposed to nervous tension, physical injury, infection, cold, heat, x-rays or anything else, are what we call *stress*. This is what is left when we abstract from the specific changes that are produced only by one or few among these agents. In my earlier writings I had defined stress, somewhat more simply but less precisely, as "the sum of all nonspecific changes caused by function or damage," or "the rate of wear and tear in the body."

syndrome.   A group of symptoms and signs which appear together.

synergist.   An agent which facilitates the action of another agent.

stressor.   That which produces stress. (See p. 64.)

target area.   The region upon which a biologic agent acts.

therapy.   Treatment.

thymus.   A large lymphatic organ in the chest. (See p. 21.)

thyroid.   An endocrine gland in the neck, which regulates metabolism in general. (See p. 111.)

tissue.   An aggregate of cells and intercellular substances forming one of the structural materials of the body. Each type of tissue (nervous, muscular, connective) has a different specific structure.

triad.   A syndrome consisting of three manifestations. (See p. 21.)

tripartite.   Having three parts.

triphasic.   Having, or developing in three stages, as, the G.A.S.

ulcer.   Inflammation and erosion on a surface.

viruses.   Living agents, even smaller than bacteria, which can cause infectious diseases. For instance, measles, mumps, poliomyelitis, and the common cold, are produced by viruses.

white blood cells.   Cells which circulate freely in the blood and do not contain the coloring matter characteristic of the red blood cells. The lymphocytes, eosinophils, and other leukocytes belong to this group. (See p. 21.)

Index

This index would have been much more concise, and easier to read, had it been based completely on the Symbolic Shorthand System (see p. 73 and H. Selye: *Journal of the American Medical Association,* vol. 161, p. 1411, 1956). Of course, it was impossible to do this without asking the reader to study all the rules of this technical code. My main object here is to demonstrate the principle of this method of classification, and therefore it will suffice to keep the following few points in mind.

In the Symbolic Shorthand System there are no synonyms, and every symbol reminds us what it stands for (e.g., A-C = antiphlogistic corticoid; DOC = desoxycorticosterone; COL = cortisol; X←Y = effect of Y on X; X:Y = relationship between X and Y; X<Y = X content of Y; X+Y = combination of X and Y).

The arrangement of symbols into phrases is not governed by syntax but by an Order of Precedence which is just as rigid as the alphabetic order that determines the position of words in a dictionary. This obviates the need for cross references, although we had to give some here for readers unfamiliar with our Order of Precedence. Even with these limitations, the symbolic expressions used in the following pages are of great help in eliminating the grammatical horrors of the usual indexing according to key words. For example, instead of "Anti-inflammatory corticoid, effect of upon allergy" (which is both clumsy and lengthy) we can simply write "A-C→allergy"; instead of "Anti-inflammatory corticoid, balance of, in relation to proinflammatory corticoid", we write A-C:P-C balance; instead of "Kidney, effect of combined treatment with desoxycorticosterone and salt upon", we write "Kidney←DOC + salt"; instead of "Sugar in blood, as influenced by insulin" (which could just as well be filed under blood sugar or hyperglycemia) we write in our synonym-free language "Sugar<blood←insulin".

About the author

Dr. Hans Selye is without question one of the great pioneers of medicine. In 1936 his famous and revolutionary concept of stress opened up countless new avenues of treatment through the discovery that hormones participate in the development of many nonendocrine degenerative diseases, including coronary thrombosis, brain hemorrhage, hardening of the arteries, certain types of high blood pressure and kidney failures, arthritis, peptic ulcers, and even cancer.

Dr. Selye was born in Vienna in 1907 and studied in Prague, Paris, and Rome. He received his medical degree from the German University of Prague in 1929 and two years later took his Ph.D. at the same university. He was then awarded a Rockefeller research fellowship which brought him to Johns Hopkins University and later to McGill University, where he became Associate Professor of Histology. Subsequently he received honorary degrees from eight other universities. Since 1945 he has served as director of the Institute of Experimental Medicine and Surgery. Dr. Selye makes his home in Montreal with his wife and four children.

Dr. Selye has written a large number of books and articles, but all of them addressed to students and specialists in medicine. *The Stress of Life* is his first book written for the general public. It gives the layman authoritative information about the medical aspects of stress in health and disease and is the first time that the creator of the stress concept has himself given the layman an explanation of his remarkable and revolutionary discoveries.